Jahangir

Praise for the Book

'A stylishly and enjoyably discursive retelling of the life of Jahangir: thoughtful and psychologically penetrating, it strips away the glitter and glamour of the Mughal court to reveal a deftly sketched portrait of Jahangir the man, in all his hedonism, inquisitiveness, refinement and intelligence.'
William Dalrymple

'A fascinating book, it not only retells the story of Jahangir with an objective eye to detail and characterization, but also tells us what the Mughal world was like in early seventeenth century India. Well written and properly researched, it is also a timely book: it recalls an India which – contrary to popular and false belief – was religiously tolerant, reasonably open and pluralistic. It was an India vibrant and opulent, the object of envy for the foreigner, be they Central Asian or Firangi. The important role of wise women in governance during Mughal times is especially brought home to the reader with great force.'
Shamsur Rahman Faruqi

'Rich in detail and narrated with great flair, *Jahangir* offers a vivid portrait of a fascinating man and emperor, bringing alive the inner workings of the Mughal court and their unforgettable world of splendour.'
Manu S. Pillai

Jahangir

An Intimate Portrait of a
Great Mughal

Parvati Sharma

Dear Mayur,

I hope very much that you'll
like this,

with much love,

Paro
nov/2018

❋ juggernaut

JUGGERNAUT BOOKS
KS House, 118 Shahpur Jat, New Delhi 110049, India

First published by Juggernaut Books 2018

10 9 8 7 6 5 4 3 2 1

ISBN 9789386228918

Typeset in Adobe Caslon Pro by R. Ajith Kumar, New Delhi

Printed at Manipal Technologies Limited

For Aftab Uncle
with love

Cast of Characters

Nuruddin Muhammad Jahangir: Fourth Mughal emperor, known as Prince Salim before his accession.

Jalaluddin Muhammad Akbar: Salim's father. Third Mughal emperor, usually considered the greatest of the dynasty.

Mariam-uz-Zamani ('Mary of the ages'): Salim's mother. Sometimes called Jodha Bai. Daughter of Raja Bihari Mal Kachhwaha of Amer (later Jaipur), sister of Raja Bhagwan Das Kachhwaha and aunt of Raja Man Singh.

Mirza* Murad: Salim's middle half-brother and Akbar's second son.

Mirza Daniyal: Salim's youngest half-brother. Akbar's third and youngest son.

Hamida Banu Begum (titled Maryam Makani, 'one who lives with Mary'): Salim's grandmother, Akbar's mother and wife of the second Mughal emperor, Humayun.

Gulbadan Begum: Daughter of Babur, the founder of the

Mughal dynasty. Half-sister of Humayun and author of the *Humayun-nama*.

Ruqaiya Sultan Begum: Akbar's cousin and first wife. Adoptive mother of Khurram.

Salima Sultan Begum: Daughter of Humayun's half-sister Gulrukh Begum. Wife and then widow of Humayun's general and Akbar's regent, Bairam Khan. Akbar's cousin and later his wife.

Man Bai (titled Shah Begum, 'king lady'): Salim's first wife and Khusro's mother. Daughter of Raja Bhagwan Das and sister of Raja Man Singh.

Jagat Gosain or Jodh Bai (titled Bilquis Makani, 'lady of paradise'): Salim's wife and Khurram's mother. Daughter of Raja Udai Singh (the Mota Raja, 'fat king') of Jodhpur.

Mihrunnisa (titled Nurmahal, 'light of the palace', and Nurjahan, 'light of the world'): Salim's favourite wife. Daughter of Ghiyas Beg and Asmat Begum.

Khusro: Salim's first son, born to Man Bai.

Parvez: Salim's second son, born to Sahib Jamal, 'mistress of beauty'.

Khurram: Salim's third son, born to Jagat Gosain and adopted by Ruqaiya Sultan Begum.

Shahryar: The more prominent of Salim's two youngest sons (the other being Jahandar, born in the same month). Husband of Mihrunnisa's daughter (and only child), Ladli Begum.

Mirza Muhammad Hakim: Akbar's half-brother.

Ghiyas Beg (titled I'timaduddawla, 'pillar of the realm'): Salim's father-in-law and father of Mihrunnisa. One of Salim's most trusted and high-ranking ministers.

Abu'l Hasan (titled I'tiqad Khan and Asaf Khan): Mihrunnisa's brother, son of Ghiyas Beg. Arjumand Begum's father and therefore Khurram's father-in-law.

Arjumand Banu Begum (titled Mumtaz Mahal, 'jewel of the palace'): Daughter of Abu'l Hasan, niece of Mihrunnisa. Khurram's favourite wife and mother of Dara Shikoh, Shah Shuja, Aurangzeb and Murad Baksh.

Mirza Aziz Koka** (titled khan azam, 'greatest khan'): Akbar's foster brother and Khusro's father-in-law.

Raja Man Singh: Salim's brother-in-law and Khusro's uncle. Son of Raja Bhagwan Das Kachhwaha. Governor of Bengal and king of Amer.

Mirza Abdur Rahim (titled khan khanan, 'khan of all the khans'): Salim's tutor and his long-term commander in the Deccan. Son of Bairam Khan and brother-in-law of Mirza Aziz Koka. Daniyal's father-in-law and Khurram's grandfather-in-law. Also related to Abu'l Hasan through a granddaughter married to Abu'l Hasan's son.

Sheikh Abu'l Fazl: A loved and trusted friend, adviser and disciple of Akbar's and principal chronicler of his reign. Author of the *Akbarnama*, Akbar's biography, and the *Ain-i-Akbari*, a history of his administration.

Abd'ul-Qadir Badauni: A member of Akbar's court, principally employed as a historian and translator. Author of *Muntakhab-ut-Tawarikh* (Selections from Histories).

Mu'tamad Khan: An officer in the imperial army and later Salim's 'secretary'. Wrote the last few entries of the *Jahangirnama*, from early 1623 to about mid-1624. Author of the *Iqbalnama*, which includes a history of Salim's reign.

Sir Thomas Roe: The first English ambassador to India. Represented King James I in Salim's court. His diary and letters from that time make up *The Embassy of Sir Thomas Roe to the Court of the Great Mogul, 1615–1619, As Narrated in His Journal and Correspondence.*

Sheikh Salim Chishti: Sufi saint of the Chishti order. Born in Delhi and spent many years studying abroad. Settled in Sikri on his return, where he foretold the birth of Akbar's three sons.

Qutbuddin Muhammad Khan: Son-in-law of Sheikh Salim Chishti and tutor to Salim. Husband of Salim's beloved foster mother and father of Khubu.

Sheikh Khubu (titled Qutbuddin Khan Koka): Grandson of Sheikh Salim Chishti. Salim's best friend.

Sheikh Ala'uddin (titled Islam Khan): Grandson of Sheikh Salim Chishti. Salim's childhood friend and his most successful governor in Bengal.

Bir Singh Deo Bundela (titled maharaja): King of Orccha and loyal friend and ally to Salim before and during his reign.

Khwaja Abdullah Khan Bahadur (titled Firoz Jang): Salim's friend and part of his rebel court.

Zamana Beg (titled Mahabat Khan, briefly khan khanan, and sometimes referred to as Madarussalatana, 'axis of the sultanate'): Salim's childhood friend and part of his rebel court.

Ali Quli Istajlu (titled Sher Afgan, 'lion-thrower'): Mihrunnisa's first husband and part of Salim's rebel court.

Rana Amar Singh: Son of Maharana Pratap, ruler of Mewar, the last Rajput kingdom to surrender to Mughal rule.

Kunwar (later Rana) Karan Singh: Son of Rana Amar Singh. Prince and then ruler of Mewar.

Kunwar Bhim (titled raja): Son of Rana Amar Singh. Part of Khurram's rebellion.

Sundar Das (titled Raja Bikramjit): First distinguished himself in Khurram's Mewar campaign and became one of his most trusted generals and advisers. Part of Khurram's rebellion.

Malik Ambar: Ethiopian soldier, general and regent in the kingdom of Ahmednagar. The Mughals' strongest foe in the Deccan.

Mirza: prince or nobleman of high rank
**Koka: a term for foster brother*

Contents

The Mughal Empire c. 1605

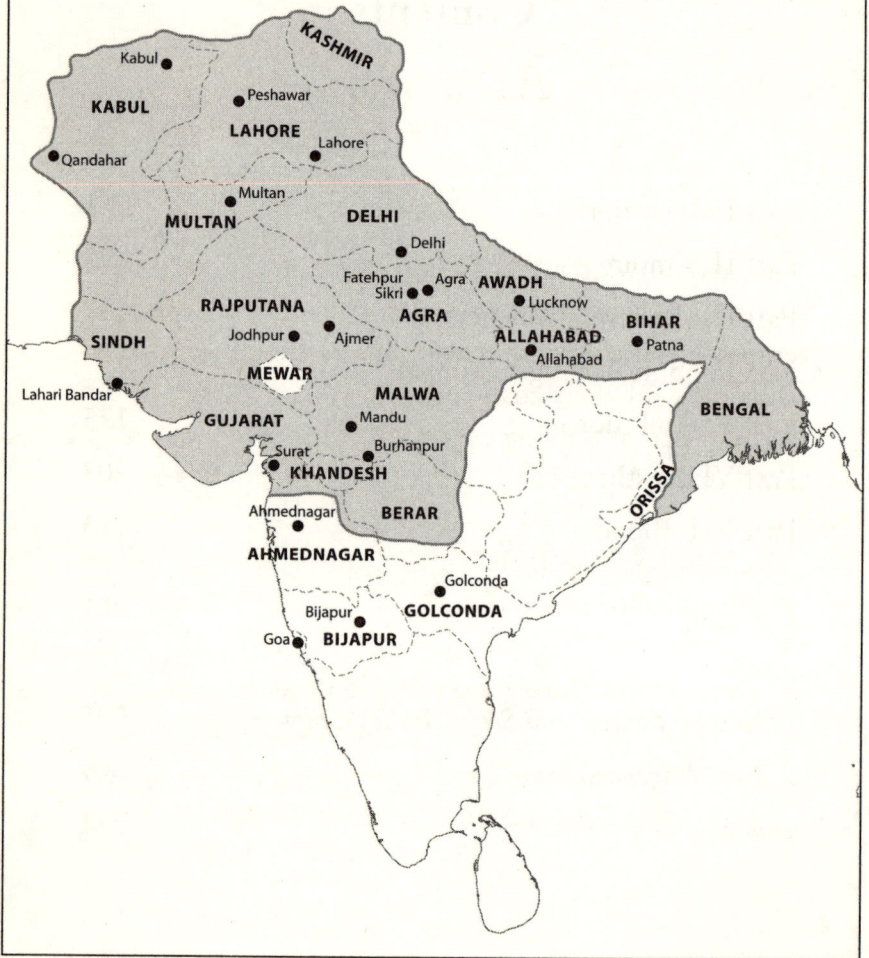

Kabul

KABUL

Peshawar

LAHORE

KASHMIR

Qandahar

Lahore

Multan

MULTAN

DELHI

Delhi

Fatehpur
Sikri   Agra

AWADH

RAJPUTANA

AGRA

Lucknow

Jodhpur   Ajmer

ALLAHABAD

BIHAR

SINDH

MEWAR

Allahabad

Patna

Lahari Bandar

GUJARAT

MALWA

Mandu

BENGAL

Surat

Burhanpur

KHANDESH

ORISSA

Ahmednagar

BERAR

AHMEDNAGAR

Golconda

GOLCONDA

Bijapur

Goa   BIJAPUR

Part I

Accession

One day in winter, Akbar, Salim and Raja Birbal went hunting. As the sun rose and the day grew warm, the emperor and the prince began to feel uncomfortable, so they took off their coats and gave them to Birbal. The sight of Birbal walking with two such heavy coats in his arms made Akbar laugh. 'That looks like an ass's load!'

'No, Your Majesty,' Birbal replied, quick of tongue, 'more like the load of two asses!'

An eighteenth-century Akbar–Birbal joke,
one of the oldest in this tradition.
Adapted from 'Popular Jokes and Political History:
The Case of Akbar, Birbal and Mullah Do-Piyaza'
by C.M. Naim

Every story of Salim begins with his father, even Salim's. 'Until my father was twenty-eight years old,' he writes in the second sentence of his autobiography, 'none of his children had survived'.[1]

His father was Akbar; and to Salim's eternal joy and torment, Akbar was one of those rare historical figures that transcend the norm so much as to gain a suffix – in his case, 'The Great'. Akbar's ambitions and achievements were tremendous; his charisma shines through any record of his reign. His eyes, says one European writer,[2] flashed bright with the light of sunbeams upon the sea. He tamed musth elephants as if for fun. His empire, following one triumph after the other, grew so large and so rich it might have toppled the balance of the globe. By the end of his reign, while it wasn't clear if Akbar believed in any kind of god, there were people (Akbar possibly included) willing to believe that Akbar himself was divine.

At twenty-eight, though, all he wanted was a child. And yet this commonplace achievement, this thing that is the course of things, he could not have. A man who had been given the world without asking, if such a man were to plead for a child, what would he not beget? Abu'l Fazl, Akbar's dedicated biographer, close friend and (depending upon one's point of view) toady-in-chief, could hardly imagine 'what sort of glorious pearl' would appear if Akbar actually asked for a boon.

Even God seemed daunted by the task at hand. 'My father,' Salim continues, 'was always soliciting dervishes and hermits', but nothing came of it. He went to holy men and he prayed, and he asked holy men to pray for him. He made a vow to his most beloved saint, Khwaja Moinuddin Chishti: *Give me a son and I will walk from Agra to Ajmer and offer you my gratitude at your holy shrine.*

Finally, one day, God relented. Some courtiers came to Akbar and told him about a venerable old sage whose austerity and spiritual power the people spoke of with awe. He, too, was of the Chishti order, he lived on a hill not far from Agra, and his name was Salim.

Akbar began visiting Sheikh Salim Chishti regularly, to pray and ask for prayers, and one day, when the sheikh was in a trance, Akbar couldn't help himself and he blurted out, 'How many sons will I have?'[3]

Perhaps he thought it better to hear a brutal truth – 'never, none' – than to suffer an eternal wait. Or perhaps, this being Akbar, the king of kings after all, he thought that by asking the question this way – 'how many', not 'will I' – he would grab the reins of fate into his own hands.

At any rate, the sheikh didn't hesitate: 'God will give you three sons,' he said.

'Then the first shall be yours, to protect and guide.'

Not lacking in reciprocity, the sheikh replied, 'Bless him. I give him my name.'

When Akbar's nameless Rajput wife – eldest daughter of Raja Bihari Mal Kachhwaha of Amer,[4] called Jodha Bai (incorrectly) and Mary of the ages, Mariam-uz-Zamani (formally), whom Akbar had married seven long years ago in the manner of kings, en route from a hunt – became pregnant, he took her to live in the sheikh's home. Partly, of course, this was so that the queen and her unborn child might be as close as possible to the sheikh's protective blessings; but partly, also, it was to keep the pregnancy far from gossiping streets and stem the tide of 'curious stories'[5] that had begun to dog the emperor's childlessness.

So it was that the Rajput queen of a Mughal monarch moved from the royal fortress of Agra into the hillside home of a Sufi saint. These new arrangements were not, as one can imagine, without their challenges. A bit of gossip from the time suggests that the sheikh's daughters-in-law were particularly unhappy by the sudden – and seemingly constant – presence of an anxious emperor in their midst. When the sheikh's sons and nephews brought up the marital strife they were having to endure at the hands of their flustered wives, they received little redress. After all, now that Akbar's own wife was lodged in his zenana, the sheikh could hardly deny the emperor access to it; and Akbar himself just laughed off their complaints. 'There is no dearth of women in the world . . . seek other wives!'[6]

The exigencies of propriety would not stand between the emperor and his heir, nor would the dark designs of fate. One day, the baby stopped kicking. At first, perhaps, the queen felt only a nagging strangeness, a sense of something missing; then, as it dawned on her, her mind fell numb and her body shivered under its skin; she could not speak and she clutched for her nurses. 'In a dither,' writes Salim, 'the nurses reported the situation to His Majesty.'

What could Akbar do? He'd promised a pilgrimage to Ajmer, he'd submitted to the protection of the sheikh, why now this final test? Perhaps he was meant to give something up, something he loved for something he craved – perhaps it was a sacrifice that was demanded of him.

Like most royals, Akbar loved to hunt, and the kind of hunting he loved most was that rare and spectacular sport of hunting with cheetahs.[7] Cheetahs, tame and trained, were among the jewels of Akbar's menagerie, riding in stately array into hunts, sitting straight-backed and alert upon carts from which they would spring after their prey when released, padding softly within striking distance to make their final, lethal leap. Much like their emperor, they rarely missed.

What did it matter now, though, the thrill of the hunt? This was time for new life, not death! As it happened, the day was a Friday, and Akbar vowed that if only his baby would move again, never again on a Friday would he hunt with cheetahs.

And never again he did: mid-morning on a Wednesday, in the monsoon of 1569, Akbar's nameless queen delivered the boy who would, one day, sit on Akbar's throne; half-Mughal, half-Rajput, they named him Salim – intact, unblemished and whole.

Reading the various accounts of Salim's birth, one gets the impression that Akbar brought it about by sheer force of will, his prayers and vows hammering at God's door like cannonballs at a fortress until there was nothing for it but to give him the son he demanded. And yes, Akbar was a man of strong will – he kept all the vows he made – but his hardest resolve was probably made after Salim was born. In deference to a popular idea that it was unlucky for fathers to meet their newborn children, Akbar did not gallop to Sikri as he must have longed to.

Instead, since there is only so much self-control a joyful father can have, celebrations burst upon Agra like lightning upon a rain-ripe sky. 'Heaps and heaps of gold were scattered,' says one writer.[8] Prisoners in dungeons across the empire were set free. For days, poets composed odes to the prince, the most stylish of which was by Khwaja Hussain Haravi – each couplet of his poem had a chronogram[9] for Akbar's accession as its first line and for Salim's birth as its second, thus beginning: 'God be praised for the glory of the king / A splendid pearl came ashore from the ocean of justice.'

'Pearl' was the favoured metaphor for Salim; in various other chronograms, he was 'a royal pearl of the great ocean', 'a pearl of the Shahenshah's mansion', 'a pearl of Akbar Shah's coffer' – each yielding the year of his birth. Not to be outdone, Abu'l Fazl titled this breathless chapter of the *Akbarnama* 'The auspicious birth of the world-illuminating pearl of the mansion of dominion and fortune, the night-gleaming jewel of the casket of greatness and glory, namely, of Prince Sultan Salim'.

Akbar's mother, Hamida Banu Begum, brought a bit of diversity to the affair by giving the newborn a magnificent ruby of 190 carats, no less. Akbar wore it in his turban while he ruled, then Salim, until it became almost a symbol of succession and, as Salim would describe it years later, a 'good luck charm' for the dynasty.

At the time of its giving, of course, what it symbolized was that without Salim there would be no dynasty. Not only had the emperor had his first child, he'd had a boy; and it was no wonder that Akbar 'issued a proclamation for enjoyment / invited the world as his guest'[10] for a celebration at which no expression of delight could possibly be too much.

Once under way, the sheikh's prophecy did not take long to come true: both Salim's younger brothers, Murad and Daniyal, were born within the next three years, though neither of them was greeted with such unbridled joy. It is apparent from Abu'l Fazl's chapter titles: 'The auspicious birth of Prince Shah Murad' he announces tersely for one, while Daniyal, the youngest, is merely the 'nosegay of fortune's Spring'.

Salim was special from the day he was conceived; and in his life, or so Abu'l Fazl hoped, Salim would be 'fortunate by pleasing His Majesty, which is a sign of pleasing God'.

Meanwhile the infant Salim, unaware as yet of all the hopes that rested on his newly breathing soul, slept and suckled, slept and suckled, nestled in the arms of his wet nurse, the sheikh's own daughter, watched over by the sheikh and his family, to whom he would be forever tied, not only by the binds of the life he'd been given, but also by the death he would bring.

The first casualty was the sheikh himself. A venerable ninety years old when Akbar first went to him, the sheikh was not, presumably, long for this world. Still, for some reason, one day Akbar asked him for his exact age and how long he would live.[11] At first, the sheikh evaded a reply: 'God – exalted be he – knows all mysteries and hidden things.' But Akbar was nothing if not persistent and the sheikh complied. It was hardly the reply Akbar would have wanted. Pointing at the infant Salim – was he, perhaps, in Akbar's lap? – the sheikh said, 'When the prince, either by instruction of a teacher or someone else, memorises something and speaks it aloud, this will be the sign of our demise.'

For a while, like a cursed prince in a fairy tale, Salim was kept from learning anything at all by heart. The prophecy was hardly likely, however, to take effect while its carrier was a baby; and inevitably, as Salim puts it, 'two years and seven months passed'. One day, Salim was alone in the harem when a waiting woman walked by. She was carrying wild rue, a flower that when dried and burnt is said to drive away evil spirits.[12] It was her habit to burn some of this incense in the prince's quarters every day, to keep him safe.

Finding the toddler all alone, she began to play and recite him some rhymes. In the process, she taught him the first line of a Persian romance, *Yusuf and Zulaikha*: 'Unfold, O God, the bud of hope; disclose / From thine eternal Paradise one rose'.[13]

Later that day, Salim, toddling innocently up to his tutor, spilled out his new-found learning. The tutor, writes Salim, 'leapt up from his place and ran to His Majesty' – while in Sikri, the inevitable happened. The sheikh caught a fever. He sent word the next day, asking if Tansen might be sent to sing to him, hoping, perhaps, that the great singer's melody would soothe the pain of his final illness, or knowing, perhaps, that he would miss that legendary voice in paradise. Having heard, one last time, Tansen's music fill the air of Sikri, the sheikh asked for Akbar.

When the emperor arrived, the sheikh had only one, final message for him. 'Farewell,' he said, and taking the turban from his own head, he placed it on Salim's. 'We have made Sultan Salim our successor and entrust him to God.'

The fever lingered; or maybe it was the tension of the sheikh's illness and Salim's own part in it that made it seem so. At any rate, the adult Salim remembers that it was 'a very, very long time' before the sheikh took one last shuddering breath of the world, and died.

Salim doesn't say who the tutor was, the one who leaped in alarm at the child prince's fateful recitation. The sheikh died sometime in 1572, when Salim couldn't have been older than three, and the custom then was to begin a boy's education when he was exactly four years, four months and four days old. Perhaps some kind of informal guardianship had been assigned. At any rate, the beginning of Salim's formal learning was an elaborate affair: amidst much feasting and celebration, the newly appointed teacher would have 'taken' Salim, literally raised him upon his shoulders in a symbolic and customary gesture. This first teacher was well into his seventies however, and his shoulders did not bear the prince very long: he barely had time to teach Salim the alphabet before he died.

Thereafter, Salim had two guardians, or ataliqs: Qutbuddin Muhammad Khan, husband of Salim's foster mother[14] and father of his best friend, Khubu; and Abdur Rahim, literary, military and diplomatic genius, who would rise to be the khan of all the khans, the khan khanan. Of course, there would have been other teachers, too, appointed for specific subjects. Salim remembers, for example, learning religion from Sheikh Abdun Nabi and fencing from a lord of the Deccan (whom an adult Salim would title Warzish 'Exercise' Khan); not to mention the extracurricular lessons he derived, like many children of privilege, from the staff – most notably, drinking from a 'wonderful gunner'[15] called Ustad Shah-Quli.

Of all his teachers, though, the one who watched him with the keenest eye was his own father. 'The wise sovereign,' writes Abu'l Fazl, 'kept his children under his own care' and Salim was therefore 'constantly acquiring various outward and inward excellences in the society of His Majesty', learning 'the rules of justice . . . the secrets of the spirit and . . . the wondrous clarifications of the heart'.

When Salim was five, Akbar took the boy along with him when he sailed down the Yamuna to quell a rebellion in Patna. It was as much a pleasure cruise as a mission of chastisement, a whole parade of boats sailing in majestic convoy, manned by sailors who could make 'the birds of the air and the fish of the water . . . dance'.[16] Often, the emperor disembarked to hunt; at night, when the ships cast anchor, there was discussion and debate and music. On the way, they even had time to stop in Allahabad, where Akbar inaugurated the building of the great fort that still stands in that city.

Not long after, when Salim was about eight or nine years old, Akbar spoke glowingly of his 'obedience, good disposition, prudence, and endurance'[17] and gave him a military rank of 10,000 zat and 10,000 suwar.[18] Given that Akbar himself became king at fourteen, putting pre-pubescent princes in charge of armies was hardly out of place; instead, in the obscure but troubled history of Akbar and Salim, what stands out is that bit of praise. Never again would Akbar express such kind thoughts about his eldest son with such abandon.

For the moment, however, this 'nursling of dominion', as Abu'l Fazl calls him, held the highest rank in Akbar's court; no amir at the time was ranked higher than 5000 zat, and the two younger princes, Murad and Daniyal, were ranked at 7000 and 6000 respectively. About three years later, when Salim was thirteen or so and Murad was twelve, the two boys were told to lead men, not just command them, and put in nominal charge of subduing a rebellion in Kabul.

It is in Abu'l Fazl's account of this campaign that one first gets a sense that something between Akbar and Salim was beginning to slip.

For one thing, it was Murad who went galloping off with the advance forces, while Akbar and Salim followed at a more stately pace. Suddenly, news arrived of a change of plan by the Kabul rebel Mirza Muhammad Hakim (who was, incidentally, Akbar's relatively unknown and undistinguished half-brother). Mirza Hakim had decided to attack the imperial forces, knowing they were led by a boy and the main army was far behind. At this, naturally, Akbar went dashing forth, but before he could quite reach, Mirza Hakim attacked – and Murad retaliated.

The battle was short and victorious and for Murad clearly a triumph. 'In spite of his youth,' writes Abu'l Fazl, '[he] showed such courage and steadfastness that veterans remembered his firmness and his exertions.'

Akbar and Murad took a moment to visit the great sights of Kabul, pay their respects at Babur's grave and admire his gardens, the proud father no doubt telling Murad stirring tales of ancestral valour. Back in the main camp, meanwhile, 'babblers' were spreading all kinds of rumours about the recent battle, suggesting that Mirza Hakim had led Akbar on a wild and dangerous chase northwards. The amirs were debating whether to hurry after them or wait for word, when Akbar and Murad rode in, the dust flying off their triumphant hooves.

The camp was greatly relieved. Salim, for his part, 'placed his head on [Akbar's] blessed feet and paid his respects' while 'the chaste ladies were filled with joy'. The family was thus reunited, yet there emerges a sense of Salim having moved a fraction to the edge of it, and Murad a little closer to its heart. It's the kind of shifting of positions that happens between siblings routinely and, as anyone who's experienced the slightest dysfunction of family knows, its consequences can be unpredictable – far more so when the siblings aren't merely vying for parental favour, but for an empire.

Was Akbar beginning to feel that his eldest son, the pearl of his fortune, lacked a flair for battle?[19] It was around this time that Salim was put under the charge of Abdur Rahim, son of the great general Bairam Khan who watched over Akbar while he was a teenage king. Abdur Rahim's own military prowess was becoming increasingly evident, as also his political intelligence, and perhaps Akbar thought he would instil some lust for the clash and clang of conquest, some love for the daily grind of rule, in Salim.

The emperor's second line of attack at engendering a sense of responsibility in his sons was to give them chores. It may not be right to read too much into this division of labour but given how Salim grew into a man defined by his delight in beauty and pleasure, it does seem fitting that his father put him in charge of marriage and birthday celebrations.[20] Murad got household management, which,

says Abu'l Fazl, leaving much between the lines, 'is equal
to the administration of a great kingdom'. And the theory
that Daniyal the youngest was Akbar's favourite finds
some support in the fact that he got religious affairs, a
subject close to the metaphysically inclined emperor's
heart.

Finally, like South Asian parents across the ages, Akbar
thought Salim might grow up once he was married. Or, as
Abu'l Fazl puts it, 'it occurred to the holy heart [Akbar]
that he ought to bring a jewel of chastity into the grasp
of that star of the mansion of sovereignty – Prince Sultan
Salim – so that by this present there might be a fresh
illumination of the hall of fortune'.

The bride, like Salim's mother, was a princess of Amer –
in fact, she was his cousin – and the marriage was fittingly
multicultural and extravagant. Among those present was
a man called Abd'ul-Qadir Badauni, a fellow courtier of
Abu'l Fazl's, and also his antithesis, rival and, if he could
only will it, nemesis. While Abu'l Fazl was devoted to
the emperor, even to his increasingly radical experiments
with religion, Badauni regarded Akbar as eccentric at best
and often as dangerously heretical. Abu'l Fazl wrote a
glowing hagiographic account of Akbar's reign; Badauni
maintained a secret diary, published long after Akbar's
death, in which he kept a detailed account of all the
injustices and blasphemies he believed the emperor was
inflicting on his long-suffering Muslim clergy.

Even Badauni, however, was impressed by the sheer
opulence of Salim's first wedding.

In the winter of 1584, when Salim was fifteen, Akbar,
Salim and the prominent nobility of the court arrived

in the realm of Raja Bhagwan[21] Das for his daughter, Man Bai. The marriage was conducted by both qazis and pandits and Badauni notes that it featured 'all the ceremonies which are customary among the Hindus, such as lighting the fire'. As is also customary among Hindus, the groom received a dowry: 'strings of horses, and a hundred elephants, and boys and girls of Abyssinia, India and Circassia, and all sorts of golden vessels set with jewels, and jewels, and utensils of gold, and vessels of silver, and all sorts of stuffs, the quantity of which is beyond all computation'; and as is customary among Muslims, the bride received a mahr (in this case, two crore rupees). And, as was customary amongst rulers, the celebration was also an occasion for giving gifts and alms. All the nobles in the baraat received horses with golden saddles; the bride's departing litter was showered with gold all the way from her father's to her husband's home. 'From the quantity of jewels and gold that were scattered,' writes Badauni, 'people's hands were weary of picking them up.'

It was during this wedding that news arrived of an imperial victory in one of the not-quite-subdued provinces, a happy coincidence that may have made Akbar imagine that, yes, marriage might well spell a new chapter in Salim's life, one that would give his father the confidence and pride of having produced a worthy heir.

Like South Asian parents across the ages, however, what Akbar didn't realize was that while the entrapments of marriage are powerful, they cannot match the enthralments of true love.

Much has been made of Salim's torrid and entirely fictional love affair with Anarkali. The most popular – and arguably most beautiful – version of this story is K. Asif's 1960 magnum opus, *Mughal-e-Azam*. Here, Anarkali is a dancing girl with whom Salim falls in love, much to his father's disappointment, disapproval and eventual fury. When the young couple will not forsake each other (*'Pyaar kiya toh darna kya'*, sings Anarkali, When you have loved, what then do you fear!), Akbar has Anarkali imprisoned and then bricked alive (though in a twist at the end, the emperor's sense of fair play overcomes his class prejudice and he allows Anarkali to escape on the condition that she leave the court forever). The story's origins are less romantic and far more salacious: they lie in the diary of William Finch who visited the tomb of 'Immacque Kelle' in Lahore sometime between 1608 and 1611 and described her as Akbar's wife and Daniyal's mother with whom 'Shah Selim had to do'. The tomb of Anarkali still stands in Lahore, but it is the only part of this tale with any solid foundation.

One way or another, the forbidden woman makes for a good story, but one can argue with far greater historical accuracy that Salim's true romance, his lifelong passion wasn't Anarkali, but alcohol.

Salim had his first drink at the age emblematic of young love, eighteen, and he tells the story with fitting nostalgia (and neglects, incidentally, to relate how his first son,[22] Khusro, was born this year, too). Ironically enough, it happened during a campaign: while the rest of Akbar's army was busy besieging a fortress in Attock,[23] trying to bring down some troublesome Afghans, the prince rode off on a hunt. At the end of a long day, that wonderful gunner Ustad Shah-Quli suggested wine might relieve Salim's exhaustion. 'Since I was young and inclined to do these things,' Salim remembers, 'I ordered Mahmud the water-carrier to go to Hakim Ali's house and bring some alcoholic syrup. The physician sent a phial and a half [about 120 ml] of yellow-coloured, sweet-tasting wine in a small bottle. I drank it and I liked the feeling I got.'

'Liked' is not the word for it: in nine years, by his own meticulous measure, Salim had progressed from these two gulps of sweet wine to 'twenty phials of double-distilled spirits, fourteen during the day and rest at night.' To clarify, he goes on, that is 'six Hindustani seers, which is equivalent to one-and-a-half Iranian maunds'.

These are the kinds of statistics that don't really need translation. Whatever the measure, Salim was obviously drinking too much, and given the dizzyingly steep gradient of his addiction it's very unlikely that Akbar didn't notice. Maybe he even expected it. The Mughals were no strangers to alcoholism. Not just Salim, both his younger brothers, too, would drink excessively. The famous story of their great-grandfather Babur breaking all his wine cups in order to induce in his reluctant Central Asian amirs a righteous urge to rule the infidel – and dusty – plains of Hindustan is incomplete without the coda that he regretted it deeply, even composing a wry little rhyme on the matter: 'While others repent and make vow to abstain / I have vowed to abstain and repentant am I.'[24] However, in Babur's case, as also in Akbar's, the urge to drink was accompanied by an equally strong ambition to thrive. Or perhaps it was the other way around: Babur and Akbar both became kings when they were little more than children, twelve and fourteen; they knew what it was to have a precarious grip on power. And they would know that wine, while it might soothe their souls, could easily wreck their hard-earned fortunes. At every lovely sip they would have been wary of seeing their gains dissolve in their cups.

Not so the fourth-generation Mughal princes. Brought up with every luxury and comfort, all Salim had to do to helm an empire was wait – and what better way to pass the time than with a jug or six of wine?

It may be that when Akbar noticed his son's growing addiction, he looked for an equal and counterbalancing increase in, say, his administrative zeal; but, just as Salim loved to hunt but not to battle, so he seemed to prefer the high of drink to the intoxication of rule. Or it may be that Akbar, like highly successful parents across time, was impatient for his son, the pearl he had laboured to bring to the world, to match him – and disappointed when he wouldn't.

Whatever it was that Akbar was thinking and feeling, a kind of inchoate resentment began to corrupt the relationship between father and son during these years, and it first erupted (as such resentments often do) in the course of a family holiday.

Having conquered Kashmir a few years ago, Akbar was keen to spend some time enjoying its delights. Accordingly, in April or May of 1589, Akbar set off for the valley with his sons, his nobles and the ladies of the court. Three thousand stonecutters and two thousand diggers were sent ahead to level the road, but it was difficult terrain even so, and when they reached Bhimber pass, where the climb from Punjab into Kashmir begins, Akbar decided to leave the main camp (and the ladies) in Murad's care, and to ride ahead with Salim and a few amirs.

When they had travelled some days ('few were able to keep up with His Majesty,' writes Abu'l Fazl) it became clear that it would be difficult for the whole imperial entourage to travel through these narrow, snowed up roads. Akbar sent Salim back to Bhimber, with instructions to escort only a few of the women as well as Salim's young son, Khusro, to the Kashmir valley, and leave the main camp in Murad's charge. The emperor himself marched on with 'fellow-travellers' even if they were, according to Abu'l Fazl (himself amongst them), 'much frightened'. Fear was not an emotion Akbar understood or encouraged, however; he was even somewhat reproving when some of his hapless retinue bought themselves snow shoes made of woven straw.

Crossing the Pir Panjal, traversing narrow ledges at over 11,000 feet, was particularly precarious. 'Shall I describe the severity of the cold?' asks Abu'l Fazl. 'Or shall I tell of the depth of the snow, and of the bewilderment of the natives of India? Or shall I describe the height of the pass, or speak of the narrowness of the path, or of the heights and hollows of this stage? Or' – and you can hear a sigh as deep as the wind blowing upon the slopes – 'shall I write of the fountains, the trees, the flowers?'

They had just managed to travel one stage when it began to snow. Stragglers either 'showed foresight and turned back' or hurried ahead and 'lost their lives on account of the snow and rain'. Even Akbar admitted this wasn't the easiest of journeys and ordered that 'tents, fuel, forage and food should be in readiness' at every stage of the way so that the ladies following behind might travel in comfort.

Somehow, with chattering teeth and muttered prayers, the emperor's men followed their unstoppable leader along the mountain pass until their wet feet and numbed bones were finally rewarded, as 'a new paradise withdrew the veil from her countenance'.[25] Delighted with the 'groves, the blossoming flowers, the glorious air, the melody of the waterfalls', Akbar sent Abdur Rahim (Salim's former ataliq, and now the khan khanan[26]) back through the pass to help Salim bring along the ladies.

Meanwhile, Kashmir showered Akbar with its charms; the cream of Kashmiri society, musicians, craftsmen, scholars, ascetics came from Srinagar to pay their respects; the beauty of the landscape increased by the day; there could not have been a more contented, happy scene.

And then.

'A cloud settled on the face of joy,' writes Abu'l Fazl in dismay. As the beauty of art and nature blossomed around him, Akbar grew ever more eager to share Kashmir with his women and his grandson, his eye on the horizon, watching for the family retinue to ride into view. Instead, what he saw was Prince Salim, all alone. The road, it seems, was too difficult; Salim had only brought the ladies a short distance before abandoning the idea, leaving them in Nowshera, barely two stages from Bhimber, and here he was, ready to present his report.

The furious emperor didn't allow his son into his sight. Instead, he shouted at Abdur Rahim: 'If the prince, owing to his evil propensities, behaved in this way, why did you allow him to exhibit such audacity?'

Even Abu'l Fazl thought Akbar was overreacting. The next morning, having fed all night on anger, Akbar called for his horse and a few men. He would go and bring the ladies himself! It was raining, the road was treacherous and slippery, but who would tell Akbar? Abu'l Fazl, left in charge of the emperor's camp, was losing his mind. When he declares that it was only through 'God's help [that] the ebullition of my disposition did not prevail over my reason and discretion' one can imagine the harassed historian trying to contain his frustration at Akbar's obduracy. It made no sense. Why 'should the Shahenshah of the Universe become so angry'? Why would he not 'accept the truthful speaking of his loyal servants'?

Somehow, at the base of the Pir Panjal, they managed to stop Akbar. Having ridden out his fury all day, he returned to camp. Abdur Rahim was sent off to the ladies, knowing better, this time, than to return without them.

Salim locked himself in his tent, neither eating nor sleeping.

In his autobiography, Salim describes his father as one might a mythical hero. His 'countenance was radiant'. He had 'the build of a lion'. He had a beautiful mole on his left nostril, a sign of 'great good fortune'. 'A divine aura' clung to him. He mentions also how his father had a 'very loud' voice, and while he adds that Akbar had a 'particularly nice way of speaking' one can imagine the slight tremors a lion-built father's loud voice might cause as it boomed through the harem where his children played.

But now, in Kashmir, Salim was twenty years old, just a couple of years younger than his grandfather Humayun when Humayun became king. Salim, meanwhile, had only made what might have been his first public decision as a grown man and he had been publicly humiliated for it. If – pacing the four corners of his tent, his father's loud voice echoing in his ears, and tears perhaps burning at his eyes – if, now, Salim hankered for a drink, one could hardly blame him.

Still, even if Salim lacked his father's flaming resolve, he did possess a kind of dogged determination, a stubborn refusal to bow out of the race. This would be evident when, years later, realizing that drink was killing him, he chipped away at his addiction and brought it down to manageable size. And it was evident now, in the days that followed Akbar's outburst.

As Akbar's rage settled and the camp resumed its march towards Srinagar, Salim began to apologize, to ask for another chance. Finally, soothed by a few days' sightseeing in Srinagar, Akbar relented. Salim charged off; the ladies were still only halfway there, with Murad and Abdur Rahim industriously repairing the road before them.

When his elder brother arrived, Murad returned to the main camp, so it was Salim who brought the women to the outskirts of Srinagar, where Akbar came to greet them with effusive pleasure.

This is how it was meant to be, and so, somehow, Salim

had made it happen. It was such piecemeal achievement of the possible that would come to define much of his life.

Another two years passed without (recorded) outbursts. Instead, there were the usual markers of time as it passes for families: marriages, births and deaths. Salim's first wife, the Rajput Man Bai, had given Salim his first daughter, Sultanunnisa, and his first son, Khusro, when Salim was in his teens. On the way back from Kashmir, Salim's second son, Parvez, was born in Kabul to another wife, named Sahib Jamal, mistress of beauty. The following year, Salim had three daughters, all by different wives, two of them on the same night, neither of whom survived; while his brothers had one child each. The year after, Akbar contracted another marriage for Salim, this one to a princess of Little Tibet,[27] but the more significant event was the birth of Salim's third son, this one to another of his Rajput wives, the daughter of Udai Singh of Jodhpur, also called the Mota (fat) Raja.

The Mota Raja's daughter was, incidentally, one of the few women in medieval history to be distinguished by her own name while she was alive, Jagat Gosain, and by a title when she died, Bilquis Makani, lady of paradise.[28] Jagat Gosain was not, however, the only mother her newborn would have. When he was born, there was equal rejoicing in the palace of Akbar's first queen, Ruqaiya Sultan Begum. Ruqaiya Begum had married Akbar in her early teens and had reached middle age without a child; she longed for an infant to raise, and her astrologer,

Gobind, had predicted that her longing would soon end and suggested that she should adopt the baby born to Jagat Gosain.

It was customary and auspicious for the Mughal emperor to name all the children born into the imperial household. Indeed, it seems to have been an imperial right to name virtually anything in the empire; as Adam named the birds and the beasts of the Garden of Eden, so Akbar, supreme lord of his lands, rechristened a particular variety of Kabul cherry 'shah-alu', king-cherry,[29] or gave the pashmina shawl the nicely alliterative name parm-narm, most-soft. So, seeing the happiness that glowed from his first wife's ageing face, the emperor gave her Jagat Gosain's newborn to raise as her own, and named him Khurram. Joy.

Another bit of what should have been just household news was that Akbar fell ill. Even conceding that a king's ill health was always a sensitive matter, kept secret from all but the most trusted men and women, and even conceding that a man like Akbar would revolt at the idea of being confined to his bed, the emperor's reaction was – as it had been in Kashmir, two years ago – bafflingly hyperbolic. He accused Salim of having poisoned him.

This was sometime in 1591, when Salim was twenty-two and Akbar was pushing fifty; and the only account of it is written in Badauni's secret diary.

Nowhere else does Badauni depict Akbar as a man subject to paranoia. Instead, he reveals an Akbar of supreme self-confidence. How else, after all, would an emperor – no matter how great his power, knowing how this horrified powerful men of Badauni's ilk – get up every dawn and worship the sun like a pagan? Badauni could hardly believe how Akbar 'devoutly turning towards the sun ... used to get hold of both ears, and turning himself quickly round about, used to strike the lower ends of his ears with his fists'. The list of outrages grew ever long. Not only the sun, he also experimented with Parsi fire worship. He wore a tilak like a Hindu. He allowed pet dogs into the harem and kept a piggery under the fort – both animals considered 'unclean' by Islam. On many days of the year, he banned any kind of animal slaughter ('many a family was ruined') and for months on end he became entirely vegetarian. Such was his antipathy to meat, in fact, that one of his many ordinances prohibited inter-dining with butchers.

These ordinances ('to recount them all would take a life-time of more than the human span,' says Badauni) reveal a mind so eclectic, an imagination so vast that it is hardly any wonder Badauni didn't know what to make of them. Sometimes, when Akbar declares 'man's reason ... as the only basis of religion', when he orders that anyone should be 'allowed to go over to any religion he pleased', that if anyone 'chose to build a church, or a synagogue, or idol-temple, or Parsi tower of silence, no one was to hinder him', it seems as if the sixteenth-century emperor were spouting the words of a twentieth-century constitution. Sometimes, when he declares that any Hindu woman who married a Muslim man must be 'taken by force from her husband, and restored to her family', that any young girl who appeared unveiled in public must set up shop in the prostitutes' quarters, he seems to be echoing the most reactionary impulses of modern fundamentalisms. Indeed, when Badauni rails against what would be called Akbar's 'Hindu appeasement' today, his words carry uncanny (not to add, ironic) echoes of the Hindutvadi discourse of twenty-first-century India: 'of Hindu infidels (who are indispensable, and of whom half the army, and country will soon consist . . .) [Akbar] could not have enough. But to other people, whatever they might ask for, he gave nothing but kicks and blows, and utterly disregarded all their devotion, and zeal, and complaisance'.

And Hindu appeasement was hardly the end of it. Not content with pronouncing new laws, Akbar announced a whole new era: the Hijri calendar was to be replaced by one that began with his accession. Then, of course, there was Din-i-Ilahi, the Divine Faith, which not even the devoted Man Singh, Salim's brother-in-law and Akbar's bravest general, could stomach. ('I am Hindu and I will convert to Islam if you say so. But no other religion do I know,' he is said to have said.) Badauni, on being told to prostrate himself before the emperor, flatly refused.

Both the new calendar and the new religion were inextricably linked to the coming of the new Islamic millennium, and the saviour of mankind, the Mahdi, who was predicted to come with it. Akbar announced the Din-i-Ilahi in 990 Hijri (1582 CE), and he was not the only Muslim ruler of that time in whom the coming millennium would produce a messianic ambition. The difference was that in Akbar's case the ambition was accompanied by what seemed like a rejection of Islam – or perhaps of any discrete religious belief.[30] As A. Azfar Moin argues in his wonderful book *The Millennial Sovereign*, Akbar combined within himself the saviours of many traditions, the Mahdi, Rama, Jesus – even the founder of his own great dynasty, Timur. The resulting controversy was not limited to the mutterings of Badauni; it was, writes Moin, 'a controversy . . . of global proportions', with the rulers of Persia and Central Asia, Portugal and Spain all keeping an eye on the would-be Mughal messiah.

Akbar's heterodoxy didn't falter; and while his opposition grew ever more disgruntled, there was little it could do. A few rebellions did arise and fail, and soon enough the resistance seems to have been reduced to wordplay. Abu'l Fazl, for example, was 'Fazlah' behind his back (a play on 'fazl', excellence, and 'fazlah', garbage). When Akbar commanded that people 'should give up the Arabic sciences, and . . . study only the really useful ones', astronomy, maths and medicine, history and literature, the underground resistance produced a disparaging chronogram: 'Decline of Learning'.

Should they dare reveal themselves to him, Akbar handled his opponents with a shrug, stints in jail or even a chuckle. There was, for example, Sheikh Abdun Nabi, one of Salim's early religious tutors. At one of Akbar's birthdays, the emperor was sprinkled with saffron, a ceremony that the puritanical sheikh found so offensive that he threw his stick at Akbar. The emperor did not react immediately, but a few days later, at Abu'l Fazl's suggestion, Akbar invited Abdun Nabi for a banquet and fed him many delicious dishes flavoured with saffron. When the sheikh had eaten his fill, Abu'l Fazl called out: 'If saffron is unlawful, why did you eat it?'[31] – at which, of course, Abdun Nabi threw his stick at Abu'l Fazl too, and no doubt the emperor and his friends spent the night doubled up with laughter. One can hear the emperor chortling through the centuries at Badauni's plight too: since the reproving scholar was employed in the royal translations department, Akbar gave him sections of the Ramayana and Mahabharata to work on. ('Such is my fate', Badauni groaned, but to his eternal credit, he completed both tasks. While the Mahabharata left him cold, Badauni seems to have almost enjoyed the Ramayana, and it says a great deal for the religious and cultural discourse of the times that a man of such conservative opinion described and understood the Ramayana as part of a larger heroic genre that included the Persian *Shahnama* and the tales of Amir Hamza.)

Still, for all the flair with which he flouted (and created) religious regulation, Akbar did live in the sixteenth century. Even today, the most irreverent agnostic might fear a final reckoning, an eternity of being proven wrong. Would Akbar not have looked for signs of being right? Besides, self-confidence doesn't imply immunity from flattery, and Akbar certainly wasn't immune. Badauni gives the example of an aged mullah who won back the emperor's favour by cooking up stories of caliphs who (like Akbar) had many wives, were clean-shaven and possessed 'many other peculiarities of the emperor', even going to the extent of making up a story about a 'Companion of the Prophet who came with shaved beard before him at which the Prophet exclaimed, "The people of Paradise will look like that!'"

Evidently, the emperor's armour was not without its chinks. Brahmins would tell him he was an incarnation of Vishnu, like Rama or Krishna. During one Shivratri, when it was Akbar's custom to eat and drink with the yogis, the ascetics told him he would live three or four times as long as a normal man. 'Fawning court doctors, wisely enough, found proofs of the longevity of the emperor,' sneers Badauni, and Akbar began to adopt all kinds of habits to increase the span of his life. Mortality, evidently, was beginning to weigh upon the emperor.

At the time of that dramatic illness, in 1591, Akbar was nearing fifty; he was older than either his father or his grandfather had ever been. Only recently, two of his closest friends and advisers, Raja Todar Mal (Akbar's finance minster and one of the 'nine jewels' of his court) and Raja Bhagwan Das (Akbar's brother-in-law and father of Salim's first wife), had died, increasing the vacuum left by Raja Birbal's and Tansen's passing some years ago.

Perhaps, then, there was some reason why an attack of colic would take disproportionate dimensions; but even so, the sheer melodrama of it beggars belief. According to Badauni, Akbar was writhing in pain and out of consciousness when he developed the notion that Salim had bribed the doctor, Hakim Humam, to kill him. 'Baba

Sheikhu ji,' he cried out in agony, using the nickname he had given Salim, 'since all this empire was to come to you, why did you make this attack on me? Why take my life so unjustly when I would give it to you willingly – if only you had asked me!'[32]

Salim's reaction was equally troubling, and he didn't even have agonizing cramps for an excuse. When it became apparent that Akbar's illness was serious, Salim ordered his men to keep their eyes on Murad; the idea being, presumably, that should their father die, the rival prince should promptly follow him to the grave.

Evidently, however, Salim's spies were slipshod; when Akbar recovered, which he did rather swiftly following his outburst, Murad and his own faction told the emperor what had happened, at which the emperor realized that he must, in Badauni's words, 'set the distance between east and west between the two brothers . . . that they might remain safe from the vain troubles of Empire' – before, that is, they killed each other. Murad was packed off with much pomp to Orchha.

Akbar's illness and its engulfing drama is a strange, almost macabre episode in the family saga. Maybe it was exaggerated gossip. Maybe it never happened at all. Certainly, Abu'l Fazl says nothing about it; nothing about Akbar's illness nor about the unpleasant intrigue. He does, however, report the news of Murad's appointment, prefacing it with a brief but suggestive discourse on Akbar's management skills. Ostensibly, Abu'l Fazl is describing the emperor's policy vis-à-vis tributary kingdoms, but might he not have been thinking, also, of Akbar's sons? 'Our sovereign lord . . . is always testing

friends and strangers, and exalting the humble. He looks
after the neighbouring rulers. If they sympathize with
mortals by administering justice, etc., no harm comes to
them, and he encourages them. Otherwise entreaties do
not prevent him from inflicting retribution. But he begins
by giving advice, and holds forth both hopes and fears.'

Was the 'exalting' of Murad an example of such hope
and fear? Watching his younger brother being granted
symbols of rule, 'a standard, a kettledrum, an umbrella and
a togh (banner)', did Salim hope for similar promotions?
Or did he fear being sent to some distant corner of the
empire and forgotten?

Could it be that his mind wandered back to Kashmir
– not the humiliation of his arrival, but a smaller incident
from just before his departure? Towards the end of his
tour of Kashmir, Akbar visited the hermitage of a well-
known ascetic called Wahid Sufi. They had a pleasant
chat, each complimenting the other on his eminence, and
Akbar was just leaving when Salim rode up. The prince
was told that he, too, must visit the hermitage and Abu'l
Fazl was told to go with him. Alone with the Sufi, Salim
dutifully asked for prayers for Akbar. 'Then,' writes Abu'l
Fazl, 'he begged his prayers for himself.' In reply, the Sufi
seems to have rebuffed the young prince, telling Salim
that he would get his due not from others' prayers but
from the lord of the world – that is, from his father.

Watching his brother being decorated and marching
off with a large army to his new fief, did Salim ask himself
when and in what way his father would ever fulfil *his*
wishes? Or did he begin to consider the possibility that,

notwithstanding the venerable Sufi, he might soon have
to grab what he desired with his own hands?

Had Salim a different temperament, history might have
taken a very different turn at this point. A prince with a
plan was never lacking for supporters, even if it was to take
on a king as formidable as Akbar. Salim was in his early
twenties, highly intelligent, certainly not lacking in bravery.
(Once, he writes, a lion[33] leaped upon the elephant he was
riding to hunt. With no time to exchange his musket for
a sword, Salim turned the gun around and hit the lion
with its butt, hard enough to throw him to the ground.)
But Salim's temperament was decidedly more indulgent
than aggressive, as one can tell from another hunting
reference in his memoirs. Describing Akbar's peerless
marksmanship with touching pride, Salim remembers his
father's legendary gun, Sangram, with which Akbar fired
the shot that won the fort of Chittor. Then, in a sweetly
oblivious boast, Salim continues: 'In marksmanship I
can be called his star pupil, for I am an avid hunter of
everything that can be hit with a gun, and I have shot
eighteen antelope in one day.' The contrast couldn't be
more stark: Akbar used his skill for the properly imperial
task of expanding territory; Salim, to enjoy himself.
Besides, the prince was eternally drunk. No matter how
many sodden nights he spent rousing himself with talk
of rebellion, the mornings after would have found him in
no condition to execute such grand plans.

On the other hand, no father–son relationship can really recover from accusations of poisoning. From that day on, a rebellion by Salim was always in the offing, surprising only his doting grandmother when it finally happened. In the meantime, though, there was all of the 1590s, including two more trips to Kashmir, a long, uncomfortable lull in which the dysfunction of the imperial family grew ever more pronounced, often to the point of tragedy.

Unfortunately, much of this drama occurs only between the lines of Abu'l Fazl's amply cushioned prose. The year after Akbar's illness, for example, in late 1592, he returned to Kashmir, this time to see the colours of autumn. On the face of it, this was a much happier journey than the last. This time, Akbar camped with the ladies in Nowshera and sent Salim ahead to judge the way. When Salim returned and said it would be dangerous to try to take the women across, Akbar agreed; the road had been bad enough in spring, it was barely manageable in autumn. Akbar's own horse slipped twice en route, the emperor nimbly avoiding serious injury. Once in the valley, both Akbar and Salim seem to have enjoyed their time together. They visited the saffron fields of Pampore in full bloom. They celebrated Diwali: 'by orders, the boats, the river banks and the roofs were adorned with lamps . . . [presenting] a splendid appearance'. Akbar and Salim both acquired Kashmiri wives.

Is there more than meets the eye, though, in this little report, buried between news of Salim's nuptials and Akbar's introduction to a new kind of indelible ink?[34] Abu'l Fazl tells us that, also, 'in this year [Akbar's nephew Mirza Kaiqubad] received some punishment. He was sent to the place of instruction of the prison. He had ignorantly given himself up to wine drinking. His punishment led to the amendment of many.'

Not, certainly, of Salim. Writing of that visit to Pampore years later, Salim remembers he was drinking 'wine . . . by the cupful'. As they might have expected, the prince and his friends got terrible headaches though Salim blames it on the scent of saffron, writing acerbically of 'bestial Kashmiris' plucking saffron without ill effect: 'it was obvious that it had never occurred to them in all their lives to have a headache.'

What, also, to make of the fact that in the following year Salim's son Khusro, then about six, was given a Brahmin tutor to teach him Hindu philosophy? Humdrum? Maybe, but given Akbar's deep interest in the subject, could it be deduced that he was grooming his grandson?

His son, meanwhile, seemed to require lessons in basic manners. When Salim's father-in-law, Bhagwan Das, died, Salim did not send any message of condolence to Bhagwan Das's son, Akbar's prized general and Salim's own brother-in-law, Man Singh. When Man Singh arrived in court after a successful campaign in Orissa, Salim was reminded firmly of his breach and told to repair it. Or, as Abu'l Fazl puts it, 'the Prince-Royal was

given leave from the hunting field' and ordered instead
to Man Singh's quarters.

Patching together the slight details that make up the
long, wearying war of attrition between the emperor
and his dissolute son, one begins to long for the clear
conflagration that might have been if only the story of
Anarkali and Salim were true. Not only because tales of
young love doomed by duty and power are so intrinsically
compelling, but also because it would be so much easier
to peg the collapse of Akbar and Salim's relationship on
one clear-cut conflict. Instead, when Salim does fall in
love, the story and its resolution is so far from causing
any serious disagreement between father and son as to
make the very idea of a romance cleaving the two apart
laughable.

In 1596, when Salim was twenty-seven, Abu'l Fazl
reports that the prince 'became violently enamoured of
the daughter of Zain Khan Koka'. Zain Khan was a foster
brother of Akbar's, a trusted and high-ranking member
of his nobility – and Salim was already married to his
niece. This close relationship between the two women
may have been why Akbar opposed the match (Abu'l
Fazl only mentions its 'impropriety'), but when Salim
insisted, Akbar gave in.

The marriage feast was held in the home of Akbar's
mother – Hamida Banu Begum – a woman whom three
generations of Mughal rulers, from Humayun to Salim,
loved and deeply respected. Perhaps the marriage was

even held through her mediation; her indulgence as a grandmother began with the 190-carat ruby she gave him at his birth and would continue in various intangible forms of even greater worth, so much so that one could argue Salim owed her the empire he would eventually gain.

For all that though, and for all that Abu'l Fazl writes cheerfully of 'a new law for joy' in the wedding's wake, the odd thing is that Salim never mentions this great love in his otherwise candid memoirs. Zain Khan's daughter was married with pomp, given a title, Khas Mahal, and pushed offstage: though she lived through Salim's reign and after, she does not survive in history beyond this anecdote.

Did Salim really love her? Was this an intoxicated infatuation? Did the fact that Daniyal had recently married not one but two daughters of high-ranking nobles (one of whom was none other than Salim's guardian, Abdur Rahim, the khan khanan) spur a competitive urge in Salim? Or was it just, as it often is, a case of grand passion leading to dull endings?

It's hard to say, and harder still to articulate without the arc of a pliable myth. Certainly, this was not a story of parental obstruction thwarting young love. But certainly, also, they did not know what to make of each other, father and son, and that is all the story we can really tell.

And yet, for all the bad blood between them, however much his father's disapproval chafed, Salim showed a marked reluctance to leave Akbar's side. Murad had already been sent to Orchha and then further south, to take charge of what would become the Mughals' eternal Deccan campaign. In 1597, the year after Salim's marriage to Khas Mahal, Daniyal was sent to govern Allahabad, armed with advice that would have appealed to the worthy Polonius ('Postpone not to the morrow the work of to-day. Reckon a good name as eternal life'[35] – and so on). Both the younger princes, once out of their father's sight, fell so hard and so deep into their addiction to alcohol that they would die of it; as if, away from His Majesty, they had embraced the bright and brief freedom of moths. Salim, however, was made of sterner stuff: *he* was drinking himself to death under Akbar's very nose.

The year that Daniyal was dispatched to Allahabad, Akbar and Salim set out on their third tour of Kashmir, this time in the summer. The whole trip was marked by implicit hostility. On the way, Salim came into Akbar's private quarters without permission (was he lurching?) and committed some undefined 'impropriety'[36] (did he slur and make a scene?) as a result of which he was 'in disgrace and not allowed to pay his respects'. Abu'l Fazl was sent to make enquiries into the prince's bad behaviour and managed to effect a reconciliation between 'the world's lord' and 'the nursling of dominion', so much so that twice in the trip Akbar showed his son what seems like great favour.

The first instance was the story of Khwajagi Fath Ullah's lucky escape. Fath Ullah had been posted on the road leading into Kashmir with orders to allow only select members of the imperial retinue to enter the valley – the idea being to prevent a flood of men, which would tax Kashmir's resources and potentially cause a famine. One of the men that Fath Ullah tried to stop was a servant of Salim's; naturally, being part of the prince's entourage, he protested, then attacked, and was killed. Word of this got to Akbar, who responded by sending Fath Ullah to Salim's tent 'in order that he might be punished'. It says something of how rarely Akbar showed his son kindness and how much Salim craved it that 'the latter was delighted at this graciousness'[37] and in his delight he let Fath Ullah off unscathed.

Of course, it is possible that Akbar was not reacting to the insult to Salim, as such, but to Fath Ullah's lack of adequate respect for the dignity of an imperial prince. That, at any rate, seems to be a clear undercurrent in the second instance of favour, the story of Khwaja Bhul's tongue. One day, it seems, Akbar and Salim were boating in the lovely Wular lake. Once again, Salim committed one of his intriguingly vague misdemeanours and Khwaja Bhul yelled out an angry message from the emperor. Perhaps, in conveying Akbar's anger, Khwaja Bhul expressed his own annoyance too. At 'his rude words' Salim lost his temper – with such force that Akbar had to 'console' his son by cutting off the tip of the hapless khwaja's tongue.[38]

It hardly seems the best way to teach a son self-control. Besides, the message was Akbar's – just as the order to guard the pass was Akbar's – and even if the khwaja added an inflection or two of his own to the imperial reprimand, or Fath Ullah carried out his duties with exaggerated enthusiasm, it doesn't seem wise of Akbar to

have sent such conflicting signals both to the prince and
to his messengers. Is it that, in Salim's spectacular loss of
temper, in the attack by Salim's servant, Akbar sensed a
potential uprising? Did Akbar, now fifty-five, flinch at
the thought?

Whatever the truth may be, if these anecdotes are
any reflection of Akbar's usual parenting then it isn't
surprising that his sons turned out spoilt and ineffective,
nor that two of them died of drink. What is surprising
is that one of them didn't.

In October, as winter began to set, Akbar and Salim took
one last look at their beloved saffron fields and returned
from Kashmir to Lahore,[39] unaware that the family was
about to suffer its first real tragedy.

Murad's nine-year-old son Rustam died.

Akbar was so inordinately fond of his grandchildren
that even Abu'l Fazl is reduced to plain-speaking: 'the
affectionate sovereign loved grandchildren more than
sons,' he writes, before inscribing another bit of revealing
observation, 'Rustam was habituated to exalted love so
that the counsels of father or mother did not become
the vesture of his heart.' In other words, not only did
Akbar clearly prefer his grandsons to his sons, his clear
preference allowed the grandchildren to disregard,
perhaps even scorn, their own parents, knowing they
had their indulgent and powerful grandfather on their
side. Even the imperial family's lexicon betrays an odd
imbalance in these relationships, and the fissures this

might have created: there was place for only one shah-baba, king-father, and that was Akbar; the grandchildren would refer to their own fathers as shah-bhai, king-brother.

One night, writes Abu'l Fazl, Rustam's 'stomach became disordered, and he grew delirious'. Two days later, the boy was dead. The court and harem wept for days. Far away in the south, Murad drank even more in his grief. Of Salim's reaction, there is no record. Did he send his brother a message of condolence? Did he mourn his nephew's death? There is only one, passing mention of Rustam in Salim's memoirs – about two decades after Rustam died, Salim was touring Gujarat and happened to have a drinking party in Rustam Bari, a garden made by Murad for his son. As it happened, the governor of Ahmedabad at the time was called Rustam, too, and so, 'because of the coincidence of names', Salim gave him the garden.

Clearly, Salim did not remember little Rustam with any great sentiment, nor did he, in what are otherwise expansive memoirs, record the grief of the court at his passing. It is unlikely, however, that he did not notice how Akbar was raising his sons' sons – and equally unlikely that he wasn't beginning to worry about it.

Rustam wasn't Akbar's only favoured grandchild, after all. There was also ten-year-old Khusro, Salim's eldest son, who would soon be grown and locked in unhappy competition with his father long after the man who invented the whole game was gone. And there was five-year-old Khurram, the boy who brought joy not only to his adoptive mother but increasingly to the emperor, too. Often, writes Salim, Akbar would say of Khurram, 'I consider him my true son.'

Whether Salim was flattered by such attention for his boys or beginning to resent it, they were not, as yet, any kind of threat. Murad and Daniyal, meanwhile, were both far away from court and doing little to distinguish themselves. For the moment, in fact, the greatest threat to Salim's chances was no one from the family at all, but rather the doggedly loyal Abu'l Fazl.

It isn't clear how such animosity erupted between the two men. It was Abu'l Fazl, after all, who helped patch things up between Akbar and Salim when the prince misbehaved en route to Kashmir. He was a favoured courtier and, had things gone well, he might have become Salim's favoured conduit to the emperor's ear. It was not as if the historian had any private axe to grind with the prince.

On the other hand, Abu'l Fazl was devoted to Akbar, and therefore to Akbar's happiness; his fondest hope, when Salim was born, was that the prince would please his father – and Salim had grown remarkably disinclined to do so.

In 1598, for example, there was an opportunity to conquer Turan, a kingdom in Central Asia that Akbar had long had his eye on. The emperor decided to send Salim, who was then almost thirty and had embarrassingly little conquest to his credit, but Salim refused. Here, finally, a note of disapproval creeps into Abu'l Fazl's narrative:

'That pleasure-loving youth,' he writes, 'could not wean his heart from India.'

But it was around this time, too, that Salim began to realize that his pleasures, having consumed most of his youth, might soon deprive him of an old age. As Salim tells it, after nine years of untrammelled drinking, 'things got so bad that in my hangovers my hands shook and trembled so badly I couldn't drink myself but had to have others help me.'

While it's almost unbelievable that Salim, at the height of his addiction, was ever sober enough to have a hangover, it's miraculous that, in the haze of his drink, he understood the danger he was in and managed to do something about it. And yet, he did. In his most wretched state, Salim called a doctor, the very Hakim Humam whom Akbar had accused of conspiring to poison him. The doctor told him 'with no beating around the bush, "Highness, the way you're drinking, in another six months – God forbid – things will be so bad it will be beyond remedy."'

Addicts are not known, however, for their ability to follow doctors' advice. Like many before and after – like his own brothers – Salim might have shrugged at the hakim's words, called for another drink and died within the year. What saved Salim was not the hakim's dire prognostication alone, but also the emergence, late in the day, of that strength of will that had enabled his forefathers' conquests – combined with another family trait, the obsessive-compulsive desire to measure, categorize and record.

Slowly and methodically, Salim began to drink less. He substituted some of the alcohol with philonium (an all-spice drug of opium, saffron, spikenard, honey, etc.); he diluted his spirits with grape wine ('two parts wine to one part spirits'); he drank only in the evenings (except the eve of Friday, a sacred day); and over the course of seven years, he went from twenty cups of double-distilled liquor to six cups of fortified wine supplement with two and a half grams of opium.[40]

Salim did, after all, want to live and to rule; he had ambition and also the will to do something about it; and he would not be indebted to a flattering courtier with a knack for lofty prose.

The unsuspecting Abu'l Fazl, meanwhile, thought he had built himself a 'choice abode in the pleasant land of *Peace with all*'. Who would have thought its roof was about to fall on his head?

For some lapse on his part (the historian does not, as ever, specify) Salim grew angry and his anger 'blazed forth' fanned by 'base and envious people'. Salim's rage alone might not have troubled Abu'l Fazl, however, if the 'untrue reports' that fuelled it had not reached Akbar's ear and – worst of all – found audience with him. Hurt and humiliated, Abu'l Fazl went into a deep sulk.

'I withdrew my hand from everything and tucked my foot into my shirt,' he writes. 'I shut my door in the face of both stranger and acquaintance.' When Akbar called him to court and told him to continue with his usual duties, Abu'l Fazl declared he would only be able to render formal service, that he couldn't possibly summon his usual zeal until a thorough enquiry had cleared him of all suspicion. Akbar tried to calm him down and dismiss his histrionics, which only agitated Abu'l Fazl more. 'I meditated my own destruction,' he writes in the throes of pathos, 'and sometimes I thought of becoming a vagabond.'

Eventually, however, the scholar put aside thoughts of suicide and exile and undertook the somewhat more hopeful task of casting his own horoscope. When the stars revealed that soon the 'veil' that had obscured the truth would be removed and that Akbar would, once again, recognize his friend for who he was, Abu'l Fazl cheered up and went back to court.

For the moment all was well, but this was not the end of the story.

What caused this temporary rift between Akbar and Abu'l Fazl isn't really clear. Henry Beveridge, translator of the *Akbarnama*, gathers from various sources that Salim may have insinuated to his father that Abu'l Fazl wasn't quite as reverential towards the emperor (and particularly the emperor's new religion) as he made himself out to be. The accusations included making copies of the Quran and continuing to treat it as a divine text – neither of which was explicitly forbidden but certainly not expected of the emperor's closest adviser and disciple. Besides, Abu'l Fazl's father, Sheikh Mubarak, had written a commentary on the Quran and not mentioned Akbar in it, a lapse that could not have gone unnoticed. Minor faults though these were, they gave Salim an opportunity, and the slight doubt that he managed to create in his father's mind was enough to make Akbar contemplate the idea of a short separation between Abu'l Fazl and the court.

So, a few months after their astrologically determined reconciliation, when reports of Murad's health became troubling, Akbar sent Abu'l Fazl to the Deccan to bring Murad home.

Abu'l Fazl was acutely aware that he was being got rid of. 'Inasmuch as the writer ... always held to his own opinion without respect of persons, and represented in an eloquent manner what was good for the State, those who sought for an opportunity and were crooked in their ways represented their own interested views. In consequence of their intrigues I was sent off ... to bring Prince Sultan Murad.'

Dutiful and possibly not disinclined to take a break from the conspiracies of court for the glamour of distant battlefields, Abu'l Fazl began his journey south.

He never came back.

Whatever promise Murad had once held, leading his father's army at the age of twelve, impressing men twice his size with his courage, that promise had long dissipated. When he went to Orchha, aged twenty-one, it was as a legitimate contender for the throne; and if he had faults, they were the faults of a ruler – excessive ambition and arrogance. As Badauni puts it, Murad 'boasted of being a ripe grape when he was not yet even an unripe grape'. In this 'over-weaning pride and arrogance', however, Badauni saw signs of Murad's 'illustrious Father' and so, even if he might never have been as popular, he might well have followed Akbar to the throne.

Following a brief triumph in Orchha, Murad was sent to the Deccan, where any kind of success would have magnified his worth in his father's eyes. Instead, he drank. He drank so much that when, eight years later, Akbar summoned both his younger sons to Lahore, in the vain hope that one of *them* might undertake the Turan mission that Salim had so high-handedly refused, Murad was too ashamed to show himself to his father.

Annoyed, Akbar declared that if his sons[41] wouldn't deign to bother themselves with conquest, he would just do it himself: first, he would march south from Lahore, set Murad straight and conquer the Deccan while he was at it; next, he would return to take Turan. The army set off on its long march, stopping, in an interesting aside, at the house of an Arjun Kuru – probably the fifth Sikh Guru, Arjan Dev – who received various favours from the emperor. The guru's relationship with Akbar's successor would be far less fortunate.

However, when Akbar reached Agra, he changed his mind. This was not typical of the emperor. When he decided on something, that thing got done. Once, he'd gone from Agra to relieve a besieged Ahmedabad, galloping about 900 kilometres in just over a week. But relieving a city under siege is not the same as helping a son battle addiction. Maybe, for once, the emperor was afraid of what he would find; 'his heart . . . [was] uneasy on account of the delay in the arrival of the princes', as Abu'l Fazl has it, and there was no lack of 'praters' telling tales. Instead, then, Akbar sent Abu'l Fazl to find out what was going on and bring Murad home.

Murad, meanwhile, grown ever more melancholy

since Rustam's death, was meandering unhappily about the Deccan Plateau, drunk and ill. He had begun to have attacks of epilepsy, which he tried to hide; he caught fever and suffered acute abdominal pain. He couldn't eat. The news of Akbar's summons brought on a fresh wave of fear, and when he heard that Abu'l Fazl was coming to get him, he panicked. To avoid meeting his father's agent, Murad devised a plan that would only make sense to a ravaged mind: he embarked on a conquest of Ahmednagar, one of the largest and most powerful kingdoms of the Deccan.[42] In pain, his mind a dark cage of muffled voices, his arms too weak to hold a sword, Murad had not even reached his target when, on the banks of a river in Berar,[43] he had a massive epileptic fit. A week later, unconscious, he died.[44]

Murad wasn't yet thirty.[45] Abu'l Fazl never reached the prince, brave and arrogant, the grape that never ripened but only shrivelled away. Of course, the historian sent a report, and it is more tragic than even Murad's wasted life that nobody in Akbar's court, not even Salim, had the courage to read the news to their illiterate king. For a whole month, Akbar was in the dark. Even the doctor – Akbar's best – who was on his way to cure Murad heard what had happened and turned back around. The emperor did not know. Eventually, it was Hamida Banu Begum, Akbar's mother, who came down to Agra from Lahore and told him.

Abu'l Fazl, who was not there and not willing to imagine his beloved sovereign in tears, writes that Akbar took the news with fortitude, comforting the women, never losing charge. But we know, as he did, that when he writes 'a world was plunged in sorrow' it was not any world but Akbar's own that had grown suddenly very dark.

Akbar drowned his grief in work. The Deccan campaign was to continue without pause, and Salim was to lead it. At the auspicious hour in which the Deccan command was to come to him, however, Salim slipped out of it. Literally: he didn't show up in court. So, instead, it was the third prince, Daniyal, who was summoned.

In his memoirs, Salim writes with evident fondness of his youngest brother. While Murad is dismissed in a brief paragraph – tall, dark and 'inclining to be portly', grave, brave and dead at thirty – Daniyal, who was also, like Salim, named after a Sufi saint, comes across as a young man of charm and light pleasures. 'It was impossible for him to hear that anyone had a good horse or elephant and not get it.' He loved Hindi songs and composed poetry. He loved guns, too, and had named his favourite Yaka-u-Janaza, One Shot to Funeral. And he loved his wife, the daughter of Abdur Rahim, called Janan Begum, who is said to have inherited much of her father's genius and to have loved Daniyal as much as the prince, 'of fine stature . . . and good looking', loved her.

Daniyal's mother, like Murad's, is unnamed. According to Salim, they were both serving girls or concubines, but there is some speculation that Daniyal was born either to Salima Begum (Akbar's cousin, wife and trusted adviser) or to the mythical Anarkali. At any rate, his mother wasn't

Rajput, like Salim's; Daniyal was far more Central Asian in appearance than either his brother or his father.

Unlike Murad, who died evading his father, Daniyal had managed to obey Akbar's summons. Even so, he dragged his feet and by the time he made it to Agra, Akbar was so angry with his son, he wouldn't give him permission to enter the court. Daniyal spent several days on the city's outskirts, pacing the banks of the Yamuna, waiting to be called. Finally, during the Nauroz festivities of 1599, Daniyal was allowed into his father's sight; and, with fervid accounts of having subdued rebels, 'civilized' Allahabad and abjured the cup, and with 'choice presents' that included 206 elephants, the youngest prince mollified the ageing emperor and they were reconciled.

A few months later, with Murad dead and Salim not willing to accept the responsibilities of governance nor to move out of sight of the throne, light-hearted Daniyal began to look like a saving grace, the only one to whom the emperor might trust his empire. The reconciliation was turning into a kind of desperate hope.

In the summer of that year, Daniyal set off for the Deccan, where he was to guard the empire's limits and expand its bounds; and where he might, should he choose, grow in the emperor's estimation and into his shoes. No wonder Akbar went beyond the usual 'weighty counsels'[46] he normally gave his sons before sending them off to prove themselves; this time, he travelled a stage of the way with Daniyal, spent a night in the camp delivering 'fresh supplications and counsels', and gave the prince a particular kind of red tent (saraca) that was normally reserved for the emperor's exclusive use.

Had Daniyal done little more than march in a straight line south, Akbar would have been delighted. Instead, of course, he swerved. He staggered. As Abu'l Fazl has it, 'he delayed somewhat on the road'. Three months later, in mid-September, Akbar, now only two years shy of sixty, got on his fastest horse and galloped towards his third son to 'urge . . . [him] to greater activity'.

Notably, Akbar did not leave Agra in Salim's care; that responsibility was given to an amir called Qilich Khan.

Akbar had been displeased with his son ever since his strategic disappearance on the day he was to get the Deccan command and had denied Salim all access to court thereafter. Eventually, it was Hamida Banu Begum who argued with her son on Salim's behalf. When he was finally allowed into Akbar's presence, Salim had the sense to make 'fresh promises of discretion and of service'. How convincing he was, how much either Salim or his father believed his vows is hard to say, but Salim was sent off to subdue the strongest, proudest and most unsubduable of the Rajput kingdoms, Mewar. Its erstwhile king, Maharana Pratap, had been amongst Akbar's most redoubtable foes, and his son and current ruler, Rana Amar Singh, was no less stubborn in his resistance to Mughal rule.

Akbar gave Salim some of his best generals, including the formidable Raja Man Singh. He even gave Salim the benefit of 'many instructive counsels' though it may have been with a hollow feeling of wasting his breath.

According to Banarsi Prasad Saksena, author of the *History of Shahjahan of Dihli*, Salim begged for at least one of his sons to go with him on the campaign, but

Akbar would not let his beloved Khurram out of his sight and he did not think it wise to send Khusro with his father. If that is true, then Akbar was already thinking of Khusro, not yet in his teens, as a rival to Salim, to be kept away from his influence and – could it be? – from his jealousy. According to Saksena, it was Parvez, Salim's second son, whom Akbar finally sent with his father, though the *Akbarnama* says all three boys remained with their grandfather and, in fact, travelled with him to the Deccan. Whatever the case may be – and poor Parvez has such a lacklustre role in history that it is quite possible he was misplaced in its annals – they were like pieces on a chessboard, Salim, Daniyal and Akbar with the grandsons he was grooming. Each must now make his move.

Akbar and Salim left for their respective campaigns on the same day, the one on a 'rapid steed',[47] the other more leisurely. Twenty days after Salim's departure, it was reported that he, like Daniyal, was 'loitering on the way' and an emissary was sent to hurry him along too. Unperturbed, Salim made it to Ajmer and set up camp; from here, he sent his troops off to do what they would with the rana. Eventually, the prince did himself venture as far as Udaipur, but even the eighteenth-century historian Muhammad-Hadi, who wrote a most favourable preface and conclusion to Salim's memoirs,[48] cannot disguise the fact that this was more a hunting tour than a military sortie.

Things might have continued in this lackadaisical way were it not for a sudden outbreak of rebellion in Bengal. Bengal was Raja Man Singh's province, and the rebellion was serious enough to require Man Singh's personal attention. Suddenly, Salim was in unsupervised control of an army, his father occupied in the south and his father's most loyal general galloping to the east. Was this, he might have wondered, an opportunity to be seized?

'Ambitious flatterers,' says Muhammad-Hadi, 'evil persons,' writes Abu'l Fazl, told him yes. For all the calumny heaped upon them by writers unable to accuse royal blood of wrongdoing, the men who now advised – and perhaps instigated – Salim were his best friends, men whom Salim held close to his heart for having been loyal to him at a time when loyalty to his precarious claim promised more risk than gain. There was Khubu, of course, Sheikh Salim Chishti's grandson and the foster brother Salim loved more than his own; there was possibly also Khubu's mother, whom, too, Salim loved more than his own ('indeed,' he says, 'she was kinder than a mother'); there was Khwaja Abdullah Khan, a hot-headed, impulsive and brave soldier; there was Zamana Beg (later Mahabat Khan), whose valour and diplomatic finesse would make him one of the most highly respected generals of his age.

One day, long into the future, some of these men would try to topple the very man they were now trying to seat, prematurely, on the Mughal throne; one day, Salim's gratitude would transform into a bitter rage. For the moment, however, all was freedom and hope. The horizon was theirs for the taking, which way should they go? Briefly, Salim thought of taking Punjab for himself, until it occurred to him that this would require a long journey and rigorous battle. Why not seize the Agra treasury instead? Part rebel force, part schoolboy army

raiding an absent father's liquor cabinet, Salim and his
cohorts set off for the Agra fort – only to be met at its
gates by the polite but firm Qilich Khan.

Qilich Khan's was not an enviable position. Having
been left in charge of Agra by the emperor, he now had
to defend it from the emperor's son. Akbar was not only
pushing sixty, he was also conducting a siege; old age or a
cannonball might have ended his life any moment, while
Salim had friends to support him, an army to command,
and a temper. A lesser man would have quailed, not
Qilich Khan. Managing to bow while standing firm,
the diplomatic amir came out of the Agra fort and paid
homage to the prince, bringing, no doubt, rich presents
to offer, but he would not let the prince near the treasury.

Muhammad-Hadi writes that Salim's friends and
advisers, growing agitated, 'insisted that if Qilich Khan
were captured, it would be quite easy to take the . . .
fortress, which was brimming with stores and treasures',
but that Salim, with greater nobility of mind, let the amir
go unharmed. For all his implied honour, however, it is as
likely that Salim was shamed into good behaviour by his
grandmother's distress as by Qilich Khan's brave stand.

Learning of her grandson's astonishing breach of filial
protocol, Hamida Banu Begum, 'seating herself in glory
in a howdah',[49] set out from the fort to meet Salim and,
no doubt, give him a brisk talking-to. Unable to bear the
thought of it, Salim took an immediate about-turn, got
into a boat and, writes Abu'l Fazl, 'went rapidly down
the river'. Qilich Khan's life was thus spared, but not
Hamida Banu's feelings. Hurt and worried, she returned
to the fort 'with a sorrowful heart', and it's unlikely that

Salim didn't realize it. After his hurried and sheepish departure, he must have sailed with guilt that night, remorse and ambition churning through his insides, to be soothed in wine.

Even so, whether it was ambition that stirred it, the prompting of friends or possibly just circumstance, Salim wasn't just running away in shame. He had set sail into rebellion, a relatively listless rebellion, yes, and one that would be interrupted by various attempts at reconciliation, but which would last, nevertheless, for the next five years and end only with Akbar's death.

About two weeks after he left Agra, in August of 1600, Salim and his men arrived in another great city on the banks of the Yamuna, Allahabad. Did Salim remember that lovely, leisurely cruise down this river with his father when he was a child? Akbar had given the city its new name then, and laid the foundations of the fort in which, with the heavy-handed irony of fate, his son, the very pearl of his prayers, would now set up a rival court.

Unlike Agra, Allahabad yielded to Salim without protest; he commandeered the fort, its treasury and the neighbouring province of Bihar; gave his men titles, promotions and estates (Khubu, for example, became Qutbuddin Khan, governor of Bihar); and declared himself king.

Typically, this was a muted declaration; and when Akbar heard of it, whether from his 'abundant loving kindness' (Abu'l Fazl) or his 'attachment' to Salim

(Muhammad-Hadi), he refused to believe it. Besides, he was nearing the end of his last military conquest, and perhaps he did not want the taste of victory sullied by the knowledge of having failed so utterly to control his own son.

While Salim settled himself in Allahabad, Akbar was camped outside Asirgarh.[50] Built of rugged black stone rising from a rocky hill as if it were the hill itself, soaring to over 2300 feet in the sky, the fort of Asirgarh looms over the hilly countryside of Khandesh[51] like a wild buffalo's hot and angry snort, stilling your breath as you approach. Of the many impregnable fortresses of India, this was one of the most difficult to capture, as Akbar discovered over the course of his siege, which lasted so long it seemed like it might never end. Camped on a low hill opposite the dark fortress, discussing strategy with Daniyal and his grandsons, with the quick-witted Abdur Rahim and the enthusiastic Abu'l Fazl, glad to be experiencing the glories of battle instead of just writing about them, did Akbar feel a certain nostalgia for his youth and the adrenaline of conquest, its challenges so much simpler than trying to understand one's own children? His grandson Khurram, then eight, had been put in the care of one Raja Salivahan, who was teaching the prince how to shoot. Watching the excited young boy at his lessons, did Akbar remember Salim's easy aptitude for the gun? Why couldn't – why wouldn't – Salim behave with the honour and dignity that must, after all, exist in him?

He sent a childhood friend of Salim's to find out. According to both Abu'l Fazl and Muhammad-Hadi, Sharif Khan the messenger carried only queries not accusations, leaving the door open wide enough for Salim to return with dignity. The prince's reaction was as disingenuous as Muhammad-Hadi's account of it: 'When the order arrived, the prince executed the forms of greeting and showed proper respect. He wanted to pay homage, however, out of farsightedness, he put his wish into abeyance, held Sharif, and refused to give him leave to return'. In sum, Salim professed his innocence and loyalty while betraying every sign of guilt and treason; and Akbar, for all that he might have been enjoying the soldierly camaraderie of his campaign, decided he must return north and continue the more wearisome battle with his son.

Asirgarh fell in January 1601. With the neighbouring town of Burhanpur, the fortress controlled access to the Deccan, and if Akbar had pushed forward he might well have changed the course of Mughal history in this elusive terrain. Instead, in April of that year, he left Asirgarh, Burhanpur and Daniyal in the care of Abdur Rahim and Abu'l Fazl and rode back to Agra. Before leaving, he told Daniyal to ask for anything he wanted, and Daniyal asked for a particular Persian horse, the best in Akbar's stable. Immediately, it was his.

In the opening pages of his autobiography, Salim writes that because he was born in the house of Sheikh Salim

Chishti, his father never called the prince anything except Sheikhu – Sheikhu baba, Sheikhu ji. For all the lavish celebration and joy that followed his birth, it is this diminutive that really captures Akbar's affection for his firstborn. It can't but make one smile. And yet, for all the clear and easy love that glows from Sheikhu ji, almost every recorded interaction between the emperor and Salim is a tortuous maze of misunderstanding, anxiety and bitterness. Almost every recorded interaction throws up the question, what if? What if, on that terrible trip to Kashmir, Akbar hadn't lost his temper? What if, when Akbar told him to, Salim had gone to conquer Turan? What if, now, when Akbar returned to Agra and Salim sent him a letter asking for permission to appear in court, what if Akbar had agreed? Instead, he said no ('the petition did not possess the glory of sincerity', writes Abu'l Fazl), while Salim, whether anticipating the rebuff or filled with Dutch courage, set out anyway – with an army of 30,000 men.

When Akbar heard of this he was, according to the political bias of the teller, either wrathful or confused; it is not hard to imagine that he was a bit of both. When Salim reached Etawah, a hundred-odd kilometres south-east of Agra, he sent the emperor a ruby, and the emperor sent him a letter, the tone of which, depending once again on who reports it, spans the gamut from conciliatory to thundering. Its message, however, was crystal clear: if you must come to me, come alone; if you come with your army, come at your own risk.

The standoff, if that is what it was, lasted only a few days. Perhaps stalemate is a better word. No matter how it ended, neither father nor son would ever, it was clear, win over or against the other. Even their patched-up peace was a failure: Salim turned his army around and Akbar offered him Bengal and Orissa to govern; but these eastern provinces, though rich, were too far from the court and also, possibly, too little too late. Instead, Salim went back to Allahabad and continued the game of being a secret king in plain view, now even ordering himself a throne and giving out more promotions and ranks.

Salim writes fondly of that throne in his memoirs; he had it brought all the way from Allahabad to Agra once he finally became emperor. It is still there today, in the Agra fort, a 'truly marvellous slab of stone', as Salim said, 'extremely black and shiny'.

In fact, it wasn't the throne but the giving of rank that both Salim and writers of the time considered his worst audacity, so much so that while he records the exact measure of his shiny black throne, Salim never admits to promoting a loyal amir. In this medieval empire, all wealth – indeed, all life – belonged to the emperor; only he could bestow a jagir, only he could tell a man what he was worth.[52] On the other hand, the men who stuck with Salim during his rebel years would have done so not only from loyalty but also from expectation of reward. Towards the end of his autobiography, Salim writes in a somewhat martyred way that 'for all the love and affection [my father] had for me, he never allowed my amirs to have titles, banners or drums' – but this doesn't mean the prince didn't give them what they wanted anyway, even though these grants were treasonous enough to arouse, for example, in Khwaja Kamgar Khan, a historian writing about Salim soon after Salim had died, a high-pitched defence of the prince. It was 'a body of seditious and turbulent people' who 'misrepresented' the facts of Salim's Allahabad sojourn, exciting the emperor by telling him Salim was conferring 'upon his servants the titles of Khan and Sultan'.

'In truth,' Khwaja Kamgar concludes, carried away by his own rhetoric, the 'love and affection' between Akbar and Salim was like that between 'Jacob and his son Joseph'.

For all Khwaja Kamgar's protestations, and for all that the love between the shahenshah and his Sheikhu was more the stuff of dysfunction than legend, there must have been something that bound them tightly enough to prevent the civil war that amirs on both sides were anticipating. Or was it only the fortuitous combination of Salim's laziness and Akbar's age that prevented a conflagration? Something, anyway, was keeping the peace of the empire, though soon it would be tested to breaking point.

Back in the Deccan, Abu'l Fazl was enjoying himself. Having spent his life with words, he had taken to the sword with surprising ease; had occupied pride of place by Akbar's side in the Asirgarh campaign; and now, pushing into the Deccan, was 'rising from rank to rank'.[53] In fact, had Salim not made his failed foray for the crown, Akbar might well have left his friend to continue what was turning into Abu'l Fazl's Deccan blitz; he was marching across the plateau with such zest that Daniyal even sent him a message telling him to slow down. But the emperor, having first sent his friend to rescue Murad and then left him behind to handle Daniyal, now wanted Abu'l Fazl back for himself. He ordered him to hurry home.

Abu'l Fazl's influence on the emperor was common knowledge and it attracted both envy and hate. Badauni, for example, described the scholar as 'officious . . . time-serving, openly faithless, continually studying the emperor's whims, a flatterer beyond all bounds'. Salim agreed, though he put it more elegantly. Abu'l Fazl, he writes, 'had ostensibly adorned himself with loyalty and sold it to my father for an exorbitant price', and of the prince himself, the historian was 'always making snide remarks'. Salim was absolutely certain that should Abu'l Fazl join Akbar in Agra, Salim never would. Therefore, Salim continues his frank and remorseless confession, 'it was . . . absolutely necessary that he be prevented from reaching him'.

Salim sent a message to Bir Singh Deo, a Rajput of Bundelkhand and raja of Orchha. 'In courage, innate goodness, and guilelessness,' writes Salim, 'he shone among his peers'. Inayatullah, who completed Abu'l Fazl's *Akbarnama* and included an account of the historian's grisly murder in it, offers a more terse description of the Bundela lord: 'highway robber'.

'I sent him a message,' Salim goes on, unabashed, 'that he should waylay the miscreant and dispatch him to nonexistence, in return for which he could expect great rewards from me'.

Bir Singh Deo agreed. Or, as Inayatullah puts it, 'that

ignorant partisan went home as quickly as possible and collected a number of bestial, savage Bundelas and lay in wait'.

What happened next can be told in one sentence or spread across pages. Salim, not surprisingly, chooses the clinical option. 'Success smiled on the endeavour, and as [Abu'l Fazl] was passing through [Bir Singh Deo's] territory, [Bir Singh Deo] blocked his path, scattered his men in a skirmish, and killed him, sending his head to me in Allahabad.'

It is from Inayatullah that we get the full and Abu'l Fazl–worthy melodrama of it.

For one thing, Abu'l Fazl knew exactly what was coming. He was in Ujjain, about to ride into the hills of Bundelkhand, when his escort told him that the road ahead was ambushed and proposed an alternative route. Abu'l Fazl refused. Nobody, least of all Inayatullah, understands why. It may be that, after his gallant victories in the Deccan, the scholar-turned-soldier thought it would dishonour him to avoid a little skirmish. Or it may be, as Inayatullah proposes, that soldiery had turned the scholar into a saint, now keen to shed the mortal coil.

So, inexplicably but inevitably, Abu'l Fazl rode into Bir Singh Deo's trap. On 12 August 1602, near the village of Antri and only 150-odd kilometres south of Agra, Bir Singh Deo and his men rose upon the horizon, the dust flying off their horses' hooves. Gadai Khan Afghan, a man who had served Abu'l Fazl since he was a child, grabbed the scholar's horse by the reins and turned it around. 'Go!' he said, or words to that effect. 'They are too many, we cannot win. Go towards Antri, *there* are men who will help! We'll keep the Bundelas at bay!'

Abu'l Fazl's reply, as recounted in all its prolix glory by Inayatullah, would have pleased the historian. 'To the noble lovers of their honour,' he declaimed, 'it is pleasanter to play away their lives with credit and to die bravely than to spend their days in cowardice, and to bring on themselves the stain of timidity. According to the code of the valiant what can be baser than to attach importance to fleeting life and give place to the enemy, and to fix one's heart on the unstable world and so gather eternal disgrace? If this be my last day – and that must happen to everyone – what remedy is there, and what counsel can one take?'

And besides, what would Akbar think of him if he fled like a coward now? Abu'l Fazl turned his horse back around.

Gadai Khan Afghan made one more desperate appeal. It was perfectly common for soldiers to flee and fight another day; there was no dishonour in it – forget all this talk of eternal disgrace – and, more critically, there was still time!

But no. 'I cannot flee from this unwashed thief,' said Abu'l Fazl, and he was still arguing stubbornly when the unwashed thief rode up. Abu'l Fazl and Gadai Khan Afghan charged into battle and both died, Abu'l Fazl falling to a spear through his chest. As he lay dying, Bir Singh Deo strode over to him and rid the writer of his head. It is said that when Salim received this ghastly trophy, he had it thrown into the latrines.

It is also said that just before the Bundela king cut off Abu'l Fazl's head, the king said to him, with grim courtesy: *Hazrat Jahangir has sent for you.*[54]

Sitting on his shiny black throne in Allahabad, Salim wasn't just disbursing titles among his men, he had given one to himself too. One can imagine the kind of snide remarks Abu'l Fazl might have made to Akbar had he been able to report the news to him – Jahangir, World Conqueror indeed. What kind of world conqueror fought fewer battles than a humble scribe?

Akbar stood on a balcony in the Agra fort, watching the pigeons fly. It was about noon on a day in mid-August, and the monsoon would have been well under way; the sky thick with clouds, the river below swelling against its banks, and gusts of cool, moist air filling the fort's large balconies, billowing under the pigeons' wings as if to lead them in a dance. As Akbar watched, entranced, he may not have noticed that Sheikh Farid, his mir bakshi,[55] was hurrying towards him. It may be that, as was the custom of Akbar's ancestors, Sheikh Farid wore a blue band on his arm to signify death. Even so, the unfortunate messenger would have had to speak the words: Abu'l Fazl was killed upon the prince's orders. His head was cut from his body. Akbar's biographer and disciple, his courtier and general, his public counsellor, his private friend was dead.

When Akbar understood what had happened, he cried out and fainted. For days afterwards, 'he had moist eyes'.[56] He sighed, he beat his breast, he cursed his son.

As Akbar mourned his friend, Salim would have been celebrating the end of his foe. It was Abu'l Fazl's absence, Salim argues, that allowed him to return to his father, 'and little by little the bad blood between us subsided'. Muhammad-Hadi has an even brighter view of the whole affair: according to him, the murder brought Salim's 'bravery and manliness' to Akbar's notice, so much so that Akbar decided to send his son 'imperial condolences' and invite him home.

It is true that Salim was home within a year of Abu'l Fazl's demise, and that he was seemingly reconciled with his father, but this was hardly because Akbar had forgiven (or, even more incredibly, been impressed by) the murder of his friend. Capturing and killing Bir Singh Deo preoccupied the emperor until he died; there wasn't a day after the historian's death that amirs were not scouring Bundelkhand for the fugitive king. No, Salim's return to grace had two main causes, neither of Salim's making: the love of his grandmother and Daniyal's relapse.

With Akbar in Asirgarh, Daniyal would have had little choice but to stop drinking. He broke his cups and vowed upon his father's head that he would give up wine; and perhaps Abu'l Fazl's presence, after Akbar's departure, kept the prince in fear of being found out, while the scholar's unflagging campaign kept him distracted from alcohol.

Hardly had Akbar absorbed the news of Abu'l Fazl's death, however, when another messenger brought news that Daniyal had broken his vow. Why, Akbar asked in reply, would the prince not 'take pity on his youth and beauty'?[57] Had he forgotten what happened to Murad?

Then, he shouted in anger, if Daniyal had the slightest love for God or his father, he would stop before he was ruined.

Meanwhile, as Akbar tried to browbeat one son out of his wretched fate, the ladies of the court conspired in favour of the other.

From Babur onward, the early Mughals shared many traits – addiction, delight in fruit and gardens, and a deep affection for the women in their lives combined with a seemingly anachronistic respect for their opinions. Babur wrote of how he consulted his grandmother on many aspects of his life and reign; Salim's future faith in Nurjahan is well known; and Akbar took the counsel of several women in his court very seriously.

These included his mother, of course, Hamida Banu Begum, whose life would make a book of its own; his aunt, Gulbadan, who wrote a history of her brother Humayun's reign, the *Humayun-nama*; and Salima Sultan Begum, Akbar's cousin and wife, a woman of renowned sagacity of whom Salim would write, 'she possessed all good qualities'. There was every reason for Salim's praise: if it hadn't been for her, the prince might never have become emperor.

As his luck would have it, all three women were extremely fond of Salim. Perhaps they saw in him the qualities that Akbar couldn't or wouldn't or didn't want to. His aestheticism, for example; his infectious enthusiasm for the beautiful and the new; his curiosity. Besides, the three women were no strangers to political upheaval. Hamida Banu and Gulbadan had spent much of their youth sharing Humayun's exile; Salima's first husband, Bairam Khan, had been Akbar's powerful regent until he was effectively deposed by the emperor. They may all three have felt that if the breach between father and son wasn't mended soon, the empire would not hold, and Akbar might end his life watching all that he had gained be lost in civil war.

They went to Akbar and argued, pleaded, begged for him to reconsider. It would not have been an easy negotiation. According to Inayatullah, Akbar never forgave Salim the murder of Abu'l Fazl. It is hard to imagine how anyone could. Finally, however, 'inasmuch as he had great respect' for his mother and aunt, he agreed to have the prince return to court. Salima offered to go and bring him herself; she took with her an imperial elephant called Fath Lashkar, a good horse and a robe of honour.

The news of Salima's embassy must have created great turmoil in Salim's rebel court. On the one hand, of course, the plan had worked! Abu'l Fazl was gone and Salim was back in favour. Or was he? Wasn't it possible that Akbar, when he saw the man guilty of Abu'l Fazl's death before him, wasn't it quite probable, in fact, that the emperor would forget whatever promises he had made in the zenana and exercise the full wrath of his majesty? His voice was loud still, though he was over sixty, and it is likely enough that Salim quaked at the thought of it raised in anger against him.

It is testament to Salim's faith in his aunt that she inspired him to courage. He rode out from Allahabad to meet her on her way, treating her with all the respect due to her and all the homage due to a representative of the emperor. He listened to what she suggested and agreed to do as she said.

Muhammad-Hadi would like his readers to believe that Salima was sent to cajole and bribe Salim back to Agra. Perhaps she did do some of that, though an elephant, a horse and a robe were hardly great inducements in Mughal terms. This was by no means, however, an easy or one-sided overture. Having convinced Salim, his aunt also had to satisfy the reluctant emperor that his son had, indeed, mended his ways. This, at any rate, is what she seems to be trying to do in a letter she sent, describing 'with fervour the beautiful tale of the devotion and sincerity of the Prince' and how she 'had cleansed the stain of savagery and suspicion from his heart'.[58] Soon, she said, she would bring him to court.

Back in Agra, Akbar heard the report without much feeling. His aunt, the venerable eighty-two-year-old Gulbadan, had fallen ill, and in the early spring of 1603 she died. As Gulbadan's eyes closed, Hamida Banu leaned forward and whispered, 'Begum jio!' It was what she called her beloved sister-in-law and friend, begum dearest, but also, in this case, begum live!

Live! If only Akbar could command it of his sons. Just weeks after he had carried his aunt's bier on his shoulder, another report arrived from Burhanpur. 'Prince Sultan Daniyal never quitted his cups and . . . had become weak and ill from constant wine-bibbing'. Akbar ordered the prince home immediately, only to receive half-baked excuses about Daniyal having to give instructions to Abdur Rahim Khan Khanan, who was conducting a campaign further south. Akbar exploded. 'His going to the Khan-i-Khanan was a subterfuge, and ... his not coming was due to his habits of drinking and self-indulgence. What need was there for the Khan-i-Khanan's receiving instructions from him? If he wrote such things again [Akbar] would be a thousand times more displeased'. Besides, what had happened to all the elephants captured in battles so far? Akbar had sent for them but the prince had only made more sly excuses. Daniyal was enjoying himself watching elephant fights, further proof, if any were needed of his 'unlucky star and perverted career'.[59]

Did Akbar pace up and down as he roared out the words of his letter, one hand on his dagger as if wishing he could hack to pieces the fiendish spirits devouring his son? Or did he want to get on a speedy horse once again, gallop and attack the son himself, shake him out of his addiction?

The court was clouded in loss and anxiety, and yet, as far as Salim was concerned, his arrival in Agra in April 1603, two months after Gulbadan had died, could not have been better timed. With Daniyal going the way of Murad, Salim was the only viable heir Akbar had left. What choice did he have except to welcome his only sentient son?

Besides, Salim had a plan to ensure the meeting was amicable. While he was on his way to Agra, he sent a petition asking if Hamida Banu would present him to the emperor, 'take his hand and cast him at the feet of His ... Majesty'. Accordingly, his grandmother came to meet Salim as he was approaching Agra. He spent the night in her palace, being reproached for his behaviour, perhaps, but kindly; his grandmother, writes Inayatullah, 'soothed the prince's terrified soul'. The next day, she took him to Akbar and, with one hand on his shoulder, thrust the prince at the emperor's feet.

Thus, three years after Salim had sailed off to Allahabad, two years after his failed coup, and eight months after Abu'l Fazl's assassination, Akbar and his firstborn were reunited. To a casual observer, it was a joyful affair. Salim brought twelve thousand gold coins and almost a thousand elephants as offering;[60] Akbar reciprocated by giving the prince one of the best elephants in the imperial stable, one that Salim had long craved. Then, with grave symbolism, he took his own turban and placed it on Salim's head.

Inayatullah does not know what to make of it. 'Ostensibly,' he writes, Akbar 'accepted [the prince's] inadmissible excuses, and held him in a loving embrace. But the fawning of the prince did not remedy the inward dissatisfaction of the sovereign'. Though the turban symbolized, perhaps even formalized, Salim's claim to the throne, Akbar 'did not approve of the Prince Royal's succeeding him'.

Such ambivalence of feeling was not new to either Akbar or Salim, however, and somehow they managed to sustain their accord for six months.

From the little detail that exists of that time, it seems both men were making an effort. Salim participated in the doings of the court. At least, there is one instance recorded by John Mildenhall, an early English traveller to India, who recounts a squabble he had with some Jesuits in

Akbar's presence. The Jesuits were, of course, Portuguese and therefore rivals of the Protestant English in both faith and trade; so it was entirely par for the course that, one day, Mildenhall launched into a long tirade against them, culminating with the accusation that, in all their years in Akbar's court, the Jesuits had not managed to procure either official ambassadors or sufficient presents for the emperor.

At this point, writes Mildenhall, 'the Kings eldest sonne stood out and said unto them (naming them) that it was most true that in eleven or twelve yeares not one came, either upon ambassage or upon any other profit unto His Majestie'. The Jesuits were tongue-tied and Akbar 'very merrie and laughed'.

For all that he was pulling their leg in court, Salim was actually very fond of the Jesuits: he knew them by name, as Mildenhall noticed; he gave them money to expand the church they had built in Agra with Akbar's patronage; he even offered them hope of his own conversion, although, as later historians have noted, and the Jesuits would discover, these hopes were soon to be dashed. Salim was currying favour with the Jesuit fathers, but not from any desire to enter their faith; it was a strategic ploy to gain Portuguese support in the event of an actual war with Akbar.

If true, this paints a rather bright picture of Salim's state at the time; strategic thinking requires both sobriety and a certain optimism about one's own future. Perhaps Akbar noticed and felt a glimmer of optimism himself. He allowed Salim's petitions in court – for example, the prince interceded successfully on behalf of one of his friends, a

Raja Basu of Mau – and he even thought of reviving the long-abandoned campaign against Rana Amar Singh.

In October 1603, during Dussehra, which was celebrated with grand military parades in Mughal courts, Akbar gave his son some of his weighty counsels and sent him off to fight the rana again. Perhaps he really believed that, this time, Salim would obey.

Salim accepted the command with alacrity, marched forty kilometres to Fatehpur Sikri and stopped. A few days later, he sent Akbar a message complaining that he did not have enough troops or supplies to continue – and Akbar's reply is the very embodiment of an exasperated sigh. Once again, it was one of the imperial women who delivered it. Shakarunnisa Begum,[61] Salim's favourite sister, came to Sikri to tell the prince that since he had left the court at an astrologically auspicious time, Akbar didn't think there was any point returning. 'It was better that he go to Allahabad and enjoy himself.'

Perhaps, after all, the Mewar campaign was a strategic ploy too; perhaps, father and son had both been missing their time apart. The prince was unperturbed by Akbar's sarcasm; instead, 'joyfully, drinking wine, and pleasuring himself, [he] crossed the Yamuna . . . and went off gaily'.[62]

It was almost as if he knew – maybe an astrologer told him – that his long and tedious wait for the empire was nearly over; in October 1603, Akbar had exactly two years left to live.

If we were to judge Akbar, paint a picture of him based only on the last two years of his life – particularly his domestic life – there would emerge a man so different from the decisive, eclectic genius of the previous sixty-one that it is almost impossible to reconcile one with the other.

In the last years of his life, Akbar's challenge was no longer conquest, the wealth of the world was already his. His passion was no longer reconciling religion with humanity, he had asked more questions than most men ever do, fuelled more debates, guessed at many more answers. India's musth elephants would need other, younger men to tame them now. Akbar's challenge, the only thing left for him to do, was to find a suitable heir – and he set about it with a seeming clumsiness that arouses a painful mix of pity and exasperation.

Just as Salim returned joyfully to Allahabad, a letter arrived from Daniyal, still in the Deccan, swearing he'd not had a drop for six months. Akbar was so relieved, he sent *him* one of his turbans, too, and, knowing how much his youngest loved horses, a 'special horse called Har Parshad'.[63] The very next month, he ordered that Daniyal receive a lakh of rupees per year from the proceeds at Cambay. Early the next year, hearing reports of Daniyal's undiminished drinking, Akbar lost his temper and sent a doctor, Hakim Fath Ullah, 'to reprove the prince'; but only a few days later, worried that too much reproving would prove counterproductive, Akbar sent a second prize horse behind the doctor, this one a gift from the Shah of Persia no less.

In all, that year, Akbar sent three emissaries to rescue Daniyal – Hakim Fath Ullah; a nurse from the prince's childhood 'who was not afraid to speak strongly';[64] and finally one Sheikh Abu'l Khair – all with increasingly urgent instructions to bring Daniyal home. All of them failed.

Meanwhile, Salim was not lacking for presents either. He was sent a special horse, too – Shah Inayat; he was given the revenue from a port in Sindh; and when he sent greetings for Nauroz and asked for a 'robe of black fox', it was promptly dispatched to him, along with another of white.

Did Akbar really believe that horses and robes and revenue was all that was needed to bring his sons in line? Or was he sending them these gifts in order to keep them – in Salim's case – content and – in Daniyal's – alive, while he worked on a secret plan?

Nobody knows if Akbar really had a secret plan, but if he did, then it vested in his grandson.

Khusro, Salim's eldest boy, is one of those tragic historical figures who is both integral to the course of events yet powerless within them. He had long been close to Akbar, which may be why he was married to the daughter of Akbar's favourite foster brother, the outspoken Mirza Aziz Koka. Not only did this bring Khusro a love that would last his life, it also gave him a powerful father-in-law. Mirza Aziz Koka, the khan azam, was wealthy, intelligent, unafraid to speak his mind – and unequivocally on Khusro's side. The sixteen-year-old prince had another formidable supporter in his uncle Raja Man Singh (brother of Salim's first wife, Man Bai, the daughter of Raja Bhagwan Das), who had little love lost for Salim. In his memoirs, Salim describes Aziz Koka and Man Singh as the 'adversarial old wolves of this eternal dynasty', writing with a wry melancholy, 'What these two have done to me, and what I have done to them, only God – and probably no one else – knows.'

Not even Akbar, who was the genesis of it. Salim does not, in his writings, come across as a man incapable of paternal love; if anything, he is susceptible to emotion, wanting to bestow affection and receive it. How must it have felt, then, to have his firstborn taken into Akbar's lap and turned against him?

At least he had his evening drink, his morning hunt. His ability to surrender himself entirely to the strange. It was in Allahabad, for example, that Salim first noticed how the koel, or black cuckoo, hatches its young; and there's something calming in just the way he describes it:

The cuckoo is a bird something like a raven, but it is smaller. A raven's eyes are black, but the cuckoo's are red. The female has white spots, and the male is totally black. The male has a very beautiful voice, completely beyond comparison with the female's. The cuckoo is really the nightingale of India, but whereas the nightingale is agitated in the spring, the cuckoo gets agitated at the beginning of the monsoon, which is the spring of Hindustan. Its cry is extremely pleasant. Its period of agitation coincides with the maturing of mangoes, and mostly the cuckoo sits on mango trees. It must enjoy the colour and scent of the mangoes. One of the strange things about the cuckoo is that it doesn't hatch its own eggs. When it is ready to lay an egg it finds an unprotected raven's nest, breaks the raven's eggs with its beak and throws them out, and then lays its own eggs and flies away. The raven thinks they are its own eggs, hatches them, and rears them. I have seen this strange thing myself in Allahabad.

Did it occur to Salim at all, as he watched two black birds compete viciously for their young, that Akbar was taking over Salim's nest? It doesn't matter. Salim, Khusro's father non-father, his shah-bhai, had the ability and opportunity to disengage himself. Khusro's mother did not.

In the summer of 1604, Man Bai committed suicide. 'What shall I write of her goodness and excellence?' asks Salim, remembering the day in May when, returning from a hunt, he found that Khusro's mother, his first wife, the Rajput girl he had married in a shower of gems so many years ago, had overdosed on opium. 'She had a mind to perfection . . .'

When Khusro was born, Salim gave his mother a title, Shah Begum, king lady. The seniormost wife of the eldest prince, the mother of his first son, Shah Begum might well have expected to see both her husband and her son ascend the Mughal throne one day. Instead, as Muhammad-Hadi has it, she witnessed 'the misguided Khusro's constant complaints of [Salim] to [Akbar]', complaints that could hardly have been spoken without the emperor's approval and encouragement. The worried queen could not reproach the emperor, but she did try to stop her son: 'she constantly wrote advice to Khusro,' says Salim, 'and tried to reason with him to be loyal and loving to me'.

As the unspoken war for the throne lurched towards its ugly end, factions consolidating around Khusro and Salim, suspicions and strategies filling the emperor's mind, Shah Begum could not bear it any more. She had always been fragile; 'several times she went berserk,' says Salim, diagnosing the fits as congenital since her father and brothers, too, were given to appearing 'quite mad' without cause. In one such moment of acute depression, unable to choose between father and son, unable to reconcile them while the emperor lived, yet able, all too well, to see how these growing fractures would break her heart, Shah Begum found a quiet room, a jar of opium and 'delivered herself of this pain and grief'.

According to most accounts, including his own, Salim loved his first wife. 'With her death, given the attachment I had to her, I passed my days without deriving pleasure in any way from life or living'; he did not eat or drink for four days; and it was only after Akbar sent him a letter of condolence (besides yet another turban 'from his own head' and a robe) that Salim's grief began to ebb. William Finch, who travelled in India soon after Salim's accession, notices the 'sumptuous tombe' built for his Shah Begum in Allahabad; and he describes her palace in Lahore as having a 'high pole to hang a light on' before it, a special honour conferred on her for having given Salim his first son. Within, the palace had a 'goodly gallery' for Salim to sit in, and its ceiling was lavishly decorated with paintings of Hindu deities ('or rather divils', as the befuddled Finch puts it, 'intermixt in most ugly shape with long hornes, staring eyes, shagge hair, great fangs, ugly pawes, long tailes, with such horrible difformity ... that I wonder the poore women are not frightened').

The picture that emerges is perfectly believable. Salim grieved for his first wife, on whom he had bestowed every honour, with whom he had taken joy in their children, in leisure, in art, for whose manic depression he had only concern and for whose death he was consoled by the emperor who, for all their differences, understood his son's pain.

On the other hand, there is the far more unsettling picture painted by Inayatullah. According to this admittedly biased historian, Shah Begum killed herself not from distress at her family's growing troubles but because 'the Prince Royal always behaved improperly to her [and] her mind became jealous'. Akbar 'was grieved at this event' not on behalf of his son but because he was 'very fond of Sultan Khusro'.

Is it really possible that Salim treated his Shah Begum so badly she killed herself to escape him? Did he blame her, perhaps, for the lapses of her 'wretched son'[65]? Reading Inayatullah's curt accusation, does Salim's tribute to his wife begin to take on an exaggerated, false air? 'She had a mind to perfection, and she was so loyal to me that she would have sacrificed a thousand sons and brothers for one hair on my head.' And yet, in the end, it was her own head she sacrificed. Was it Salim, somehow, who forced her to?

From all that exists about Salim till this point, one would extrapolate the answer 'no'. Drunkenness, laziness, self-indulgence, these aren't necessarily oppressive qualities. But then, as if on cue to complicate matters, it is exactly at this time that the first and most lurid of Salim's cruelties streams out of Allahabad and into the emperor's ear.

It began as a love triangle.

One of the prince's court recorders fell in love with a khanazad, that is, a man who was born into royal employment, and was therefore possibly of higher rank than the servant boy with whom he, in turn, was besotted. In a rather cheerful solution to their quandary, the three men decided to run away together. By all accounts they were headed to Daniyal in Burhanpur, a decision that begins to make more sense in light of the historian Beni Prasad's revelation that the recorder was suspected of conspiring against Salim.

Still, Salim's reaction when the three men were caught and brought before him was brutal, even by the harsh standards of his times. He had the recorder skinned alive before his eyes; he had the khanazad castrated; and the lowly servant beaten to death.

Even Muhammad-Hadi doesn't deny it, though he does try to divert the focus of the tale to how it was used by the 'self-serving with a hundred embellishments' to create further discord between Akbar and his 'darling son'.

What these embellishments were, one may gather from Inayatullah. The prince, he writes, 'did not keep his lips from the wine-cup for a moment' and he had begun to mix opium with his drink; and when this 'double intoxication . . . had taken hold of him, and when the brain was dried up, and his disposition unsettled, he for slight offences ordered unfitting, capital punishments'. According to Muhammad-Hadi, Salim's ill-wishers added that when recovering from these bouts of demonic fury, the prince would be sunk in stupor, alone in 'a corner . . . as active as a design on a carpet or a picture on a wall'.

Both Inayatullah and Muhammad-Hadi agree that Akbar was shocked. 'We have conquered a whole world by the sword,' he is said to have exclaimed, with, perhaps, mocking allusion to Salim's grandiose title, 'but until today we have not ordered so much as a sheep to be skinned in our presence!'

'Because the emperor was worried about him', writes Muhammad-Hadi, because 'his holy heart was deeply displeased by these . . . wickednesses', says Inayatullah, Akbar decided that enough was finally enough. He would go to Allahabad, ostensibly on a hunting expedition, and give Salim one last chance to repent. If he didn't, then the prince would soon realize that an ageing emperor's wrath held more terrors than his callow savagery ever could.

Finally, it seemed, a reckoning was at hand; finally, all the bad blood was going to spill. And then . . . there is no other explanation for it: the God and the sheikh who had brought Salim to life conspired to save him.

On the night of 21 August 1604, at an hour astrologically determined, the emperor set sail from Agra towards Allahabad. The journey had barely begun, however, when his boat got stuck. Akbar spent the night on ship, wondering if this was an omen. Still, not wanting to abandon the mission, he pitched camp on the riverbank next morning while the boat was dug out. That day, it began to rain. The monsoon winds were high, the rain was unceasing, the soldiers didn't have tents and for three days the camp was drenched in distress until, in the manner of omens, a third portent arrived. The emperor's mother was ill.

At first, Akbar didn't believe it. He sent Khurram and a doctor to his mother, but he knew how much Hamida Banu loved her grandson and he knew she was perfectly capable of feigning a tactical illness. This time, he would not let his anger dissolve in her love. But again, the messengers came. Hamida Banu was very ill, the doctors had given up. Akbar must hurry before it was too late.

The emperor rushed to his mother's bed. Already, she had closed her eyes and could no longer speak. He called to her, again and again. There was no reply. All the emperor could do was weep.

'Who shall describe the grief of His Majesty?'[66] He shaved his head, his moustache; he took off his turban and 'donned the garb of woe'. Hamida Banu Begum would be buried in the tomb of her husband, Humayun, in Delhi; Akbar was the first to carry her body on the long journey there. Having walked with her awhile, he returned to the fort and spent the day alone and silent. When he emerged that evening, to dismiss the guards, his grief had turned into a still serenity. His last order before retiring was that the court servants need not dress in mourning the next day. It was Dussehra, after all; they should celebrate.

In Allahabad, meanwhile, the news reached Salim.

In his own writings, Salim rarely talks of his time as a rebel prince. He does not talk of how much he drank or did not, he does not defend or deny his alleged cruelties. He mentions the black throne, he talks about the cuckoo, and he reveals, almost by chance, that while in Allahabad he made a vow that when he was fifty, he would give up hunting with guns. He does not explain why he made the vow. Was it a prayer, a sacrifice, for a long life – *if* he lived up to fifty, he would give up the gun? Or was he making a pact for more immediate gain – give me the throne now and *when* I get to fifty . . .

He does not say when he made his vow, either. Was it now, when he heard of Hamida Banu's passing? Her death and Salim's reaction to it was, as Salim would later write, one of the most decisive moments of his life.

Many later historians have argued or implied that Salim was excessively susceptible to others' strong opinions. Salim himself states otherwise, claiming that 'in councils on state affairs and government I usually act according to my own opinion and understanding'. Now, for example, 'contrary to the advice and approval of all my faithful servants', he decided to go to his bereaved father and condole with him. Whatever one might make of Salim's wider claim to independent thought and action, in this particular case he would certainly have decided on his own. The decision was not without grave risk, especially for his advisers. It was only days ago, after all, that Akbar had been advancing with an army upon his wayward son, and it was Hamida Banu, once again but for the last time, who had saved him. Not only had Salim lost his grandmother, he had also lost his most influential supporter. The factions that despised him were now that much stronger. To walk alone into the imperial snake-pit would be risky for Salim; and for his faithful (as also treasonous) friends, it might well be terminal.

When, in early November 1604, Salim left Allahabad for Agra, many of these friends, too, melted away. But the prince was not deterred. Armed only with several hundred gold coins, elephants and a large diamond, and accompanied by a handful of his most loyal and fearless courtiers, Salim continued on his way. It was, he writes, the best path he could have taken, 'for through that very act I became emperor'.

His wisdom was not immediately apparent, however, even if Muhammad-Hadi writes cheerily of how Akbar 'rejoiced in his grieving heart' to see his 'fortunate son', while the 'ambitious hypocrites' of Akbar's court were 'stymied and gnashed their teeth'.

In public, yes, Akbar and Salim met cordially, even affectionately. Akbar rose and hugged his son; he accepted his offerings and even those of the men who came with him. No sooner had father and son retired from the court and entered the privacy of the women's quarters, however, than Akbar turned with pent-up fury on Salim.

Ignorant! Wayward! Presumptuous! How often had Akbar turned his face from Salim's evil? How often had he not listened to what he heard? How often erased the truth from his mind! And all Salim could do in return was spend more of his time with his wretched friends, more of his time indulging himself, all of his time soaked to the marrow in wine! Enough, it was enough! Today Salim would learn what it meant to test his father's patience!

Some accounts suggest Akbar hit his son, though his words were hard enough.

'The prince cast his eyes on the ground and answered with streaming eyes.'[67] Unmoved, Akbar called the guards and had them lock Salim in a small room in the harem, with strict instructions that he was not to get a drop of wine. 'This,' writes Inayatullah, with something like pity, 'was the hardest of punishments.'

The prince did not endure it with fortitude. Akbar may have thought that by locking him in the harem he would be keeping Salim from his Allahabad co-conspirators, but he had forgotten all about Salim's secret weapon. Women.

His sisters, his stepmothers, all were as anguished by Salim's pitiable state as Salim himself. Every day they came to the prince, in sorrow and sympathy, and every day they carried his lamentations, his remorse and his pleas to the emperor. It was not the kind of attack Akbar was trained for; he lasted only ten days. Salim was set free and, after expressing a vague intention of confining him to his own palace, Akbar restored Salim to his previous rank and gave him back his lands and his men.

At sixty-two, Akbar was losing his nerve. He was also – and this may have had much to do with his wavering vis-à-vis Salim – losing yet another son.

For all the emissaries that went to him, the doctor, the nurse, the amir, for all the swift horses, the turbans, the words of counsel and courage, Daniyal never did give up drinking. Even so, his life wasn't in complete collapse. As late as 1604, he had a son, and contracted a strategically sound marriage with a Deccani princess of Bijapur. Until the very last year of his life, he managed to give up drink for the month of Ramzan. Even in that last year, in the spring of 1605, he sent three elephants to Akbar for Nauroz, though he was still shy of appearing in court himself. According to one report,[68] this was no longer because he was ashamed of his drinking, but because he did not want to be in the fort while Salim was there too. But the idea of Daniyal worrying about Salim plotting against him, though disturbing, is laughable. Daniyal was doing a perfectly good job of plotting against himself.

Daniyal's more-or-less functional existence until his pitiful end may owe itself to Akbar's constant and relentless watch over his son. Whether effectively or not, with his messengers and his letters and his threats and his gifts, Akbar tried; and just the thought of his father's restless anxiety may have kept Daniyal this side of comatose. Eventually, however, Akbar went too far: he blocked the prince's access to drink altogether.

Wracked with withdrawal and too far from his father to plead with him as Salim had, Daniyal turned to his servants. *Bring me wine by any means!*

It was the means that killed him. While some of his servants smuggled him liquor in animal intestines, his intrepid musketeer poured liquor into Daniyal's favourite gun – One Shot to Funeral.

The thirsty prince drank long and deep from its muzzle, neither noticing nor caring for the iron rust dissolved into the alcohol. 'What thought of headache,' Inayatullah sighs, 'has the devotee of wine?'

According to Salim, his brother died before the muzzle had left his lips; Inayatullah says he lasted forty days, 'benumbed'. All he could say, the only word he could utter as he lay dying, was 'wine'.

When Akbar heard the news, he said nothing at all.

As a star gathers pace before it explodes, the endgame for empire began to play itself out at dizzying speed. Soon after Daniyal's death, Akbar went to meet Salim in secret. He took a boat across the river, where Salim was camped with his supporters in preference to sharing space with Khusro and his faction within the Agra fort. Akbar went without telling anybody, spent three hours with his only remaining son and returned. Did they talk about Daniyal? Hamida Banu? Abu'l Fazl? Akbar had not forgotten his hunt for Bir Singh Deo – his stronghold in Orchha had recently fallen and the raja had barely escaped. Or did they decide to put the past behind them? Was it weighty counsels the emperor came with, for Salim to follow when Akbar was gone?

Maybe it doesn't really matter. Whether it was an encouraging conversation or not, Salim wasn't going to give up his claim to the empire no matter how much Akbar favoured Khusro; and he would have reasonable hope that Akbar, for all his blasphemies, would hesitate to commit the breach of openly passing over his own son for the throne. Besides, Salim had received a letter of prophecy to bolster his hope. Sheikh Husayn Jami had dreamt of the founder of his order, Khwaja Baha'uddin, declaring, 'Soon Sultan Salim will mount the throne, causing the world to flourish'.[69]

There were other signs of support for Salim, too. 'When I was a prince,' he wrote, 'I heard from the sages of India that when the time of [Akbar's] rule was over, one named Nuruddin would succeed to the rule' – and one can imagine that these might have been disgruntled clerics, hoping for a Nuruddin, light of faith, to restore their world to its usual order. As Akbar's heresies (and rumours thereof) grew ever more scandalous, Salim had not been lax in playing to the disenchanted gallery of conservative Muslim fears. Recently, it had been rumoured that after the conquest of the mighty Asirgarh fort Akbar had ordered that its Jama Masjid be destroyed and replaced with a temple. Jahangir, sitting on his throne in Allahabad, had even issued farmans censoring his father's anti-Islamic decrees, declaring that 'it was improper on his part to have acted in this manner'.[70]

Akbar, meanwhile, was casting tokens of hope in every direction. With one hand, he promoted both Khusro and his uncle Man Singh, gave the former his own drum and banner, and made the latter Khusro's guardian. With the other, he put Salim in charge of running the empire, ordering that no mansab, rank, would be given without the prince's seal. And finally, having stacked the scales of his son's and grandson's fortunes with seemingly meticulous care, Akbar threw it all up to chance.

The house of Timur had a long and fascinated love affair with elephants. Once creatures that inspired awe and fear (Timur's greatest challenge in conquering Delhi was to stop his soldiers from fleeing at the sight of these animals advancing upon them), elephants became the noblest symbols of Mughal majesty, their long trunks raised in salaam the most thrilling salute an emperor could receive. Elephants in the stables of Akbar and Salim were so highly prized, writes one John Jourdain of the then fledgling East India Company, that the most valued amongst them, the ones, that is, that the emperor chose to ride himself, had 'two or four younge elaphanntes for their pages and two wives', and would appear thus in procession, 'very Ritchlie trapped with velvett, Cloth of gould and other Ritch stuffes'.

To acquire great elephants, swift and strong, to tame them and ride them and to watch them fight, these were the great pleasures of a Mughal monarch's life; the stretch of ground between the Agra fort and the Yamuna river was reserved for such entertainments.

On 20 September 1605, Akbar ordered the most memorable and portentous elephant fight of his reign. The battle was to be between Salim's magnificent Giranbar, an animal never yet defeated, and Khusro's Apurva. A third elephant, Ran Mathan, was brought from Akbar's own stable to play the role of tabancha, an elephant referee meant to disentangle the fighting elephants should their mahouts lose control.

Why Akbar dreamt up this obviously provocative and quite foolish plan no one can say. Was he thinking of the epic tests that prove a man's worth? Of Rama and Janaka's bow, of Arjuna and the eye of the fish? Was he too full of doubts, in these last moments of his life, to make a difficult decision? Was he hoping fate would choose for him? Salim doesn't mention the fight in his memoirs; nor does the *Akbarnama*, as if this last indiscretion of Akbar's was too great for even Inayatullah to explain. Muhammad-Hadi just calls it 'very strange'.[71]

At the time though, everyone would have known that, inexplicable though Akbar's idea was, it might well and forever break the balance between the two contenders for his throne. Salim and Khusro certainly knew it: while Akbar sat in the fort with young Khurram by his side, the two rivals rode their horses upon the riverside maidan, to cheer their fighters on.

For a moment, the Mughal court held its breath. And then the battle began.

No animal on earth can bring down a grown elephant; to watch two of these titans charge at each other, their wrestling trunks, their piercing tusks, flapping their ears in rage as their feet pound the earth till it shakes, it would have been a mesmerizing sight. Thomas Coryat, a writer and travelling Englishman whose great ambition was to have a picture of himself upon an elephant printed in a book, calls it 'the bravest spectacle in the worlde' the elephants seeming to 'justle together like two little mountaines' likely, unless parted, to 'exceedingly gore and cruentate one another by their murdering teeth'.

For a while, perhaps, the audience was lost in the battle, forgetting the omens it held.

Then, Salim's Giranbar began to win. With every blow he pushed Apurva backwards, trumpeting victorious rage, until it was clear that the referee Ran Mathan would have to come and separate the two pachyderms. But as soon as Ran Mathan stepped into the fight, Salim's supporters, as if possessed by Giranbar's resolve to crush Apurva until he never dared stand again, began to throw mud and stones at Ran Mathan's mahout. The poor man drove his elephant towards Giranbar, streaming blood from his brow.

At this, Muhammad-Hadi tut-tuts: 'Khusro and a group of his chatterboxes ran to [Akbar] to report with great exaggeration the audacity of [Salim's] men and the wounding of the elephant keeper, making a mountain of a molehill.' Akbar, having seemingly convinced himself that a fight like this could proceed decorously, was furious. And he proceeded to make the situation even more tense by sending Khurram, then only about thirteen years old, to scold his own father. 'Tell your Shah-bhai that Shah-baba says the elephant bout is yours. What is the reason for violence?'

Confronted by Khurram, Salim denied any hand in his supporters' misbehaviour; he even allowed Khurram to give the order for the fight to be stopped.

But who would tell Giranbar? Having lost interest in his inadequate opponent, Khusro's Apurva, Giranbar was charging at the imperial referee. Ran Mathan and his bleeding mahout were holding up as best they could but it was clearly time to try some other tested means of separating elephants: fireworks. No matter how many charkhis were lit, however, Giranbar's blood wouldn't cool; he continued to charge until Ran Mathan, defeated, ran into the river. Giranbar followed, the waters of the Yamuna tossing under his onslaught. It was only when a large boat came between the two beasts that their battle was finally ended.

So, too, was Akbar's.

The emperor who never lost in a field of war had been defeated by his own machinations in the scrabble for succession. Barely two or three days after the chaotic end of his ill-planned test for an heir, Akbar fell ill. His doctor, Hakim Ali, seems to have spent many days doing very little.[72] Describing Hakim Ali in his memoirs, Salim is, maybe understandably, equivocal: 'He was a peerless physician', he says, but 'his diligence was greater than his understanding'.

For eight days after Akbar fell ill, Hakim Ali did nothing. When Akbar became gravely ill, his dysentery 'a bloody flux',[73] the doctor gave him medicines that made him worse; ten days later, when Akbar was critical, Hakim Ali disappeared entirely, either scared of Akbar's anger or the harem's wrath, and sought the protection of Sheikh Farid, the mir bakshi who had brought Akbar news of Abu'l Fazl's death. 'Bravo,' writes Inayatullah bitterly of Farid, 'for the stony-heartedness of that amir who applied himself to his protection!'

Meanwhile, the cold war for succession grew flaming hot. Man Singh and Aziz Koka – *those old wolves* – plotted to put Salim in jail and Khusro on the throne. Salim,

camped across the river, was half prepared to flee and ill-
prepared to fight. Khurram, still as a crocodile between
these whirling eddies, sat by his grandfather's side even
though his mother sent him countless messages, telling
him to flee; such storms were no place for a boy. And
Nature, intractable, gave Salim two more sons, Jahandar
and Shahryar.

Someone had to make the first move. It was Man
Singh and Aziz Koka who did, and they made a mistake.
Instead of declaring a coup, they called for a council. In
itself, this was unprecedented; amirs would normally play
a supporting role in such matters, it was up to family blood
to assert its claims. But Man Singh and Aziz Koka were
men of as much stature and will as Akbar himself, and
besides, they were his closest surviving friends. They knew
that they knew what he wanted, and what he wanted, they
were sure, was for Khusro to reign.

The council said no. In particular, Sayyid Khan Barha
said no. The Sayyids of Barha were a clan spread across
twelve, barha, villages of what is now Muzaffarnagar,
renowned, writes Beni Prasad, for both 'religious zeal and
martial honour'. Salim would call them 'the outstanding
brave men of their time' and his memoirs are littered with
praise and promotions for various valorous men of their
tribe. Even Aziz Koka, writes Salim, 'always used to say,
"Barha sayyids are the bulwark of the empire." And it's true.'

The most flavourful sense of the pride of these Sayyids,
however, comes from this eighteenth-century joke told by
the poet Mir: 'People asked a sayyid from Barha, "How
long has it been that you sayyids settled in Barha?"

'"Five thousand years," he replied.

'They said, "But 'sayyid-ness' is traced from the Prophet, peace be upon him, and the whole world knows how long ago he, the most select of men, lived."

'"He was a sayyid of one kind,' the fellow replied, 'and we are of another."'[74]

In short, Sayyid Khan Barha was not a man to be taken lightly. He took on the two conspirators as he would have a contingent in war. To supersede a son while he was alive and able went against every ethical and moral principle on which the Mughal dynasty was founded. No matter how Man Singh and Aziz Koka denounced Salim's incompetence, Sayyid Khan Barha would have none of it. Finally, gathering his supporters, he walked out of the council and effectively broke it.

Beating drums of victory, the Sayyids of Barha crossed the Yamuna and joined the prince. As news of his powerful supporters spread, more and more amirs arrived to pay homage to their future emperor; eventually even Aziz Koka came to Salim and pledged allegiance.

The next day, Salim met his father for the last time. They did not speak. Akbar couldn't any more, although all through his growing weakness the emperor had made himself stand upon his usual balcony at the usual hour, to give the people their usual darshan of their ruler. With his heir before him, Akbar signalled that Salim wear his turban and his robe, that he bind Akbar's own dagger around his waist. He gestured all of this and he watched him do it; then he closed his eyes.

On a Thursday in the third week of October 1605, a full
week's mourning after his father died, and a long and
restless thirty-six years after he'd been brought into this
world – through Akbar's incessant prayers, the Chishtis'
intercession and God's mercy – Salim did what he had
been born to do.

No longer Salim, no more Sheikhu baba, he ascended
the throne as Nuruddin Muhammad Jahangir, the light
of faith, conqueror of the world, and ready to take his
place in history.

He became emperor of Hindustan.

Part II

Empire

It was a Hill
Of Paradise the highest, from whose top
The Hemisphere of Earth in cleerest Ken
Stretcht out to amplest reach of prospect lay.

. . .

His eyes might there command whatever stood
City of old or modern fame, the seat
Of mightiest empire, from the destined walls
Of Cambalu, seat of Cathian Can,
And Samarcand by Oxus, Temir's throne,
To Paquin of Sinaen Kings, and thence
To Agra and Lahore of Great Mogul . . .

John Milton, *Paradise Lost*, Book XI (1667)

They say the past is a foreign country, so perhaps it is fitting to look at the world that Jahangir ruled through the wide eyes of the farangs who travelled to its shores. For many of these Europeans, this wasn't just a six-month ship ride into the relatively unknown – it was a journey into fantasy. Pietro Della Valle, for example, an amiable Italian who came to India in the 1620s, recounts a conversation with the captain of his ship, in which the two men discussed not whether but where unicorns may be found.

Both as it was imagined and as it actually existed, the Hindustan that Akbar ruled and passed on to Jahangir was, to European eyes, magnificent and exotic – and for modern Indians, looking into that past can be a mildly hallucinatory experience, both familiar and incredibly strange.

Over a lifetime of winning battles and friendships, Akbar had brought all the various kingdoms of the north Indian plains – Mewar holding out – into the folds of his empire; he ruled, also, the ports of Gujarat; the busy rivers of Bengal; Multan, Sindh and parts of Balochistan,

Kabul, Qandahar and Kashmir, not to mention his final acquisitions in and around Burhanpur.[1]

Sir Thomas Roe, England's first ambassador to an Indian king, spent about four years in Jahangir's court, and described the emperor's territory as 'farre greater than the Persians, and almost equall, if not as great as, the Turkes. His meanes of money ... above both.' Roe's chaplain, the Reverend Edward Terry, hailed the 'Great Mogol' as the 'greatest knowne king of the East, if not of the world'.

In modern terms, the Mughal empire was a superpower,[2] it is hard, even now, to begin to describe it. There was, of course, the sheer abundance of the land itself, what more than one European calls the 'fatness' of its soil. 'The land abounds,' writes Terry, 'in singular good wheate, rice, barley, and divers other kindes of graine to make bread', and an 'abundance of other good provisions' to eat it with. There were fruits of every kind, melons, mangoes, oranges, dates, grapes, figs, and Terry's favourite ananas, the pineapple of which he provides this lovely description: 'a pleasing compound made of strawberries, claret wine, rose-water, and sugar, well-tempered together'. Meat was equally plentiful. Besides the cow, which was forbidden (though substituted by buffalo, 'like beefe, but not so wholsome'), 'it were as infinite as needlesse ... to write of their geese, duckes, pigeons, partridges, quailes, peacocks, and many such singular good fowle ... bought at such easie rates as I have seene a good mutton sold for the value of one shilling ... one hare for the value of a penie'. A man needn't pay even that if he chose to catch his own dinner. 'The whole kingdome is as it were a forrest, for a man can travell no way but he shall see [deer, hares, fish and fowle], and . . . they are every mans game'.

Thomas Coryat, the first English backpacker on Indian soil, accomplished the no mean feat of walking from Aleppo to Ajmer; it took him ten months and cost him three pounds, 'victuals beeing so cheape . . . that I oftentimes lived competentlie for a pennie sterling a day'. Future men and women of his ilk would (and do) echo Coryat's extolment of the cheapness of travel in the East, but this was not then, as it is now, a corollary of eastern poverty; if anything, it was a mark of its riches. 'No part of the world,' writes Coryat, '[yields] a more fruitful veine of ground than all that which lieth in [Jahangir's] empire'. The only place that could possibly compare with it, in Coryat's imagination, was the Garden of Eden.

This prelapsarian wealth wasn't confined to the fruits of the soil, however. There was also the bounty of mineral wealth hidden underneath it. In Patna, for example, a trader called Robert Finch watched how 'they digge deepe pits in the earth, and washe the earth in great bolles, and therein they find the gold'. There was plenty of silver, too, but the empire's wealth wasn't confined to these precious metals either. As Edward Terry would remark, Mughal Hindustan didn't need to dig out its own silver, 'being so enriched by other nations'. Streams of silver were flowing into the empire, he said, 'as all rivers to the sea'.

Other Europeans would put it in other words. William Hawkins, an Englishman who was briefly in Jahangir's employ as his 'English khan', wrote that 'India is rich in silver, for all nations bring coyne and carry away commodities for the same; and this coyne is buried in

India and goeth not out'. Francisco Pelsaert, a Dutch merchant, described the predicament of his cash-poor compatriots having to slash prices for their Indonesian spices, arm-twisted by 'crafty Hindu merchants' who realized how the Europeans were desperate to sell, needing ready money for all the Indian goods they wanted to buy. The balance of trade was so heavily tilted in favour of India (and the East, generally) that European governments tried to limit the amount of bullion their trading houses could take abroad. Thomas Roe gets to the heart of it when he evokes the plight of the English king's empty mint 'which . . . cryes like a hungry belly against this trade'.

As long as India had more to sell than it needed to buy – and there was very little, at the time, that Europe could offer the empire, 'no Comoditye,' writes Roe, 'that will prove staple and certaynly vendable' – Europe could only watch as its treasuries emptied, its coins rolled East. If, Roe warned, England did not, and quickly, think of an alternative, 'our state . . . must fall to the ground by the weaknes of its owne leggs'.

Just because India was not interested in European goods, however, did not mean that it was not a sizeable market for imports. In fact, as Roe would discover, the Indian emperor and nobility were used to the very best from across the globe. Having arrived in India as a representative of King James I, with a mandate to secure favourable trading contracts for the nascent East India Company, Thomas Roe spent much of his time in the Mughal court trying to maintain – more accurately, manufacture – an equivalence between his own king and

Jahangir.[3] It was a doomed enterprise, mostly because the poverty of the ambassador, and therefore his king, was all too apparent, especially when it came to the gifts Roe gave the emperor and his amirs. 'The Presentes you have this yeare sent,' wrote Roe in one of his many such complaints to the Company, 'are extremly despised by those who have seene them'. The velvet lining of the coach was faded, the knives 'little and meane', the magnifying glasses and telescopes cheap, the pictures not worth a second glance. 'Here are nothing esteemed but of the best sorts,' he continued, 'good Cloth and fine, and rich Pictures, they comming out of Italy overland and from Ormus; soe that they laugh at us for such as wee bring'.

By contrast, the Persian ambassador who came to Jahangir while Roe was in attendance brought with him a whole caravan of gifts, including twenty-seven Persian and Arabian horses, twenty-one camel-loads of wine, seven of velvet, one of Persian brocade, daggers and swords set with gems, guns, rubies, carpets and so much more that just the giving of gifts took over a week; or, as Roe noted bitterly, 'The Play will not bee finished in ten dayes'.

Not surprisingly, Persia was also a key partner in the Mughal empire's thriving international trade. In fact, the Italian Pietro Della Valle saw his first Holi celebration in the Persian city of Isfahan, which had a large community of Hindu traders. And no wonder: every year, 14,000 camels went from India to Persia via Qandahar, itself a strategically important town on the border between the two empires, and a hub of trade in the region. Another hub was Aleppo, and Persian caravans to India often came via this Syrian city; the caravans could be the size of small towns themselves. Thomas Coryat travelled with one and describes it as having 2000 camels, 1500 horses, 1000 mules, 800 asses and 6000 people! Merchants would also arrive from Kashgar, then a Central Asian kingdom and the entry to the famously secretive Chinese empire. No more than ten or fifteen merchants at a time were allowed into China, so caravans would camp in Kashgar, waiting their turn. Far more open were the port towns of the Red Sea and the Persian Gulf, Mocha, Hormuz and Bahrain; the busy trading town of Pegu, now in Myanmar; and the archipelagos of Southeast Asia.

Once in the Mughal's realm, merchants had their pick of big cities, busy with trade, Agra, Lahore and the ports of Cambay and Surat foremost among them. The roads, wide and tree-lined, were well equipped for travellers with wells and caravanserais (though not entirely free of bandits). In Gujarat, Jahangir noticed low walls along the way, meant for porters to rest their loads on, so they might 'take a breather and then easily get under way again without anyone else's assistance'. Merchants travelled on camels and mules, on speeding bullock carts, loud warning bells hanging from the animals' muscular necks, and often by ship.

It is a truth commonly acknowledged that India produced no real maritime power except the Cholas; less well known is the fact that Indians were great sailors, if not so much on the sea, then certainly on the country's rivers. The Ganga flowing to Bengal and the Yamuna through Agra carried an immense traffic of ships laden with goods.[4]

Most contemporary descriptions of these goods read like Ali Baba's sigh at the first sight of his cave. From the Mughal realm, of course, the most valuable export was cloth: the muslins of Dhaka, the silks of Patna, the brocades of Banaras, the shawls of Kashmir had no comparison in the world. The empire also produced opium and other drugs, pepper, sugar and rice, vermilion, lac and, of course, indigo. In return, the empire consumed every kind of rarity and luxury that was available, from Qandahar's heeng (asafoetida) and Kabul's fruit to Malabar's coconuts; porcelain and musk from China, rubies and sapphires from Burma, diamonds from Vijayanagar and the island of Java, pearls from Bahrain and the Hainan island in the South China Sea. Camphor from Borneo 'was dearer than gold', writes Ralph Fitch, and white sandalwood from Timor in great demand because it was used as an anointing paste. Spices came from the Maluku Islands and gave them the sobriquet they carry still; the best pepper from Cochin; benzoin (or benjamin) from Thailand; ivory and amber from Africa – and not much more than woollen cloth from Europe.

There was little use for woollen cloth in the heat of the north Indian plains. Muqarrab Khan, who was Jahangir's governor in Surat for some years, tried to help Thomas Roe by telling him he was bringing 'too much Cloth and ill swoordes and almost nothing else; that every body was weary of yt'. Soon after, Roe got a message from his merchants in Agra telling him they hadn't sold a thing in three months and could barely afford to eat.

Driven by aching bellies, both literal and metaphorical, locked in bitter competition with each other for whatever small corner of the Indian coast they could ply their ships on, European traders would begin to realize that it wasn't the diamonds of Golconda, the gold of Patna, that would enrich them – though they would get that, too – but the vast Indian market. If only India were no longer 'able to subsist and flourish of it self, without the least help from any neighbour' as Terry has it. If only Indians would hanker after European goods . . . wouldn't that be nice, to till the fatness of Indian soil towards the fattening of European wallets?

For the moment, though, this was no more than a dream, less likely than unicorns. During his five years in India near the beginning of Jahangir's reign, William Hawkins, the English khan, estimated the empire's annual income at over 56 million pounds; England's, by comparison, was less than half a million. In fact, therefore, there was no comparison and so most travellers didn't make it; instead, they wrote urgent observations of this magnificent land – as if to tell the world back home, *Look, this too is possible!* – often with wonder, often with disdain, and usually with a mixture of both: scorn disguising the envy that the wonder aroused.

In the winter of 1605, when Jahangir finally ascended the Mughal throne, he was as splendidly unaware of the turmoil of fascination and greed that his empire was arousing across Western Europe as a lion may be of the machinations of ants. That is not to say, however, that he wasn't aware of the precariousness of his position. Akbar's death had shaken his realm. A young Jain merchant called

Banarasidas fainted when he heard the news, fell down and hurt his head. 'The people felt suddenly orphaned and insecure without their sire,' Banarasidas wrote. A. Azfar Moin,[5] who tells the story of Banarasidas in *The Millennial Sovereign*, adds that across the empire, 'bazaars shut down, people buried their jewels, put on old clothes, and expected the worst'.[6]

Jahangir's accession, a week after his father's shattering death, would have been a grand affair, but the new emperor would also have known that he must belie the fears of his people urgently, or risk losing the throne he had gained by the breadth of a hair. As, indeed, he almost did.

A contemporary painting by Abu'l Hasan shows a scene of the Agra fort crowded with celebration; men and women heralding the new reign with trumpets and drums; horses and elephants jostling for space; some of the men prostrate in thanksgiving, others gazing with wide eyes; every kind of hat one can imagine, conical and flat, feathered and peaked, turban and fez, one man even carrying a basket of chickens on his head – and above it all, high upon the gate of the fort, a stately peacock standing serene against a blue sky.

Amid the crowd is a man in a black cassock and flat-topped black hat, probably one of the Jesuit priests who undertook prolonged missions to Akbar's and Jahangir's courts. By the Jesuits' account, the new emperor had 'ordered a dais, very splendidly adorned . . . and he came forth and took his seat thereon. The people brought gifts to him, and all shouted . . . "Hail King."'[7]

Padishah Salamat!

Barely had the cry stopped echoing through the

narrow, crowded streets of Agra, when a whisper arose in its wake – *Sultan Shah! King Sultan!* Sultan Khusro and his supporters, outmanoeuvred once, were gathering again. Not even six months after Jahangir became emperor, his eldest son revolted.

But first, the lull. As night began to fall, Jahangir went into the private chambers of the fort, no doubt to continue a more intimate celebration with the men who had stuck with him so loyally over the course of his seemingly endless princehood. The next morning, he would begin his rule.

The Agra where Jahangir began his reign was one of the largest cities in the world, with 'so many buildings', writes the new emperor, that 'several cities of . . . Persia, Khursan, and Transoxania' would fit in it. It wasn't as well planned or attractive as, say, Lahore, and it had exploded during the long years of Akbar's rule, much of which was spent in this city, growing somewhat organically around the Agra fort.[8] Most of its glamour came from the massive fort and the mansions of the nobility that flanked it along the banks of the Yamuna. The city was thus shaped like a half-moon, the prime waterfront property forming its flat edge to the east and more modest homes its western bulk. The riverside, with its beautiful homes and elegant inhabitants, was, in the words of the Dutch trader Francisco Pelsaert, 'very gay and magnificent'. The bulk of the city, on the other hand, was built close and dense, houses often three or four storeys tall, Hindu and Muslim,[9] well-off and poor all jumbled together in such congestion, said Jahangir, 'that one can scarcely pass in the lanes and markets'.

It was a bustle not bereft of hazard. Both fire and sickness could spread with frightening speed; once, Jahangir found himself exiled from his own capital for months because of a virulent plague. William Finch describes a conflagration that lasted for about six weeks in the summer of 1610, 'fires night and day, flaming in one part or other, whereby many thousand houses were consumed, besides men, women, children and cattell, [so] that we feared the judgement of Sodome and Gomorrha upon the place'.

Still, this being a city of the garden-loving Mughals after all, hazards like fast-spreading fires were offset by a 'luxuriance of groves all around', which, said Pelsaert, made it look more like 'a royal park rather than a city'. Jahangir gives a vivid description of the many sweet smells that wafted through the town in which he grew up: of the delicate scent of yellow champa; of keora 'sharp and heady' and jasmine-like rae bel; of maulsari, growing mild and profuse upon its 'stately, harmonious and shady' trees. The trees themselves were no less varied, many from other parts of the world, from cypresses and pines of temperate climes to sandalwoods from 'the islands'. Mangoes ('my particular favourite,' says Jahangir) grew abundantly here, of course, but the Mughals had planted other fruits, too – every year, for example, the Gulafshan garden, laid by Babur, yielded thousands of sweet pineapples.

Not far from the fort was Agra's main market, where every morning one would find 'horses, camels, oxen, tents, cotton goods, and many other things', while across the river, in Sikandra, there was a custom house where ships and bullock carts would come and go heaped with goods from and for all parts of the empire and beyond, from cotton and carpets to butter and grain.

The man in whose name, under whose protection and for whose profit all this frenzied activity continued and expanded – Emperor Jahangir – began his reign with what would become a sustained effort to give his people the two things that a busy economy needs most: justice and peace. The Jesuits say that Jahangir declared himself the Adil Padishah, Just Emperor; and by his own account, Jahangir's first act as king was to command the creation of a Chain of Justice. In this, he may have been inspired by his grandfather Humayun, who had installed a drum near his hall of public audience, which anyone present could beat should he need the emperor's adjudication. Jahangir's chain was both more flamboyant and expansive: 120 kilos of pure gold strung twenty-five metres from a tower in the fort to a stone pillar by the river below. Anyone, he declared, 'who had suffered injustice could have recourse to the chain' and its sixty golden bells would peal their grievance directly to the emperor's ear.

Whether or not anyone ever did so is perhaps beside the point. From the beginning of his reign, Jahangir wanted to position himself as a saviour of the downtrodden, distributing both justice and prosperity – so much so that ten years later he would commission a startlingly propagandist painting of himself shooting arrows at a shrivelled old man representing poverty.

Having ordered the Chain, Jahangir broadcast twelve benevolent decrees: he ordered the building of sarais and wells on deserted roads to drive out bandits, and of imperially funded hospitals in large cities; he guaranteed inheritance of property without state interference and commanded that proceeds from property without heir be used for public infrastructure; he forbade the searching of traders' cargo without their permission, the use of civilian houses as barracks, and the cutting off of ears and noses as punishment. In continuation of what Badauni had considered Akbar's policy of Hindu appeasement, Jahangir forbade animal slaughter on the day of his accession (Thursday), of Akbar's birth (Sunday), and, each year, for a number of days equal to the years of his own life (that number to increase, naturally, with every passing birthday). To please the mullahs, Jahangir banished certain un-Islamic taxes and also the manufacture and sale of alcohol.[10]

On this last point, however, he couldn't help inserting a caveat that is not only an indication of the emperor's playful mind, but also, perhaps, of how seriously his new decrees would be taken, even by his own self. Having prohibited 'wine, spirits, or any sort of intoxicant or forbidden liquor', Jahangir confesses, quite charmingly, that he is doing so 'despite the fact that I myself commit the sin of drinking wine and have constantly done so from the age of eighteen'. There follows a brief but precise chronology of his alcoholism and de-addiction, ending with a regal disregard for the facts: 'these days I drink solely to promote digestion'.

Whether or not this and his other decrees were implemented with any rigour would have depended not only on the emperor's enthusiasm to have his bidding done but also on his administrators' will to do it: imperial orders, though issued with great force, were implemented with bureaucratic compromise. There was one decree, however, in which Jahangir may have taken a keen and personal interest: this was the twelfth and last, and in it, perhaps, lay the key to Jahangir's strategy for peace.

'I ordered generally that my father's servants' ranks and jagirs would remain as they were. After these preliminaries I increased the rank of each one according to his worth, but not less than twenty percent and up to triple and quadruple.' In other words, there would be no reprisals, only rewards.

Even to men whom he mistrusted or even feared, Jahangir showed favour. Raja Man Singh, who had lobbied for Khusro, was reconfirmed as governor of Bengal and given robes of honour, a jewelled sword and a horse besides, even though, writes Jahangir discreetly, 'on account of several things that had happened he did not expect this favour'. Qilich Khan, who had conscientiously defended the Agra treasury from the rebel prince, was made governor of Gujarat. Even those turncoat friends who had taken Jahangir's side when he set up his rebel court in Allahabad despaired as the rebellion grew ever more protracted and, losing faith in Jahangir's spirit while fearing Akbar's wrath, abandoned him, received gracious acceptance from the new emperor. As Jahangir writes of one such friend, Khwaja Abdullah Khan, 'despite such disloyalty, I reconfirmed him in [his] rank … if he had not committed that one fault, he would be without blemish'. Even Abu'l Fazl's son received a robe of honour, and his mission to hunt out Bir Singh Deo was tactfully forgotten.

For the Bundela raja himself, and others like him who had been unstinting in their loyalty, Jahangir's accession was the dawn they had long been awaiting. It did not disappoint. Bir Singh Deo was given a rank of 3000; the emperor never forgot the debt he owed him, and year after year his rank would increase. Sharif Khan, Jahangir's childhood friend and the ill-chosen messenger Akbar had sent to Allahabad to set his son straight, but who had, instead, joined Jahangir's rebellion, was made amir-ul-umara, amir of all amirs, 'higher than which there is no title'. Zamana Beg, another childhood friend, received a threefold promotion and the title Mahabat Khan. Sheikh Hussain, 'very nimble and quick in service' and the man Jahangir most trusted to bleed him when he was ill, was titled Muqarrab Khan and sent on the sensitive mission of bringing Daniyal's family back north from Burhanpur and of apprising Abdur Rahim, the khan khanan, of his new ruler's (and former student's) plans. Khubu, Jahangir's best friend, foster brother and Sheikh Salim Chishti's grandson, would soon receive rewards beyond his dreams; and various other sons and grandsons of the saint, whom Jahangir counted among his closest companions, were given high ranks and titles, particularly Sheikh Ala'uddin, 'a very manly and good person at heart', who was titled Islam Khan and would work wonders in consolidating Mughal rule in Bengal during Jahangir's reign. 'His loyalty to me is so great,' wrote the emperor with foresight, 'that I have exalted him by addressing him as "son".'

The full extent of Jahangir's strategic generosity may be gauged by the fact that even for his eldest son, whose loyalty he had most reason to suspect, the emperor had only kind-hearted plans. Khusro was given a mansion and a lakh of rupees to renovate it with.

This was, after all, the beginning of a new era; together, Jahangir and his subjects were entering a new world, his world, and even if there were reservations on both sides, Jahangir, at any rate, was willing to put his aside; willing to make a promise of peace and fair play; even willing, if he must, to undertake the crucial imperial obligation he had resisted so far: conquest.

Within weeks of his accession, Jahangir had given his second son, Parvez, command of a fresh campaign against Rana Amar Singh of Mewar; and soon the emperor was jotting down an ambitious to-do list that led from victory in Mewar to a conquest, led by Jahangir himself, of the Mughals' holy grail, Samarkand,[11] and ended with triumph over the Deccan. In sum, Jahangir would bribe for loyalty and he wasn't above battling for it either; and even if he might never command the devotion his father had, he would settle for acceptance. It wasn't, he might have thought, too much to ask.

Not only did Jahangir not ask for much, on the first Nauroz after his accession, he even gave back the gifts his nobility brought for him. Nauroz, new day, is the ancient Persian new year, and it became – with Dussehra, Diwali, Shab-e-Barat, Shivratri, the two Eids and the emperor's own birthday – a favourite festival of the Mughals, celebrated over nineteen days every March. 'In my father's time,' writes Jahangir, 'it was customary for the great amirs to give a party every day and arrange rare offerings of all sorts of jewels, gem-studded vessels, precious textiles, elephants and horses, and persuade His Majesty to attend' – and to accept their gifts. In March 1606, Jahangir ordered the usual grand arrangements. The walls of his durbars were hung with beautiful cloth; musicians, singers, 'dancing gypsies and charmers of India, who could steal away the hearts from angels' were gathered to entertain. Their audience was given leave to drink their fill. However, while Jahangir ensured that revelry did not lag, he demonstrated remarkable renunciation when it came to those gifts, writing that as he was 'inclined to the welfare and ease of military and civilian alike', he 'gave back all the gifts except a little bit from a few intimates'.

In itself, this may not seem very significant. What need had the emperor, to whom everything already belonged, for gifts? But gift-giving was integral to the Mughal economy and polity in more ways than one; and for Jahangir himself, it was a source of personal aesthetic and intellectual pleasure. When one sees the sheer joy with which Jahangir would receive the many gifts he got in years to come, one realizes how keen he must have been, that March, to bring all the variously embroiled mansabdars into his own camp. It was a sacrifice he would make only one more time, and in vastly happier circumstances. This year, however, he would realize that no sacrifice could guard against the lure of power.

Ever since his father's victory in their race for the throne, Khusro had been, in Jahangir's words, 'preoccupied and distracted'. Jahangir's claim that he went out of his way to 'remove the worries and concerns from [Khusro's] mind' may well be exaggerated, but no matter how hard he tried, it is easy to imagine, even sympathize with, Khusro's frustration. He was barely eighteen years old and had been *this* close to the crown, supported not only by the crowds of ambitious amirs who gravitated towards rival centres of power, but also by his powerful uncle and father-in-law and, most of all, his charismatic and beloved grandfather. Now, anticipating a future that held little but a new mansion and the prospect of waiting endlessly, like Jahangir had, for his own chance to rule, perhaps unable, also, to bear the thought of submitting to a father he had long been taught to regard as debauched and unfit for power, Khusro cracked.

In April 1606, two weeks after Nauroz, Khusro and a few hundred soldiers rode out of Agra as if to visit Akbar's grave in Sikandra. They didn't come back. That night a lamplighter – noticing, perhaps, the ominous darkness of Khusro's quarters – told one of Jahangir's viziers that the prince had fled. The vizier rushed to Sharif Khan, the amir-ul-umara, who 'came in a tizzy'[12] to the emperor.

Jahangir, whose own rebellion had been such a laid-back affair, wasn't expecting this; he ambled out of the harem thinking Sharif Khan had come with news from the provinces. When he heard what had really happened, he didn't know how to react. Should he go himself, should he – since Parvez had left to chase the rana – send young Khurram? Sharif Khan said he would set out immediately if the emperor commanded it, but asked what if Khusro wouldn't be persuaded, what if he chose to fight? *Do what you must*, said Jahangir, *a king knows no bonds of blood.*

No sooner had Sharif Khan left, however, than Jahangir had second thoughts. Khusro was *his* own blood, after all, and what had Sultan Salim done to a favoured envoy of his father's? 'God forbid,' writes Jahangir, poor Abu'l Fazl's bloodied head rising visibly in his mind, 'God forbid that they should think up a plot against him [Sharif Khan] and do away with him!'

He sent reinforcements, and rode out himself the next day, leaving in such a hurry that not only did he forget to ask astrologers for an auspicious hour for the chase but he even forgot his morning opium.

Jahangir's hurry isn't explained by his fears for Sharif Khan alone, no matter how poetically just that might be. No; not only was the slowly ripened fruit of his patience being snatched from him, he wasn't at all sure by whom. Sharif Khan himself, after all, had betrayed Akbar's trust. All the men Jahangir depended on had betrayed Akbar's trust. Who was to say they would not betray his?

As one of the Jesuits observed, 'all was confusion in the palace'. Waking to find that the emperor had galloped away with practically no escort ('encumbered by no one and nothing', he writes himself), the amirs hurried to their horses and chased after him. Jahangir was right, however, to set off as promptly as he did. He says so himself. Just as he had gone to Agra to meet his father after Hamida Banu Begum died, this was a critical decision Jahangir made without – even against – the advice of his amirs. The Jesuits, too, agree: according to them, the new emperor was already less popular than his rebel son. It would take all his determination and luck to stem the tide from turning against him.

Perhaps nothing illustrates the general lack of faith in Jahangir's fortunes as clearly as these two incidents from the tree-lined roads that led from Agra to Lahore, on which father chased son, fickle amirs in tow. The first is the story of the impulsive Hasan Beg. As he was passing Mathura, Khusro came across a nobleman from Kabul, one Hasan Beg Khan Badakhshi, who, along with some two or three hundred of his tribesmen, was en route to Agra, to pay homage to the new emperor. Upon learning of Khusro's rebellion, however, he joined it straight away, embarking upon a rambunctious rampage through the countryside which, at least in Jahangir's telling, did little to boost Khusro's popularity. (Hasan Beg's nonchalant defection was hardly abnormal, it seems. A few days later, in Panipat, Khusro would meet another capricious amir, Abdul Rahim, and promptly make him his vizier.)

The emperor, for his part, gave all the Badakhshi tribesmen in his army a prompt and generous bonus, lest they decide to defect to their fellows in Hasan Beg's camp; besides, he also ordered that money be distributed to 'the poor and Brahmins along the way', in order to purchase some of the goodwill Khusro was squandering through his riotous new friends.

The second incident is that of the failed prophecy. While some rajas and amirs would, no doubt, have kept their newly made vows of loyalty, and while others would have shown a more calculated allegiance to their own advantage, a great many would have been merely confused. One of this number was the zamindar of Bikaner, Rai Singh Bhurtiya. When Jahangir set off on his urgent pursuit, Rai Singh did not immediately follow. Instead, he looked for advice.

Amongst the many religious orders that Akbar patronized was that of the Jains, and as it happened a leader of the Sewra sect, Man Singh, was then in Agra. Rai Singh went to the priest and asked him how long he thought Jahangir's reign would last. 'The black-tongued beggar,' writes Jahangir sardonically, many years later, 'said, "At most two years."' At this, Jahangir continues, Rai Singh 'the idiot went off to his homeland without leave'; though from the zamindar's perspective, of course, it would have been eminently sensible to disengage from whatever chaos was descending upon the empire and wait it out in Bikaner. Fortunately for Rai Singh, Jahangir did not hold this against him, though for the Sewras he conceived a great antipathy, and eventually expelled them from his realm. Man Singh, meanwhile, contracted leprosy soon after his misjudged prediction – a fact that Jahangir records with evident satisfaction – and, years later, when Jahangir called him to court out of the blue, the monk was so terrified he committed suicide.[13]

For the moment, however, Man Singh was not the only religious leader from whom advice was being sought, nor the only one to underestimate Jahangir's chances. Among them was Sheikh Nizam Thanesari, who not only met Khusro, blessed the rebel and travelled awhile with him, but was self-assured enough, thereafter, to go and meet Jahangir. Not amused, the emperor sent the sheikh ('one of the great imposters of the age') to Mecca – a popular euphemism for exile. Guru Arjan Dev, the fifth Sikh Guru, poet and compiler of the Adi Granth, met a grimmer fate.

Whether because Akbar had shown the guru favour – once even visiting his hermitage – whether from kindness for Akbar's grandson or sympathy for Khusro's cause, Guru Arjan Dev met the prince, blessed him and put a protective tika on his forehead; perhaps, he even gave him some money. A few months later, 'when this was reported to me,' says Jahangir, 'I realized how perfectly false he was and ordered him brought to me.' The guru's property was confiscated and he, himself, was imprisoned and then killed.

For the moment, however, the fates of all these men, and the fates, most of all, of Khusro and Jahangir hung in a delicate balance; one bit of luck here, one mistake there, and history would be forever changed.

Fortunately for Jahangir, he had all the luck and his son made all the mistakes. For one thing, though he hurtled with all speed to Lahore, Khusro didn't reach the city before news of his rebellion did and its gates were closed against him. Even so, over the course of the nine-day siege that followed, Khusro's forces expanded; Lahore was a great town and its capture promised rich plunder. The Jesuits caught in the city, for example, were in a state of panic: Armenian merchants had stored some goods in their houses and, should the rebellion succeed, the poor Fathers feared they would be ransacked, and possibly killed.

Soon, Khusro's army had about twelve thousand men, and was confident enough – it was reported to Jahangir –

to plan a surprise attack on the imperial vanguard rushing towards them. Though it was already dark and pouring rain, the anxious emperor and his army marched all night to catch up with the endangered advance forces. At noon the next day, they were still way behind, not yet across the Beas river, but Jahangir had decided to restore himself with a pot of biryani. He was just about to eat when news arrived: battle had begun! Taking only a mouthful for luck (although, he confesses, 'I was very desirous of eating the biryani'), Jahangir began to ride without even waiting for his armour, carrying just a spear and a sword to fight with, barely fifty men scurrying behind him.

This was not the day that Jahangir's luck would be tested, however. Barely had the emperor and his ill-prepared troops crossed the Beas when an amir called Shamsi Toshakchi (forever after Khushkhabar – good news – Khan) arrived with news of victory.

The imperial vanguard may have been outnumbered but it was far more disciplined than Khusro's ragtag mercenaries. Besides, the emperor had those Sayyids of Barha on his side: having fought to put Jahangir on the throne, now they died to keep him on it. Barely fifty or sixty of these men, writes Jahangir, killed over a thousand Badakhshis, and though the Sayyids were 'themselves cut to shreds' they demoralized (and diminished) Khusro's troops so much that when a reserve contingent rode into battle – *Padishah Salamat!* – the rebels 'went to pieces'.[14] Khusro even dropped a precious jewel chest he always carried with him.

Soon the eighteen-year-old with little experience of leading men in battle, let alone in battle against a mighty empire, fumbled again. Many of his remaining supporters wanted to make an immediate about-turn, return to Agra and capture the capital while it was unoccupied; others suggested they go east and seek protection and counsel from Khusro's uncle Raja Man Singh; and Husain Beg wanted to go back home, and suggested Khusro come with him to Kabul. The prince chose Kabul.

Maybe he was thinking of his grand-uncle Mirza Hakim, who had rebelled against Akbar, lost to Murad yet continued to rule the distant province of Kabul in relative peace thereafter. Maybe Man Singh in Bengal was too far away. Whatever his reasons, Khusro made a bad decision: he had only to announce that they were off to Kabul and all his Indian troops vanished, unwilling to travel so far and so uncertainly from home. Since most of the Badakhshis had been killed by the Sayyids of Barha, this left Khusro with barely a handful of soldiers, besides Husain Beg and that vacillating amir from Panipat, Abdul Rahim.

Jahangir, meanwhile, wasn't resting on his laurels. He sent his best commanders, including Raja Basu (on whose behalf, as prince, Jahangir had interceded with Akbar) and Mahabat Khan, armed with plenty of troops and plenty of money to pay them with, to hunt out Khusro wherever he might go.

The rebel prince and his allies, tired, outnumbered and growing desperate, rode as fast and long as they could to the north, so exhausted at the end of the day that they fell into a dead sleep wherever they lay. 'No one of the party took the slightest heed of his comrade', writes an anonymous historian from that time, telling a story he claims to have heard from Khusro himself.[15] 'The horses also lay neglected on the ground. After a short time, a jackal came and seized hold of [Khusro's] foot, but his boots saved him from injury.'

To be nibbled at by jackals may seem bad enough, but the once favoured prince's fortunes would plunge much further. One fateful night, in a village on the banks of the Chenab, Khusro and his men were looking for boats to take them across. They had just negotiated a deal when the village chaudhary came by and recognized them. Now that it was clear which side was winning, helping Khusro would have been suicide, and the chaudhary wasn't interested in such martyrdom. The rebels were already on the boat, pushing themselves off its banks when the chaudhary grabbed the steering pole from the boatman's hands. Not all the bribes and threats in the world would persuade the gathered villagers to return the pole nor another boatman to join the crew. Husain Beg shouted curses and aimed angry arrows at the stubborn crowd, but what could he do? The rudderless boat meandered off with the current and – guided by the spirits that had long protected Jahangir – into a sandbank.

And there he sat, the young rebel with his furious adherents, helpless as the sun rose on his wretched plight, until imperial soldiers arrived to arrest him.

Khusro's feet were bound in velvet-coated fetters. Perhaps this indulgence, traditional in the house of Timur, eased the terror in his heart, but it is unlikely. The emperor received the rebels in a garden on the outskirts of Lahore, the auspicious hour for entering the city having not yet come. Khusro was brought before him. He tried, despite his chains, to fall prostrate. Instead, he was made to stand between his two 'commanders', Husain Beg and Abdul Rahim. He was 'trembling and weeping', writes Jahangir, but whatever effect this might have had on his paternal self, the emperor was unmoved. 'The whole court awaited in suspense the sentence of the King', writes a Jesuit. They did not wait very long.

Jahangir's wrath exploded. 'He upbraided [Khusro] in the most bitter terms' – *What brave captains you picked!* Then, turning to his two supporters, he continued with bitter sarcasm, *What a fine and great king you chose for yourself!*

Khusro, in his terrified convulsions, was unable to utter a word. Husain Beg tried to speak in his own defence; he was promptly silenced. Abdul Rahim, wiser, said nothing.

What a fine sight you are!

The sight would soon turn into a gruesome spectacle. The prince was led away by guards, his 'amirs' to a greatly more horrifying end. Husain Beg and Abdul Rahim were wrapped, naked, in animal skin – the Badakhshi was stuffed into a freshly killed ox, Abdur Rahim into a donkey – and mounted backwards on asses they were paraded through the city. Husain Beg died of suffocation; Abdul Rahim, perhaps because donkey skin is more porous, perhaps because he had supporters in the crowd who gave him water, survived. Even so, as the Jesuits recount in disgusting detail, 'the moisture engendered fleas and vermin, so that he was tormented worse than before'. Besides, as the day grew warm, the donkey hide began to rot, emitting 'such an evil smell that none would go near him'.

Miraculously, however, not only did Abdul Rahim live to tell the tale, he even continued in Jahangir's service and, though forever after referred to as The Donkey by the emperor, he eventually regained his old position.

Khusro's punishment lay before him. Literally – when Jahangir finally entered Lahore, he had the road from the garden to the city embellished with some two hundred men from Khusro's army, impaled or hanged. Khusro, shackled upon a puny, bare elephant, was made to ride through this grisly procession, 'a spectator by compulsion of this tragic sequel to his ill-judged adventure'.[16]

It says a great deal for Khusro's ambition, and even more so for his popularity and Jahangir's lack of it, that barely a year after this humiliating end to his disastrous rebellion, the prince was plotting again – and had managed to garner four hundred noblemen, no less, to his side.

Jahangir spent about ten months in Lahore, catching his breath and re-evaluating his strategy. For example, he seems to have decided to abandon his policy of rapprochement vis-à-vis Raja Man Singh and Aziz Koka – Khusro's uncle and father-in-law, those 'two old wolves' – though neither man had participated in Khusro's rebellion.

To Man Singh, then governor of Bengal, he sent a robe of honour, and then his replacement. Khubu,

Qutbuddin Khan Koka – Jahangir's closest friend and son of the nurse whom the emperor described as 'kinder than a mother' – had been 'hoping for such a day for years'. Finally, now, he was given a rank of 5000, a robe and jewelled sword, two lakh rupees and the rich governorship of Bengal.

Aziz Koka was sidelined in a more dramatic fashion. Somehow, an old letter that Aziz Koka had written disparaging *his* foster brother, Akbar, fell into Jahangir's hands. In itself, the letter's contents would not have surprised anyone, least of all Akbar; Aziz Koka was as outspoken as he was flamboyant. When he travelled the three-odd kilometres from his mansion to the Agra fort, he would have 500 torchbearers line the way to light his path. Once at the fort, he was likely to flare in indignation at Akbar's policies, and it wasn't uncommon for the late emperor to forbid his visits altogether. Once, in exasperation at Akbar's new faith, Aziz Koka went off to Mecca; there, he was so annoyed by the sharifs who guard the holy city that he returned and promptly joined the Din-i-Ilahi.

It was a fractious yet friendly relationship and Akbar had remained fond of the irascible amir no matter what the provocation. Jahangir, however, chose to use his letter to humiliate the man; he summoned Aziz Koka to court, handed him the letter and made him read it aloud. As Aziz Koka obeyed, with whatever dignity he could summon, 'every one of those present at court . . . reviled and chided him'. Then, it was the emperor's turn. 'Yea,' he proclaimed, with an unattractive show of resignation, 'what can be done with original disposition and innate nature? Since your clay was mixed with the water of disloyalty, what else could come of it?'[17]

What came of it was that Aziz Koka was deprived of his jagir, a punishment that may have fallen short of Jahangir's fancy but to which he acceded, he says 'on account of certain considerations'. These may have been the intercession of Salima Sultan Begum, Akbar's widow and among the most respected women in the harem, the woman who had once travelled all the way to Allahabad to bring Jahangir back to his father. Arguably, if Jahangir now wore his father's crown, it was partly thanks to Salima. The Mughal ladies often observed court proceedings from behind a screen and some accounts tell of how, as the emperor was contemplating Aziz Koka's fate, Salima called out for Jahangir to come and listen to the women's views. These were decidedly in favour of a man who, though blunt, had always been a loyal friend to the imperial family, and Aziz Koka was thus set free.

Inevitably, as some fortunes declined, others revived. Parvez, the emperor's eternally overlooked second son, enjoyed one of his few moments in the light of his father's good opinion. With his elder brother so thoroughly disgraced, Parvez was given money and jewels, even wedded to a daughter of the late prince Murad. Young Khurram, too, received a promotion, banner and drums and a jagir. And finally, for the weary emperor himself, there was a hunt. For three months and six days before the Nauroz of 1607, Jahangir rode off into the forests of Punjab to enjoy various kinds of hunts – with 'gun, leopards, trap and qamargha'.

Of the many methods of hunting the Mughals enjoyed,

the qamargha was perhaps the most elaborate.[18] Long before the day of the hunt – days, even weeks, in advance – soldiers would be sent to encircle a large tract of forest land (in one instance, 50,000 soldiers were arranged in a circle almost 100 kilometres in diameter). Slowly, methodically, the soldiers would advance, not allowing a rabbit to escape until they had created a much smaller hunting ground densely packed with animals. Now, the emperor would arrive, and for the first few days only he would be allowed to hunt. When he had killed his fill ('When I was thoroughly sick of hunting', as Jahangir put it), the amirs, then their servants, and finally the soldiers would all get their turn. Luxury, of course, was integral to the exercise; as the emperor and his nobility hunted, servants scurried about, ensuring their enjoyment. Cup-bearers served wine and refreshments on trays of gold, lamplighters arrived with torches when dusk began to fall – all the while trying to avoid getting in the way of either a hunter or his prey. Once, for example, Jahangir tells of a lamplighter called Salih who, turning a corner with his torches, 'bumped into [a] lion. With one swipe of its paw the lion sent him flying. He fell to the earth dead.' At another time, it was Jahangir himself who had a servant executed and two others hamstrung for interrupting him as he was taking aim.

On Jahangir's first hunt as emperor, however, only animals seem to have been killed: 581, to be precise, of which Jahangir took 158 himself – mountain sheep and mountain goats, wild asses, nilgai and other kinds of antelope . . . One of these last, writes Jahangir, when its belly was pierced by a bullet from the emperor's gun, uttered such a cry as had 'never been heard before from an antelope not in rut' – thus giving us the first instance of what became one of Jahangir's favourite declarations through his memoirs, 'Since this experience was not a little strange, it has been recorded.'

In fact, much of what Jahangir writes in these months before Khusro's second rebellion reveals facets of the emperor that would appear more and more clearly over the years. Through others' accounts of his princehood, Jahangir was indolent, drunken, sometimes cowardly or vicious. In his own words, in the infectious enthusiasm with which he recounts the many years of his reign, there begins to emerge another vision of the man: his sentimentality and his precise observations; his whimsy and his lifelong adherence to a certain idea of justice; his visceral appreciation of beauty.

And, besides, a kind of disingenuousness.

Akbar's death and Jahangir's accession hadn't caused domestic upheavals alone. Persia, the Mughals' closest and most powerful neighbour, saw in this sudden disturbance its chance to regain Qandahar, which had long been a sore subject between the two empires. (Briefly, the Persian shah had 'loaned' the city to Humayun as a temporary base during his exile and Humayun had forgotten to give it back. Two generations later, Qandahar was considered as much Mughal territory as Kabul – but only by the Mughals.) If Khusro's rebellion had been successful, or perhaps even lasted a little longer, the Persians might have won the border town; instead, the rebellion was squashed and the exploratory Persian forces were driven away.

Meanwhile, having celebrated the second Nauroz of his reign in Lahore, Jahangir remembered the grand plans of conquest he had made the previous year: Parvez in Mewar, Jahangir himself leading back-to-back campaigns in Samarkand and the Deccan. Now, however, the Samarkand venture was downgraded to a 'hunting tour of Kabul'. Since Kabul was halfway to Qandahar, this may have been a Mughal show of strength in the region. However, though Kabul was also en route to Samarkand, plans for conquering that city were not mentioned again.

In late March 1607, the emperor and his retinue set off on a leisurely march to Kabul, the city once ruled by his great-grandfather Babur. With Khusro in chains, his supporters either dead or cowed, Jahangir was at ease; free, for example, to stop by a tower built to honour a favourite trained antelope, Hansraj, who had assisted the prince Jahangir on many hunts. (Antelopes, like cheetahs, were trained to 'hunt'. A contraption was tied to their horns by which they could lock horns, literally, with other antelopes and make them captive.) To further honour the dead animal, the emperor ordered that all antelopes of this area be held forbidden henceforth, 'like the flesh of cows for the infidel and like the flesh of pigs for Muslims'.

Some three weeks later, the imperial train passed through a village called Bhakra, just a few days short of Rawalpindi. All the way to the village, they rode alongside a stream, both banks of which were a riot of 'oleander flowers like peach blossoms, very colourful and in full bloom'. What else was an emperor to do with such a sight?

He ordered all those with him to decorate their turbans with oleander bouquets – anyone who didn't would forfeit his turban. Thus, writes the emperor, pleased, 'an amazing field of flowers was . . . made!'

Jahangir's fancies were not limited to decorating his mansabdars, however. A week or so later, he spent three days on a lake in Hasan Abdal (near Taxila), drinking wine and learning to fish with a particularly tricky kind of net called sufra or bhanwar jaal. When he caught a dozen-odd fish in one throw, Jahangir showed them truly imperial favour – releasing them into the water with pearls pinned to their noses.

From the antelope memorial, the flower-bedecked nobles, the bejewelled fish, one might imagine an emperor either whimsical or effete, childlike or childish, depending on one's perspective and inclination, and if his memoirs comprised such anecdotes alone, the debate about his character, too, might have remained at this somewhat insubstantial level. Every so often though – as here, between the flowers and the fish – there is a passage such as this:

> Along the road there were many palash flowers in bloom. This flower is peculiar to the forests of Hindustan. It has no odour, but its colour is a fiery orange. The base is black, and the bush is about the size of a red rose bush, although sometimes it gets larger. It looks so beautiful you can't take your eyes off it.
>
> Because the air was so fine, a patch of cloud was screening the light and heat of the sun, and a gentle rain was falling, I was taken by a desire to drink wine.

In short, the road was traversed in the utmost good spirits and joy.

Jahangir transfixed by the colour and beauty of palash in bloom, Jahangir painting such a picture of gentle drizzle from a blue sky, 'a patch of cloud ... screening the light and heat of the sun', that one can almost feel the drops of rain, taste the celebratory wine, this is Jahangir the poet, the aesthete, a man with such a highly developed sense of beauty that its truth – and his truth, in a way – is immediately apparent.

Of course, another of his truths was that he was an emperor – a seventeenth-century emperor of the most powerful empire of the time. He was powerful in a way that may be impossible to imagine today; powerful in a way that would make a man, even if he were capable of near-epiphanic response to flowers and rain, pathologically narcissistic. How else, after all, to explain this story from that very trip: a few days after the beautiful drizzle, Jahangir camped by a small pond near Rawalpindi. The locals told the emperor that they had long believed that the pond held alligators. 'Therefore,' they said, 'no one dares go in.' The emperor wanted to check for himself. First, he threw a sheep into the pond. The animal swam across unharmed, so he ordered one of his servants to follow suit. At the end of the day, the emperor was possibly pleased to have shattered Rawalpindi's baseless fear of alligators, but the poor servant's heart may have been pounding all night.

Still, of what interest is a man, let alone an emperor,

who does not contain multiple truths? Another of Jahangir's would become apparent when he reached Kabul.

Kabul held Babur's grave as it had once held his heart; and Jahangir referred to the province as 'home', literally 'vilayat'. The fascinating etymology of this word goes thus: originally, as Jahangir uses it, it meant homeland,[19] the land of one's ancestors and also, specifically, the land of the ruler's ancestors. Over the centuries, however, its meaning has taken a 180-degree turn; in common parlance, now, vilayat means the opposite of home – abroad. Partly, the change may have happened during British rule, when the land of the ruler's ancestors was England; and 'England' is, in fact, the strict definition of vilayat today. But partly, also, the changed meaning must have derived from changed context – as, over the centuries, Kabul became foreign and Lahore, Delhi, Agra became home.

During this visit, for example, it would become amply clear that the fourth Mughal's heart belonged to Hindustan.

Not that Kabul didn't have its enchantments. There was the pleasure, of course, of its gardens, all of which had been built by one or another of Jahangir's ancestors, from Babur to Hamida Banu Begum. The most beautiful of these was Shahrara Bagh, especially its pavilion, which was built by Babur's aunt: a construction 'so delicate that to place one's foot on it with shoes on would have been distasteful and unnatural'. The garden had two particularly grand chinar trees, which Jahangir named Farahbakhsh and Sayabakhsh (joy- and shade-giver). He also installed a large white slab of stone between them, and had it inscribed with his lineage all the way to Timur.[20]

Far more than Timur, of course, it was Babur who defined the Mughals' connection to Kabul; his spirit pervaded the city's gardens and architecture. Jahangir was especially taken by a lovely drinking spot that Babur had built himself below a mountain south of Kabul: a stone dais with a round basin at one end to hold his wine. Jahangir had a companion 'throne' built to face Babur's, with its own wine basin; then ordered both basins filled and their contents consumed.

Gardens, pavilions, wonderful views – and, of course, fruit. The melons that Babur had so enjoyed. Grapes. Apricots, particularly the ones that grew on 'Mirzai', a tree grafted by Jahangir's uncle Mirza Hakim. Peaches, large and full of juice. The cherries that Akbar called shah-alu – Jahangir loved to pick these from the tree, where they hung 'like butterflies . . . chunks of round ruby suspended from the branch'. Once, he ate 150 of them at a go.

This is what Babur had missed most during his brief rule in India. Cool streams, shady trees, crisp and juicy fruit. They tried to soothe him with mangoes, which he found passable enough, but oh, what would he not have done for a good melon.

And now, Jahangir. With the kind of perfect mirroring that can only be achieved in real life,[21] Jahangir writes the one sentence that says more than a dozen books could of how 'Indian' the Mughals had become: 'the excellence of the fruits of Kabul notwithstanding, not one is as delicious as the mango in my opinion.'[22]

Mango loyalist and aesthete, sentimental and cruel, Jahangir was yet another thing: a fond parent. While it may not be strictly true that, as Jahangir claims, he kept Khusro in 'utmost luxury and comfort' while captive,[23] he did feel a paternal urge to share Kabul's beauties with his son; one sunny day in June, he had the shackles removed from Khusro's feet and let him walk in the lovely Shahrara Bagh.

Khusro's antipathy to his father, however, had only grown; the brutal punishment of his supporters hadn't cowed the prince, as it might have a less audacious man, but given him a fresh burst of anger and ambition. A painting from before Khusro's fall shows the young prince bringing wine to his father. The two men share their Rajput features (unlike, for example, the distinctly less dark and more Central Asian prince Parvez, holding a tray of fruit in the painting).[24] They also share a look of stubborn pride.

Perhaps the emperor should have anticipated what was coming. By his own account, one of his amirs had recently accused another, Fathullah, of saying that Jahangir should have given Lahore to Khusro instead of fighting him; a charge that Fathullah denied, 'and both sides resorted to an exchange of oaths'. Jahangir didn't suspect anything then; certainly not that, barely two weeks later, he would be ordering Fathullah's death.

In August 1607, Jahangir was planning a series of hunts before his departure for Lahore, describing how he saw a large spider eat a snake, and cheerfully comparing the relative tastiness of sheep, Barbari goat and ibex meat, when he heard that Khusro was planning to have him assassinated.

Between four and five hundred mansabdars were in on the plot, which was to kill Jahangir while he was hunting. In fact, the assassins were even then lying in wait.

For a while, the emperor's mind was a ferment of all the 'various tortures' by which he would have them executed – stinking, flea-ridden donkey hide would appear positively cosy in comparison to what he would do now. Then, Jahangir had second thoughts. Indeed, this ability to have second thoughts may well have been what helped him become emperor and then remain so. Second thoughts had stopped him from charging against Akbar's formidable army from Etawah; and second thoughts, now, stopped him from precipitating what might have become a widespread rebellion. To kill four or five hundred well-connected young men, no matter how satisfactory, 'would occasion a tumult and chaos in the royal camp'. Jahangir decided against it. Instead, only a handful of ringleaders – Fathullah included – were arrested and executed, and the emperor pretended he didn't know the full extent of the conspiracy.

As for Khusro himself, Jahangir doesn't admit this but all other accounts agree – he was blinded.

This was not the end of Khusro. He lived well into the last years of Jahangir's reign and made more than occasional appearances in accounts of it. However, his second failed rebellion did, in a way, spell the end of his ambition, just as it propelled his younger brother Khurram's rise.

Even though Akbar was grooming Khusro as his heir, it was Khurram whom he is said to have thought of as truly special. From his very birth, he had been a source of joy, and 'little by little,' writes Jahangir, 'as his years progressed real potential was noticed in him. He served my exalted father more and better than any of my sons, and my father was very pleased with him and his service. He always commended him to me. Many times he said, "There is no comparison between him and your other sons."'

Of course, Jahangir could well have written this as a subtle denigration of Khusro, and later, as Khurram's power increased so did the history written in his favour. But it could also be that the boy really was exceptional. There is something oddly compelling about that intense vigil he maintained by his dying grandfather's side. Jahangir, for his part, betrays a real affection for his son, Baba Khurram as he calls him.

They were not unalike, father and son: both enjoyed hunting and beauty; and in some ways, Khurram was even more a child of the soil on which he was born than Jahangir. He had no interest in learning Turki, for example, the language of the Mughals' Central Asian ancestors. In a rare instance of agreement, both Akbar and Jahangir bemoaned the fact, Jahangir even complaining to Ruqaiya Begum, Khurram's adoptive mother, of his lassitude.[25] They needn't have worried. For most of his life, Khurram would prove himself an excellent judge of what was useful to know and what wasn't.

In Kabul, now, Khurram was about fifteen and, just a few months ago, he had been engaged to Arjumand Banu Begum, a young girl who would become the love of his life. In other words, Khurram was almost a grown man, and he was ready to begin participating in the affairs of the world around him.

It was Khurram, then, who first heard of Khusro's assassination plot. His divan came to him with the news, and Khurram rushed to tell Jahangir, thus catapulting his own worth in the emperor's eyes. Neither father nor son could have known, however, just how high Khurram's star was about to rise, nor how low it would one day fall.

Part III

Believer/Unbeliever

I found him sitting on his throwne, and a begger at his feet, a poore silly ould man, all ashd, ragged, and Patched, with a young roage attending him. With these kinde of professed Poore holy men the Country aboundes, and are held in great reverence . . . This miserable wretch clothd in raggs, crownd with feathers, couered with ashes, his Maiestie talked with about an hower, with such familiarity and show of kindnes that it must needes argue an humilitye not found easely among kinges . . . . and after many strange humiliations and Charetyes rising, the ould wretch not beeing Nimble, hee tooke him up in his armes, which noe Cleanly bodye durst have touchd, embracing him; and 3 tymes laying his hand on his hart, calling him father, hee left him, and us, and me in admiration of such a virtue in a heathen Prince.

Thomas Roe, *The Embassy of Sir Thomas Roe to the Court of the Great Mogul, 1615–1619*, Volume 2

Jahangir's thirty-six years as a prince abound with narrative but little detail. One can piece together the ambitions and jealousies, the bitterness, the triumphs, but only from stray anecdotes, often couched in wary prose. By contrast, his twenty-two-year reign, bookended by rebellions at its beginning and end, is largely a plateau of peace, prosperity and the emperor's various pleasures – all of it recounted in fabulous detail. Jahangir's memoirs, or more accurately, his diary, written as it was in real time, is a treasure of observation and anecdote. Amongst contemporary writings, this is also the most comprehensive account of his life and times, although there's much it doesn't mention.

Jahangir doesn't write a word, for example, about the various Europeans who, now, began to stream into the Great Mogul's realm. The Portuguese Jesuits, of course, had been around since Akbar's time, but the Dutch and English East India Companies were founded only a few years before Jahangir's accession and many men from these countries now began to appear in and around the Mughal court; and many of them wrote accounts of what they saw. These accounts comprise the earliest European descriptions of Mughal India, and although their accuracy is often suspect, they do that one thing only travellers' writing can do: they tell us what surprised them. And, arguably, what surprised them the most was to find in Jahangir a ruler of great religious eclecticism, and his empire a land of extraordinary religious freedom.

Just before Jahangir left for Kabul from Lahore, the Jesuit mission that was waiting on him gifted him a Persian translation of the Bible, a gift that pleased him so much that, say the Jesuits, he 'kept it in his hand till he withdrew' from the durbar. The emperor's enthusiasm for Christian theology – and particularly Christian iconography – was well known; the rumour that he was Christian himself[1] (or might soon become one) circulated widely, at least among European writers, before and after his coronation. There was even a theory that the emperor was uncircumcised.

Their confusion is understandable; they came, after all, from a continent where people were being executed for belonging to different sects of the same religion (the antipathy between Catholic and Protestant amongst these visitors is as great as their combined mistrust of the 'Moor' and 'Gentile'). But here was Jahangir, his palaces decorated not only with paintings of his family and his amirs, but also of Hindu deities on the one hand and Jesus Christ on the other. In the Agra fort, for example, the Jesuits were amazed to see that the ceiling of the jharokha balcony where Jahangir sat for his daily darshan[2] was decorated with paintings of 'Christ our Lord, very perfectly finished with an aureola, and surrounded by angels'. A painting of Jahangir holding an image of the Madonna is still one of the best-known portraits of the emperor. In Lahore, when the Jesuits celebrated Christmas in their church, building a little manger that many people came to see, Jahangir sent them 'choice candles of white wax to be burnt before it, and some of his own beautiful pictures to add to the ornament'.

Some months before Christmas, the mission had organized a procession for the Passion of Christ, their self-mortification drawing crowds of 'Gentiles who gazed in astonishment . . . shuddered at the sight of the blood so willingly spilled . . . eager to see what the end would be'.[3] A few days later, on the celebration of Easter there were fireworks ('which they make very well in this country') and another 'grand procession'. The priests and their newly minted flock walked through the streets of Lahore, some of them carrying a cross decorated with flowers, others with candles and paintings, musicians playing oboes as they advanced, and – a fact that never ceased to amaze Europeans – proceeding 'as serenely and devoutly as though they were . . . in the land of the most catholic of kings'. It was a freedom that the Jesuits attributed to 'the glory of our Lord, and the exaltation of our holy faith', rather churlishly ignoring the more temporal liberality of the emperor and his people.

The Italian Pietro Della Valle put it in rather more 'secular' (and oddly modern) terms: 'in India there is Liberty of Conscience, and . . . a Man may hold or change what Faith he pleases, not the least trouble being given to any person touching Religion in the Dominions of the Moghol'. Not only, in fact, might a person profess any faith, he might even rail against another's without undue trepidation. The backpacking Thomas Coryat, though usually delighted by his travels in the East, was occasionally inspired by a parochial passion against Islam. Once, by Edward Terry's account, Coryat went racing up the minaret of a mosque in Agra and, before anyone could stop him, proclaimed a redrafted kalma, 'La ilaha illallah Hazarat Isa Ibn-Allah!' – that is, No God but God and Christ the Son of God – a blasphemy that might have cost him his life except that 'here,' writes Terry, 'every man hath libertie to professe his owne religion freely and ... to dispute against theirs with impunity'.

Another time, Coryat records how he delivered such a fiery speech to a Florence-returned Muslim in Multan that even though Coryat railed in Italian, a crowd of hundred-odd gathered around them, for whose benefit the Muslim translated the Englishman's thoughts on 'Mahomet and his accursed religion'. Once again, and Coryat himself admits it, 'if I had spoken thus much in Turky or Persia against Mahomet, they would have rosted me upon a spitt; but in the Mogols dominions a Christian may speake much more freely'.

This is not to say, of course, that there was never any friction between Indians and the farangs. English sailors were particularly prone to drunken gaucheries, causing acute embarrassment to their superiors. William Finch, for example, was glad to see the back of 'one Thomas Tucker, which in drinke had killed a calfe (a slaughter more than murther in India)', while Thomas Roe could barely contain his frustration at a sailor who peeped into a covered doli to see what was inside – 'for what Civill

Town will endure a stranger by force to open in streetes the close Chayres wherin their weomen are Carried (which they take for a dishonor equall to a ravishment)?'[4]

Even in these two cases, however, the offending sailors escaped unscathed. Religious heresies, social misdemeanours, these were forgivable, even negotiable; if there was a rigidity in Indian society, its focus was not so much belief but that seemingly inescapable concept of purity.

Not everyone calls it 'caste'. Pietro Della Valle, for example, describes the 'scrupulous' division between 'races' considered more or less 'noble': "'tis a pretty sight to behold,' he writes, 'how upon meeting in the street the ignoble not onely give place, but dance wildly up and down for fear of rushing against the noble, and polluting them in any measure; which, if they should not do, the Noble, and especially the Souldiers, would make them do it to the Musick of blows'.

So stark was this prohibition against 'impure' touch – whether of bodies or even shared utensils – that Della Valle and his fellow Europeans improvised a drinking game from their bemusement, toasting each other à la Indienne (without touching lip to cup, that is), 'and he that cannot do it right either wets himself, or falls a coughing and [hiccuping], which gives occasion of laughter'. Some years previously, a less amused Thomas Roe had dismissed an enterprising Englishman's idea of building public waterworks in Agra with the impatient explanation that 'noe Cast here will drinck of the water, but fetchd by his owne Cast'.

The attachment to purity was not limited to any

religion either. In Goa, writes Della Valle, Brahmin converts to Catholicism had sent a deputation of Jesuits to the Pope, asking whether they might continue to wear their 'Ribbon' – that is, their sacred thread – and the argument that the Jesuits were making on their behalf was that the ribbon wasn't so much a sign of religion but a mark of 'honour' so that even 'Mahometans . . . have in recompence of great and honourable services enjoy'd this priviledge'.

Thomas Roe, meanwhile, would discover that it was easier to get Jahangir to excuse him the formal prostration due the emperor than to get any of his nobility – whether Hindu or Muslim – to eat with him. Only once, near the end of Roe's embassy, did Jahangir's brother-in-law, Asaf Khan, invite the ambassador for dinner. The evening was pleasant, the food and drink plentiful but, for all his hospitality, Asaf Khan would not eat with his guests.

Having lived in India for years now, Roe didn't protest. 'They eate not willingly with us,' he said, perhaps recalling the time when, some years ago, another amir called Mir Jamaluddin Hussain[5] had invited Roe for a meal without eating with him. On that occasion, Roe did protest, telling the amir that 'without his Company I had little appetite'. Embarrassed, Mir Jamaluddin ate a few nuts with the Englishman but soon excused himself, saying 'his Countrymen would take it ill if hee eate not with them'. A few days later, when Roe invited the governor to his own home, Mir Jamaluddin was clearly uncomfortable. He only had a few gingerly bites, and only of those dishes that he was assured had been made by a Muslim cook. As he was leaving, however, the amir turned to the ambassador and asked him if Roe would send some of the dishes he hadn't tasted to his home. Roe's cooks had made a few baked meats, Mir Jamaluddin had never seen the like, and he was keen to 'dine on them in privatt'.

The endearingly secret curiosity of Mir Jamaluddin's appetite is, perhaps, key to how purity was understood in this world: it was not so much what one ate but that there were some things one did not eat, and therefore some people one did not eat with, that defined the relative 'nobility' of one's race.[6]

Insofar as these ideas – one might even call them instincts – were embedded in his realm, they were also embodied in the thoughts and actions of the emperor. Jahangir had no objection whatsoever, for example, to the consumption of pork. There's no record of him eating it himself, but it was common knowledge that he enjoyed receiving swine as gifts. Soon after Thomas Roe landed in Gujarat, he was approached by some Indian traders-cum-officials wanting to buy 'English Swyne for the Mogull, in which beast he takes infinite delight, having had two from one ship the last year'. Jahangir himself was exceedingly generous when it came to gifting pigs to the Christians in his realm, from the Jesuits to the English ambassador, even asking how they cooked their presents. Thomas Roe complained of the sheer number of 'wild hogges' he got from the emperor – and far too few trade concessions, he would have muttered – but Jahangir's enthusiasm was undiminished. Once, hearing the ambassador was ill and craving wine, he sent him five bottles of his own, plus 'a fat Hogge, the fattest I ever saw' which had come to Jahangir from the Portuguese. It was delivered to Roe at midnight 'with this message: since it came to the King it had eaten nothing but Sugar and Butter.'

The emperor enjoyed his own food, too. He was particularly fond of, for example, rohu fish, which he considered the very 'best kind of fish in Hindustan'. Once, on his way from Mandu to Gujarat, Jahangir had been deprived of this fish for almost a year when one of his military commanders, Rai Man, caught a tasty rohu. 'One was caught today!' the emperor exclaimed in his diary. 'I really enjoyed it and gave Rai Man a horse as a reward.'

While on the subject of fish, however, Jahangir made it clear that he only ate fish with scales, though he insisted this had nothing to do with the Islamic (specifically Shiite) law to that effect. 'Shiites don't know why they don't eat fish without scales or why it is haram,' writes the emperor. He himself had got to the bottom of the matter: unlike fish with scales, fish without ate carrion. 'Therefore eating fish without scales is repugnant to my nature.'

It was this rationalist Jahangir, however, who, when he was introduced to the Magh people of the Arakan kingdom[7] and realized that they 'eat every part of every kind of sea and land animal' and that 'in their religion nothing is forbidden, and they eat with anyone' derided them as 'a bunch of animals that look like human beings'.

Indeed, this idea of purity of food and company was so deeply ingrained in the emperor and his world that 'sullying' a man could even be a form of punishment. When, for example, a provincial prince called Kalyan was accused of having murdered the parents of his 'Gypsy Muslim' lover, Jahangir ordered that his tongue be cut off and condemned him to eating the rest of his meals with 'dog keepers and outcasts'.

When it comes to religion itself – Jahangir's own religious ideas and beliefs, that is, and not the 'liberty of conscience' of his realm – the emperor's actions present an even more complicated story. His mother was Hindu and so were many of his wives; his father was sceptical to the point of heresy; the two sons he was closest to, Khusro and Khurram, had more Hindu blood in them than Muslim. Thomas Roe puts it best when he writes that Jahangir was 'bred up without any religion at all' – though he might also have added that the emperor would certainly have been bred with an idea of the near divinity of his own lineage. The absolute and everyday power that Jahangir exercised is clear from another of Roe's anecdotes; if, during the course of his evening durbar, Jahangir fell asleep – often, more accurately, passed out – immediately, the 'candles were poppd out' and the courtiers crept away, 'blindfold dismissed'.

As sleep for the emperor was darkness for all, so religious decrees must defer to his whims. Thus, for example, since Jahangir had ordered that no animals be killed on Thursdays, when Bakrid once happened to fall on that day, the ritual sacrifice was duly postponed. On another occasion, while touring Pushkar, the aesthetically minded emperor took exception to a statue of Varaha, the boar-headed incarnation of Vishnu, and promptly, in his words, 'ordered the hideous thing smashed and thrown into the tank'. Then, being told of a yogi who preached from a hill nearby, and having decided that the man was a charlatan, he ordered his ashram destroyed too – 'the yogi driven away, and the idol that was in the dome smashed'. Finally, having evidently developed some deep antipathy towards Pushkar, Jahangir decided to prove that the tank was not bottomless as commonly believed, and had it measured. 'In no place,' he writes with satisfaction, 'was it more than twelve ells [ten metres] deep.' While they were at it, the emperor's men also measured its perimeter: it was, he writes, about six kilometres in circumference.

Why would Jahangir, whose religious zeal wouldn't fill a pamphlet, display such aggression in Pushkar? Was it because he had just arrived in nearby Ajmer to rally his troops in their resumed conflict with Rana Amar Singh of Mewar? This was still in the early years of his reign, and he was still as disinclined as ever to actually lead a campaign. The temple in which that Varaha statue once stood was built by Amar Singh's uncle Rana Shankar, and though Jahangir was fond of the uncle (whom he described as 'a great amir in our state'), perhaps the emperor was conducting a proxy war upon his nephew through the statue?

The measuring of the tank is more easily explained: there was nothing Jahangir wouldn't have measured and recorded, from a particularly large peach to his favourite elephant or the exact number of animals, arranged by type, that he had hunted down. 'Whatsoever he doth, either without or within, drunken or sober,' writes William

Hawkins, the English khan, 'he hath writers who by turnes set down everything . . . so that there is nothing passeth in his lifetime which is not noted, no, not so much as his going to the necessary; and how often he lieth with his women, and with whom; and all this is done unto this end, that when he dieth these writings of all his actions and speeches which are worthy to be set downe might be recorded in the chronicles.'

Then what is the chronicler to make of that poor yogi? It's hard to say, but this we know: the yogi was no sooner chased away than he was forgotten. A far greater space was occupied in Jahangir's world by another Hindu ascetic called Jadrup Gosain.

Jadrup was a Brahmin who lived in a cave near Ujjain – which, too, Jahangir had measured. (It was tiny; even 'a skinny person would have great difficulty getting in'.) Jadrup's asceticism impressed Jahangir greatly: how could a man sit in this dark, narrow cave, naked except for a loincloth, meditating all alone without even a fire to warm him in the winter? As for what he ate and who he ate with, there was simply no contest: Jadrup went to Ujjain once a day to beg exactly five morsels of food from three of the seven Brahmin families he had shortlisted for the honour. He even swallowed without chewing 'lest he derive any enjoyment from the taste'.

Jahangir met Jadrup when passing through Ujjain on his way to spur yet another campaign, this time in the Deccan. He went to the cave not once but twice, for three hours each. Thereafter, the ascetic appears many times in his memoirs, and each time because the emperor had a 'great yearning' or 'another overwhelming desire' to meet him. They always conversed alone, always for hours, and Jahangir always returned from these conversations strangely elated. 'Without exaggeration,' he once wrote, 'it was hard for me to part from him.'

Perhaps there is some indication of how religion was understood, both in Jahangir's mind and his times, in the way the emperor describes Jadrup. The entrance to his cave, for example, was 'shaped like a mihrab'; and the Brahmin was learned in 'the science of the Vedanta, which is the science of Sufism'. Such conflation of mosque and cave, of Vedanta and Sufism is not unique, of course, but it is so seamless here, so natural that it comes as almost a shock when Jahangir does assume a difference between Hinduism and Islam.

In the autumn of 1620, on his way south from Kashmir, Jahangir stopped in Rajaor, the population of which had converted to Islam during Firoz Shah Tughlaq's rule over two centuries earlier. Even so, writes Jahangir, 'the heretical customs of pre-Islamic times still continue among them'; these included an Islamicized version of sati, in which widows were buried alive with their husbands.

Sati was not prohibited under Mughal rule, though it was carefully administered. Any woman who wished to commit sati required the local governor's consent, with the governor obliged to ensure that she wasn't being forced into it. Like many European travellers, Francisco Pelsaert claims to have witnessed a sati. One of his neighbours declared she would burn with her husband, and Pelsaert was part of the crowd that went to watch her do it. Before she climbed upon the pyre, however, the woman would have to get past the usual bureaucratic hurdles. So, having put on her best clothing and jewels, with musicians and singers by her side, the woman went to the governor.

The widow was young and pretty, says Pelsaert, and the governor 'urged many sound arguments' to try to dissuade her, even offering her an annuity of five hundred rupees 'as long as she should live'. She was unmoved; not 'all the King's treasures' would make her change her mind, she declared, so finally, since 'she was taking up far too much time' and since governors were 'not allowed by the King's orders to refuse these requests', he agreed.

Governors, of course, were only representatives of the emperor; it was common enough, according to William Hawkins, for widows intent on burning to come to Jahangir himself for permission. 'When any of these commeth,' writes Hawkins, the emperor 'doth perswade them with many promises of gifts . . . if they will live', but never successfully. Eventually, Jahangir would give in, yielding 'his leave for her to be carried to the fire'.

Evidently, sati was not a custom the emperor approved of, though he never banned it either. Was this because he was wary of interfering too much with entrenched custom, or because he did not think he had the locus to interfere with specifically *Hindu* custom? From his proclamation in Rajaor, it would seem the latter – here, he immediately outlawed widow burial on pain of death. For good measure, he also prohibited the giving of Muslim brides to Hindu men, another of the 'heretical' practices of the town. 'Taking them is all well and good, but giving them to Hindus – God forbid!'

Why he should have felt this way is an utter mystery to a modern mind. Jahangir was half Hindu himself, his sons even more so; his uncles, brothers- and fathers-in-law numbered many Rajputs among them. His brother, Daniyal, though born to a Muslim mother, was raised in a Rajput home. And yet, just as whom you ate with defined your 'race', so, it seems, whom you married your daughters to defined your pride.

Many years earlier, in the first few years of his reign, Jahangir had converted three of his nephews (Daniyal's sons) to Christianity. The boys were 'christened solemnly', writes William Finch, 'conducted to church by all the Christians of [Agra] to the number of sixtie horse'. The English khan led the procession 'with St. Georges colours carried before him . . . letting them flie in the court before Sha Selim himselfe'. At the end of the day, three Mughal princes, Tahmuras, Baisanghar and Hoshang, rode back to the palace Don Phillippo, Don Carlos and Don Henrico. Among the several theories on why Jahangir took this unprecedented step is that he had a notion of acquiring Portuguese brides for the boys and thought that Christians would agree more readily to their women marrying Catholic Mughals. (From all accounts, they did not.)

In fact, seen through such discrete incidents, the emperor appears bafflingly contradictory in character – and yet, from the cracks between the anecdotes, there emerges a man so wholly neither one thing nor another that he will not make sense when viewed through any one lens, but only, perhaps, through a kaleidoscope.[8]

The princes were converted because Jahangir had

flirted with the idea of converting himself, *and* he enjoyed Jesuit company and loved Christian art, *and* he had a hankering for a bit of pageantry, *and* he thought, having just survived a double rebellion, that conversion would disqualify the princes from the throne . . . and that they might like Portuguese wives as consolation.[9]

Or take his tour of Kangra years later, in the winter of 1621. The fort had been captured some months ago by Raja Bikramjit; in its long history, this would be the first time that Kangra had a Muslim ruler. When Jahangir arrived, he took some mullahs with him to, in his words, 'carry out whatever was in accordance with the precepts of the Muhammadan religion'. As it turns out, this involved doing what 'had not previously been done there since the bastion was built, like the call for prayer, reciting the khutba, slaughtering a cow, etc'.

What is surprising about this is not that Jahangir had a cow sacrificed, even though all accounts – including that of Thomas Tucker to his friends, no doubt – agree that killing cows was forbidden across the realm. Pelsaert even adds that, in legislation that would have pleased gau-rakshaks of today, cow slaughter was 'strictly forbidden by the King on pain of death'. It isn't surprising, however, that Jahangir would flout his own rule; no one rule of the emperor, after all, was greater than the emperor's rule itself. What is surprising is that, in having done what had never been done before, Jahangir was, in fact, ordering a type of ceremony that Kangra's Hindu kings would have found all too familiar – that of ritual purification.

There is one more source of the complicated and fascinating workings of Jahangir's mind, however, that paints, literally, another picture. This is the rich collection of art produced by Jahangir's atelier, a collection unparalleled in Mughal history for its sheer breadth and beauty, but also notable for the many symbolic secrets it holds.

As A. Azfar Moin has argued, Akbar's claim of being the promised messiah of the new age – the religion he founded, the disciples he inducted into it – was very much part of the legacy he bequeathed to his heir. This legacy, moreover, was not of the emperor as a near-divine saviour alone, it was of the emperor as a near-divine saviour of *all* faiths. There was, of course, a great deal of political logic in this idea: an emperor-messiah who was tied to just one sect or religion would reduce not only the number of his disciples, but also the number (and devotion) of his subjects.

Jahangir, argues Moin, both adopted and adapted his father's legacy. As Akbar had promised his people sulh-i-kul, 'peace for all', so Jahangir now claimed to be the mazhar-i-kull, a 'universal manifestation', and vowed, says Moin, 'that just as God was concerned with all his slaves, [Jahangir] too was concerned with all of God's slaves'. There is even some evidence that Jahangir continued his father's practice of initiating disciples into his own 'cult'.[10] For one, Jahangir says so himself in his memoirs, writing of one Sheikh Ahmad Lahauri whom the new emperor appointed to bring him 'aspirants and the devoted' and to advise him on whom he should 'offer my hand and to whom I should present a portrait'. The presentation of a portrait was an essential part of the ritual of initiation; and the disciple was thereafter expected to always wear it on his person.

One of the most startling theories that has emerged from the study of this aspect of Jahangir's rule is that the emperor may, in fact, have inducted Thomas Roe – the straight-backed ambassador who wrote with such authority about Jahangir's lack of religiosity – into his service. Even more ironically, the theory emerges from an incident that Roe describes himself, though clearly without grasping the full import of his experience.[11]

Briefly, it was thus: Jahangir's passion for art was widely known and Thomas Roe was growing desperate for suitable presents to give the emperor. One day, the ambassador decided to part with a small painting of his own. Jahangir was pleased, but when he showed it to his assembled courtiers, a painter amongst them boasted that he could easily make a replica that no one, not even Roe, would be able to tell from the original. Immediately, Jahangir proposed the wager to Roe who, after some effort at wriggling out of it, agreed. A few days later, Jahangir summoned the ambassador. They had a convivial chat – 'with many passages of jests, mirth and brages concerning the arts of his Countrye, he fell to aske mee questions: "How often I drancke a day, and how much and what? What in England? What beere was? How made? and whether I could made it here?"' – and Roe was told to return that evening. When he did, the astonished ambassador was presented with not one but five replicas of his gift, each so good that it took Roe a long while and great effort to find the original among them.

Afterwards, amid much laughter by the emperor and promises of reward for the painter, Roe happened to say that he hadn't expected such talented work since the one painting he had bought in India – a portrait of Jahangir – was not very impressive. At this, Jahangir appeared genuinely upset that Roe hadn't asked *him* for a portrait, and Roe, always determined to make a show of not accepting presents, kept repeating that if Jahangir must give him a portrait, let him give it for King James. Eventually, the emperor put an end to the matter by declaring, 'your king doth not desire one, but you doe: therefore, you shall have it' – and ordered one to be made forthwith.

Another few days passed until, once again, Roe was called to court. There, amid great ceremony, he was given a small portrait of Jahangir, set in a gold frame and hung from a gold chain that was strung around the ambassador's neck. Then, he was prompted to do the sijda, the full prostration that was expected of new disciples in Akbar's time (and of all subjects in Jahangir's), but when the ambassador protested, Jahangir indicated that he was to be excused.

So it was that Thomas Roe returned home, pleased and possibly a little confused. He knew that he had been granted a great favour, that no one was allowed to wear the emperor's image 'but to whom it is given' – but he certainly didn't suspect that he had just been bound by sacred ties to Jahangir.

Roe's obliviousness may have arisen, partly, because Jahangir did not rely on the Din-i-Ilahi as much as Akbar had to express the idea of his messianic self. Instead, he used art – particularly his allegorical portraits such as, for example, one that shows Jahangir preferring a Sufi saint to kings, or one that shows Jahangir 'shooting' poverty.

It was here, in these paintings, that 'Jahangir performed his miracles', argues Moin, as he provides an eye-opening analysis of the destruction of poverty.

In this image, Jahangir is dressed in extravagant purple, standing upon a globe, with a lion and lamb curled up beneath his feet to represent the peace of his reign. Above him are two winged cherubs holding a jewelled crown; in front of him another cherub holds out arrows for the emperor. Behind this cherub, in a cloud of darkness, stands a skeletal, white-haired old man, biting his own fingernails in fear. With a smile of satisfaction on his face, Jahangir has just shot an arrow into the old man's left eye, and has strung his bow with another.

The old man is poverty or, as the inscription on the painting says, 'dalidar'. Moin notes the use of this Hindi word, derived from the Sanskrit 'daridra', in an otherwise Persian inscription, and argues that this links the painting with the festival of Diwali in which, traditionally, families welcome Lakshmi, the goddess of wealth, while expelling her sister Daridra, the goddess of poverty. Diwali is also considered the beginning of a new year, an idea that the commentary suggests, too, when it describes Jahangir as shooting an 'arrow of kindness' to destroy dalidar and create 'the world anew with his justice and fairness'.

'But,' writes Moin, 'neither this painting nor the

memoir explains why the king must perform this renewal ritual for the world. Nevertheless, a clue may be found in the association of the Diwali festival with a key symbol of Hindu kingship: Rama.'

If the idea of Jahangir portraying himself as Rama seems far-fetched, it is worth noticing one last element of the painting. Below the globe is another bearded man floating upon a huge fish – this is Manu, who may be considered iconic of Brahminical Hinduism, riding upon Matsya, the first avatar of Vishnu.

If the 'destruction of Poverty' is so full of symbols and clues as to be almost overwhelming, there exists another, less well-known painting that presents the matter more simply. In this, Jahangir is sitting out in the open, on what looks like a veranda or terrace. Above him, the skies are blue and two cherubs hold an embroidered cloth as a canopy above the king. Jahangir is bare-chested, he wears nothing but a loincloth, and he is seated cross-legged in the lotus position. As Ebba Koch describes it, the Mughal emperor is here an 'Indian deity or ruler' – and this is, she exclaims, 'the most Indian (and eccentric!) depiction of a Muslim king one could possibly imagine'.[12]

Hindu deities are incomplete, however, without their consorts. By his side, therefore, sits that other great mystery of Jahangir's life, whose relationship with the emperor is even more enigmatic than the emperor's relationship with God – his begum, Nurjahan.

Part IV

Sun Amongst Women

On the grave of this poor stranger,
let there be neither lamp nor rose.
Let neither butterfly's wing burn
nor nightingale sing.

Epitaph on Nurjahan's tomb,
quoted in *Nur Jahan* by Ellison Banks Findly,
translated by Wheeler M. Thackston

In 1621, when Jahangir toured Kangra, he had only six years left to rule. These would not be his best years, but perhaps, through the course of them, he took consolation in the fact that the previous sixteen had passed, on the whole, wonderfully well. The empire had teetered a bit with Khusro's rebellions at the beginning and Jahangir had experienced two severe personal losses within the first two years of his reign, that of his beloved foster mother and of Khubu. 'What can I write to express my grief and sadness over this terrible news?' Jahangir had written at the time. Only the death of his own father, he says, had affected him as deeply.

Still, for all the pessimistic prophecies and disapproval of his ways that marked Jahangir's accession, his reign was surprisingly successful. Partly, of course, this was thanks to Akbar, who left behind such a stable, prosperous and well-administered empire that it might have taken an equal effort of will to dismantle it. Partly, Jahangir's own largely conciliatory and generous approach to governance helped to keep his realm at peace. And finally, the emperor's success owed a great deal to his advisers, first amongst whom was the family of a Persian immigrant called Ghiyas Beg.

In 1577, Ghiyas Beg did not know what the future held for him, nor if, indeed, he had a future at all. His father had been a high-ranking minister in Persia; Ghiyas Beg was less lucky. In 1577, like many Persians escaping political upheavals before him and after, Ghiyas Beg and his family – his wife, Asmat Begum, and their three children – were travelling with a caravan led by one Malik Masud, hoping for a fresh start in Hindustan. They had two mules between the five of them, hardly any money and, to top it all, Asmat Begum was pregnant. She delivered a baby girl along the way, in Qandahar, but the family was so desperately poor that they decided to abandon her. They left her under a tree, hoping, perhaps, that a more fortunate family would find her. The caravan, uncaring, continued its long march.

As they walked, Asmat Begum couldn't stop herself from turning, looking for the tree that was, for now, her child's only protector. As soon as they lost sight of it, she burst into tears. *I cannot,* she cried, *I cannot.*

Perhaps Ghiyas Beg was thinking the same thing. Perhaps he thanked God for his wife's tears. He made no argument; he did not try to rationalize; instead, he turned around and hurried back to their newborn daughter. She was lying where they had left her, a black snake wrapped around her tiny form.

Carefully waving the reptile away, Ghiyas Beg picked up his daughter and carried her to his wife. Asmat Begum wept once more, this time with relief and joy. They named her Mihrunnisa, sun amongst women, and continued their journey, little knowing that they were carrying a queen into her realm.

Modern historians agree that the story of Mihrunnisa's abandonment is more legend than fact; her family's hard beginnings are not. Another child at this time was a burden on their already straitened means and they may have asked Malik Masud, the caravan leader, for help. Later, they also asked Malik Masud to introduce Ghiyas Beg to Akbar's court.

A gregarious and generous, intelligent and cheerfully corrupt man,[1] Ghiyas Beg did fairly well under Akbar, rising into the upper-middle echelons of the bureaucracy so that, at Jahangir's accession, he had a mansab of 700 zat and was divan of the royal workshops. Mihrunnisa's career, meanwhile, was following what was, presumably, the usual course for women of the nobility. In the mid-1590s, at seventeen, she married a swashbuckling Persian soldier called Ali Quli Istajlu. Ali Quli, like Mihrunnisa's father, had fled the Shah of Persia. In Hindustan, he had been part of Abdur Rahim Khan Khanan's army and had impressed the general so much that Abdur Rahim recommended him to Jahangir when Jahangir was still a prince. It was from the prince that Ali Quli received the title by which he would henceforth be known: Sher Afgan, the lion-thrower.

Sher Afgan had been by the prince's side when, in Ajmer, Jahangir had the idea of ransacking his father's treasury; quite likely, he had stood by the prince as he

argued with Qilich Khan outside the gates of Agra and
been part of his fleet when he sailed hurriedly down to
Allahabad – and here, Sher Afgan had served in the
prince's rebel court. Given all this, Sher Afgan might
well have formed part of the new emperor's inner
coterie. Unfortunately, however, Sher Afgan had been
amongst those men who had beaten a strategic retreat
when it seemed as if the prince's rebellion would fizzle
out under the glare of Akbar's indignation. Jahangir may
have forgiven these men upon his accession, but he did
not forget. Still, he writes, he was 'manly enough . . . to
overlook [Sher Afgan's] faults' and gave him the decent
– if distant – jagir of Burdwan in Bengal. And so, for the
moment, Sher Afgan, Mihrunnisa and their newborn
daughter Ladli Begum settled down in the provinces, as
the pages of history slowly turned.

Ghiyas Beg, meanwhile, was at the very heart of things.
When Jahangir became emperor, Ghiyas Beg's mansab
was doubled from 700 to 1500, he was made co-vizier of
the empire and titled I'timaduddawla, pillar of the realm.
But promotions were par for the course at Jahangir's
accession; no one could have predicted how high this
particular pillar would rise. Not even I'timaduddawla
himself: his seemingly good beginning in Jahangir's
employ soon hit a very rocky spot.

Not only, in 1605, did I'timaduddawla receive
several promotions, in March 1607, after Jahangir had
returned from his successful campaign against Khusro,

the emperor's younger son, Khurram, was engaged to
I'timaduddawla's granddaughter. Arjumand Begum was
the daughter of I'timaduddawla's younger son, Abu'l
Hasan, and her liaison with the imperial family cannot
but have been a great favour to the Persian immigrant and
his family. Only months later, however, I'timaduddawla's
older son, Muhammad Sharif, was discovered to be one of
the ringleaders of Khusro's assassination scheme in Kabul.
Muhammad Sharif was executed and I'timaduddawla
himself, naturally, came under a shadow. Khurram and
Arjumand's engagement wasn't broken, but their alliance
was indefinitely postponed – it would be another four
years before they were married.

At least two modern historians, Ellison Banks Findly
and Banarsi Prasad Saksena, have argued that there is
more to this postponement than meets the eye. In fact,
there was yet another significant event that happened
in 1607. It did not happen in Lahore, however, nor in
Kabul, nor anywhere near the emperor and his family – it
happened in faraway Burdwan.

The province of Bengal, though one of the richest
in the Mughal empire, was also very difficult to govern.
Its climate and terrain were inhospitable, and its sheer
distance from the court – whether in Agra or even further
away in Lahore – encouraged rebellion. Now, for example,
Jahangir received reports that Ali Quli 'Sher Afgan' was
fermenting trouble in his jagir. The flighty Persian soldier
had already tested the emperor's patience and Jahangir
sent a stern message to his friend Khubu – who had
recently replaced Man Singh as governor of Bengal – to
dispatch Sher Afgan to court.

Khubu rode out to Burdwan with his men, many of whom, incidentally, were recruited from Kashmir. The governor and his troops were approaching Sher Afgan when the Persian called out for them to stop. Khubu's orders were only to send Sher Afgan to court, but perhaps Sher Afgan thought he had come with more lethal intent. Whatever the reason, Sher Afgan persuaded Khubu to approach him without his guard, and when he came within reach Sher Afgan lunged at him with his sword so that, in the expressive words of the contemporary historian Mu'tamad Khan, Khubu's 'bowels gushed out'. Khubu – 'to me ... like a dear son, an affectionate brother, and a devoted friend' – collapsed, calling for vengeance, and died. Khubu's men, writes Jahangir, 'fell on Ali-Quli, chopped him to pieces and dispatched him to hell'.

Both Mu'tamad Khan and Jahangir, however, are silent on what was, in historical terms, the most important result of this tragic fracas. For that, we have the account of one of Khubu's Kashmiri guards, Haider Malik. The man who struck the blow that killed Sher Afgan, writes Haider Malik, was called Yusuf Khan. Having killed the man who had so brutally murdered his commander, Yusuf Khan galloped off to Sher Afgan's fortress, his blood in boil, intending to plunder his home and that of his newly widowed wife, Mihrunnisa.

When Haider Malik realized what was happening, he chased after Yusuf Khan and made it to the fortress in time to rescue Mihrunnisa and her child; the two of them spent the next forty days of mourning safe under the protection of Haider Malik and the other Kashmiris in his contingent. At the end of the mourning, a message arrived from the emperor. Sher Afgan's widow was to come to Agra with her child; she would earn her keep (or pass her time) as lady-in-waiting to the venerable Salima Sultan Begum.

Findly, who describes Haider Malik's account at length in her book,[2] offers the theory that only a little while before he sent Khubu to Sher Afgan, Jahangir had seen Mihrunnisa at the engagement of Khurram and Arjumand, who was, after all, Mihrunnisa's niece. Then, having fallen violently in love, he had Sher Afgan murdered and his wife inducted into the imperial zenana. Saksena has a slightly different take: according to him, Jahangir met Mihrunnisa *after* she had begun serving Salima Sultan, not before. Then, enamoured, the emperor began his long wooing of the reluctant widow, a wooing in which Khurram and Arjumand became unwitting pawns as Jahangir held Arjumand's wedding hostage in order to 'persuade' her aunt to marry him.

The idea that Jahangir loved Mihrunnisa long before he married her is not unique to these historians, of course. There are old and far more salacious stories about the two, including that Mihrunnisa knew and seduced Jahangir while he was still a prince, that Akbar opposed the match, that Mihrunnisa lived only to fulfil her ambition of becoming queen. On the other hand, there is no real evidence to support these tales, and no lack of theories to refute them. As the historian Beni Prasad has pointed out, there is no contemporary account – not even a whisper at a time when whispers were rife – of any scandal between the emperor and another man's wife. And besides, Jahangir was emperor after all – if he wanted another man's wife, he could have her. There was no need for such elaborate strategies nor for the sacrifice of his best friend.

His own father, Akbar, had done so. That ever-reliable narrator of backstage gossip, Badauni tells of how Akbar once decided he should ally himself with some of the Delhi nobility. As it happened, the emperor's eye was caught by a 'wonderfully beautiful' woman of the city. As it also happened, she had a husband, to whom she was 'a charming wife without a peer'. This did not, however, cause the emperor any pause: Akbar sent his proposal, and 'that virtuous lady entered the Imperial Haram' – while the hapless husband went off to the Deccan, never to be heard of again. No one except Akbar had a choice in the matter because, as Badauni explains, 'it is a law of the Moghul Emperors that, if the Emperor cast his eye with desire on any woman, the husband is bound to divorce her'.

Of course, this wasn't a particularly popular law. When news spread that Akbar was thinking of taking one or two more Delhi brides – just to keep the city's nobility on an equal footing – a slave boy shot an arrow at the emperor from a Delhi roof. Akbar took the hint and abandoned the idea.

Whether or not one believes the stories of Jahangir's extramarital dalliance – even if he was, already, besotted with Mihrunnisa's many charms – Jahangir himself could hardly have known, as he mourned Khubu's death, that the demise of his most trusted friend had set in motion a process that would bring him an even closer companion, the closest, in fact, of his reign – the ingenious, beautiful

Mihrunnisa, daughter of Ghiyas Beg, widow of Sher Afgan, and soon to be Jahangir's beloved Nurjahan.

Depending, once again, on whose perspective one chooses, Nurjahan was either ambitious and manipulative – siphoning power from an increasingly addled emperor to the advantage of her own family and designs – or a woman of wisdom, as beautiful as she was efficient, strong in the interests of the empire, kind towards the dispossessed, and as much in love with Jahangir as Jahangir was in love with her. As for Jahangir's feelings for his most well-known wife, there is no doubt about it: whenever he writes about his Nurjahan Begum in his memoirs, it is with palpably deep affection.

Sher Afgan was killed in March 1607 and, according to the most dry – though perfectly likely – accounts of the affair, Jahangir met his widow four years later, during the Nauroz celebrations of March 1611. The story is that they met during one of the playful 'bazaars' that were organized during Nauroz, in which noblewomen would 'sell' their wares to the emperor, 'an unusual situation', as the modern author Bamber Gascoigne describes it, that allowed for 'an undercurrent, equally unusual in harem society, of flirtation'.

They were married two months later, in May. Mihrunnisa, the sun amongst women, would now become Nurmahal, light of the palace, and soon, Nurjahan, light of the world. Her powers would grow apace with her titles.

Indeed, the undeniable influence that she exercised on the emperor – whether for better or worse – is evident in the immediate surge in her family's fortunes.

In April or so of 1611, I'timaduddawla's rank was still 1500, stuck there since Jahangir first promoted him at his accession in 1605. Now, the emperor's father-in-law to-be received his first promotion in six years: to 1800. A few days later, he was promoted again 'for his loyalty and long service' to a rank of 2000 and given a bonus of five thousand rupees. At the end of July, only weeks after the wedding, I'timaduddawla became the head vizier of the empire. His son and Nurjahan's brother, Abu'l Hasan, the father of Khurram's prospective bride, was titled I'tiqad Khan and given one of Jahangir's favourite swords (called Sherandam, lion-bodied), and soon he would receive the title by which he is best known – Asaf Khan. The year after, in 1612, Sultan (no longer Baba) Khurram was promoted, too, and his long-deferred marriage to Arjumand Begum finally took place.

Naturally, none of this went unnoticed in court. 'Now one Gaihbeig,' writes William Hawkins, the English khan, 'was made chiefe Vizir, and his daughter marryed with the King, being his chiefe queen or paramour. This Vizirs sonne [i.e. Asaf Khan] and myselfe were great friends, he having beene often at my house, and was now exalted to high dignities by the King.' These high dignities were just the beginning. For a sense of the speed and scale at which the new queen's family's fortunes burgeoned, Findly makes this helpful calculation: before 1611, not one person in Nurjahan's family had been made governor in any Mughal province; in the fifteen-odd years between her marriage and the end of Jahangir's reign, a dozen governorships went to her kin.

Nurjahan's influence, then, is irrefutable. Its causes are less clear. Is it really possible that Jahangir lost his heart and his head so completely to his wife that he just gave away all the power he had so long craved? Or is it possible that Nurjahan had such a flair for governance that Jahangir found it both convenient and advantageous to share his rule with her? Could it also be, perhaps, that as the emperor lost more and more of his oldest and most trusted friends, he became increasingly reliant on those that remained?

Khubu and his mother had died all too soon. In the winter of 1612, the year after he married Nurjahan, Jahangir lost two other close companions, Sharif Khan, the amir-ul-umara, and Salima Sultan Begum, who died within a month of each other. The year after, Afzal Khan succumbed to an illness that had produced boils and lesions all over his body. Afzal Khan was Abu'l Fazl's son, and it says a great deal for what might be called Jahangir's sociability[3] that the son of the man he had had killed became one of his most hard-working and trustworthy amirs. The year after that, in early 1614, news came that, despite appearing perfectly healthy, Islam Khan had passed away.

Islam Khan was, like Khubu, a descendant of Sheikh Salim Chishti; and he had been sent in Khubu's place to govern Bengal in 1608. He had done a fantastic job; no one, wrote Jahangir, 'had ever exhibited the competence he had'. His death was as much a loss for the empire as it was a personal bereavement for the emperor. And besides, the story of his mysterious demise adds another strand to the esoteric bonds of life and death that tied Jahangir to the Chishti clan.

In 1612, soon after Khurram married Arjumand Begum, Jahangir contracted his first noteworthy illness. 'Because a congestion of blood had started to dominate my constitution,' he writes, 'upon the advice of physicians, I had about a seer of blood let from my left arm.' The man who did the bloodletting was another of Jahangir's trusted friends, Muqarrab Khan – he received a jewelled dagger as reward – and the emperor, for whom naming things was almost as much a compulsion as wine, was so pleased by the effects of the cure that he declared that bloodletting be called 'lightening' from then on.

Despite his cheer, Jahangir didn't quite recover; and in 1614 he had a relapse, serious enough that Jahangir says, 'I kept my condition hidden from most of my intimates and cohorts, lest harm befall the country and subjects'. This was not an exaggerated fear: William Finch describes how, while he was travelling from Agra to Lahore, a rumour spread of the emperor's death. At this, 'many rogues with that false alarme were abroad'. The law was after them, 'some two thousand horse and foot in their pursuit', but the rogues and the faujdars seem to have created more tumult than they resolved, towns burning in their wake. The imperial state might well have had many pillars, but it had only one head, and this precarious balance was best left undisturbed. Therefore,

Jahangir writes, 'I made no one of the harem privy to this state other than Nurjahan Begum, the one I thought had more affection for me than any other.' It was only when he became visibly weak that Jahangir called the doctors; at their bidding (or was it Nurjahan's?) he even gave up drink for a few days, though muttering that this only 'increased my weakness and lassitude'.

Finally, seemingly at death's door, the emperor had no recourse but to appeal to the power that gave him life itself. 'One night, racked with fever, I went to the exalted khwaja's shrine' – that is, the shrine of Moinuddin Chishti in Ajmer, where the imperial camp had recently arrived – 'and prayed to God . . . for my health'. Twenty-two days later, he was entirely recovered.

Jahangir pierced his ears in thanksgiving, 'a lustrous pearl in each ear' proclaiming him a disciple of the khwaja; he did not know that, far from him, another disciple of the Chishti order, Islam Khan, had given up his life for the emperor's.

It would be years before Jahangir heard what had happened. Islam Khan had not only divined his friend and ruler's illness, he had also had a vision that only a sacrifice of something 'dear and precious' would keep Jahangir safe. First, Islam Khan thought of sacrificing his son; then he decided to give up his own life. Immediately, 'the arrow of his prayer . . . struck its target'. Soon after, he died.[4]

For the moment, however, Jahangir was unaware of the sacrifice that had saved him; all he knew was that another old friend had died while he grew ever closer to his most affectionate wife.

Part V

Ambition

My affection for this son of mine is so great . . . that I
cannot disappoint him in anything.

Jahangir, *Jahangirnama*

'I never saw so settled a Countenance,' Thomas Roe once wrote of Sultan Khurram, watching the prince leaf through some letters, 'nor any man keepe so Constant a gravety, never smiling, nor in face showeing any respect or difference of men; but mingled with extreame Pride and Contempt of all.'

Thomas Roe did not like Khurram very much. It was to the prince – and to his father-in-law, Asaf Khan – that the ambassador had to go to negotiate the trade concessions he had come to seek, and these discussions were never as pleasant as Roe's conversations with the emperor. Khurram was suspicious of the English agenda in Hindustan and he made no attempt to disguise his misgivings with, for example, banter about beer. Instead, his manner was so forbidding that Roe confesses he once drank 'some powerfull wyne' to give him courage before a meeting with the prince.

Roe's description would have been nothing if not biased, therefore, but there is something in these words that brings alive the single-mindedness of purpose that seems to have defined Khurram's life. The boy who had sat by his grandfather's side, immovable as conspiracies swirled around him, the child in whom Akbar is said to have discerned signs of greatness – glimmers of his own self, in fact[1] – had grown into a man of impressive will and ambition. And, whether by coincidence or otherwise, it was shortly after his marriage to Nurjahan's niece, Arjumand, that Khurram began to succeed with dizzying speed, so much so that much of the history of Jahangir's reign is also the history of Khurram's rise.

Only about six months after Khurram's wedding, in the eighth year of Jahangir's reign, Khurram (now 'my lucky son') was given command of the Mewar campaign. In one way or another, this campaign had been ongoing since Jahangir's accession, led by several of his most able commanders, including his old friends Mahabat Khan – who fought so well that rumours grew among the Rajputs that he was Rajput himself – and Abdullah Khan. Currently, it was in the hands of the outspoken Aziz Koka. From the very beginning, however, when Parvez led the first Jahangir-era expedition to Mewar, Rana Amar Singh's capitulation had become as much a question of protocol as of military defeat. The rana was clear he would never himself pay obeisance to the emperor, but he had offered to send one of his younger sons to do so. Jahangir had been willing to accept but he would not be satisfied with younger sons; he wanted the eldest prince and heir of Mewar, Karan Singh, to bow to him.

These negotiations were interrupted by Khusro's revolt, but the empire had now been stable for years. Jahangir's days and nights passed, in Roe's words, 'as regular as a clock that stricks at sett howers'. This clockwork routine

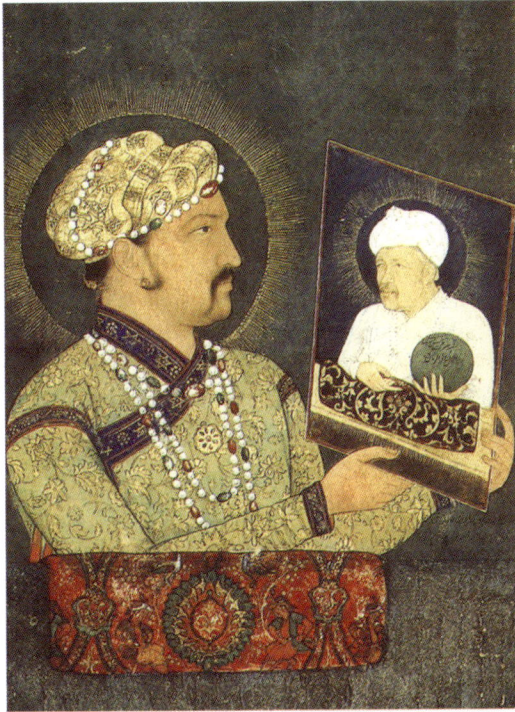

Top: Jahangir contemplating a portrait of Akbar holding a globe, c. 1614. Attributed to Abu'l Hasan and Hashim.

Bottom: Jahangir weighing Prince Khurram, c. 1615. Jahangir had his son Khurram weighed against gold and silver and other metals for his fifteenth birthday. As was the custom, these coins were then distributed as alms. Khurram is seated on a scale made of gold set with rubies and other jewels. Beside the prince is Jahangir's commander in the Deccan, Abdur Rahim.

Top: Akbar hands his crown to Shahjahan, while Jahangir looks on, c. 1631. Commissioned during Shahjahan's reign and attributed to Bichitr.

Bottom: The Maharana of Mewar, Amar Singh, submits to Prince Khurram during Jahangir's reign, c. 1615–18. Over the generations, various ranas of Mewar had been defeated in battle by Mughal forces, but none had been subdued until Khurram's successful campaign. Obtaining Rana Amar Singh's fealty was something that even Akbar hadn't managed to achieve: this was the very mission that Jahangir had twice disdained as a prince. To have won, even if by proxy through his son, delighted him. Attributed to Nanha.

Jahangir in a loincloth, c. 1620. In what the art historian Ebba Koch describes as 'the most Indian (and eccentric!) depiction of a Muslim king one could possibly imagine', Jahangir appears bare-chested, dressed in a dhoti, seated cross-legged and, in the manner of Indian deities, accompanied by his consort – most likely, Nurjahan.

Metropolitan Museum of Art, New York

Jahangir watches an elephant fight, c. 1605. Mahouts control the elephants as an audience looks on. One of the riders drops his ankush (a metal rod used to control elephants). To the right, servants hold fireworks on poles, prepared to help deflect the elephants if necessary. Jahangir and his horse appear in red and gold in the foreground. Just before his demise, Akbar ordered a bout between two elephants: one belonged to Jahangir, the other to Khusro (Jahangir's eldest son). The fight came to symbolize their struggle for the throne. Attributed to Farrukh Chela.

Top: Salim kills a rhinoceros and a lion, c. 1600–04. This painting was part of a shikarnama (hunting album). From the age of about twelve to fifty, according to his memoirs, Jahangir killed 17,167 animals and birds (out of a total of 28,532 hunted down in his presence). The sheer enormity of the number is leavened, somewhat, by the specifics: Jahangir's tally included eighty-six lions but 10,348 pigeons.

Bottom: Jahangir triumphing over poverty, c. 1620–25. From the beginning of his reign, Jahangir wanted to position himself as a saviour of the downtrodden, distributing both justice and prosperity. He commissioned a propagandist painting of himself shooting arrows at a shrivelled old man representing poverty. Attributed to Abu'l Hasan.

Top: The dying Inayat Khan, c. 1618. A hard-drinking mansabdar called Inayat Khan fell so ill that he asked for permission to leave the imperial retinue and go home. The emperor gave him leave, but first he ordered that a painting of his be made. Jahangir exclaimed, 'Whereas painters employ great exaggeration when they depict skinny people, nothing remotely resembling him had ever been seen.'

Bottom: A spotted forktail, by Abu'l Hasan. An inscription states that the emperor's servants hunted this bird, though not whether they caught it or killed it. The mysteries of nature were an endless source of wonder for Jahangir who would have been a 'better and happier' man, according to Henry Beveridge, if he had been the 'head of a Natural History Museum' instead of an empire.

Top: Jahangir holding a picture of the Madonna, c. 1620. This is one of the best-known portraits of Jahangir, whose court was replete with paintings of Hindu deities and Christian iconography. European visitors, accustomed to sectarian strife back home, were amazed by Jahangir's eclecticism and the religious freedom of his empire.

Bottom: Jahangir converses with Jadrup Gosain, c. 1620. Jahangir met the Hindu ascetic Jadrup when passing through Ujjain on his way to spur Khurram's first campaign in the Deccan. He went to the ascetic's cave twice and for three hours each time. The ascetic appears many times in Jahangir's memoirs thereafter, often because the emperor had a 'great yearning' or 'another overwhelming desire' to meet him. Jahangir always returned from these conversations strangely elated. 'Without exaggeration,' he once wrote, 'it was hard for me to part from him.'

In 2011, this six-foot high, life-size portrait of Jahangir sold for a staggering 1.42 million pounds – the most expensive Mughal painting ever sold – at an auction in London. The portrait, attributed to Abu'l Hasan and dated 1617, is painted with watercolours and real gold.

began at dawn; as the sun rose to light the world, so Jahangir appeared on his jharokha balcony for the morning darshan, casting his own majesty upon his subjects and letting his realm know that its ruler was well. Then, the emperor retired for a two-hour nap, after which he ate breakfast with the women. At noon, Jahangir would appear on the jharokha balcony again, not to be seen this time but to watch, for a few hours, whatever spectacle had been arranged for him. Elephant fights were a regular entertainment, as also bouts between other kinds of animals. The afternoons were reserved for the public durbar.

In the hall of public audience, Jahangir sat on a slightly elevated platform, under a canopy of velvet and silk to keep out the sun. While all the amirs then present in the city were required to attend, only the most high ranking, including Khurram, were allowed to stand near the emperor. Besides the amirs, two men stood on either side of Jahangir to fan him; another stood a little below, swatting flies. This small group was enclosed by a wooden railing; and a similar railing marked off a somewhat larger section of the hall, into which only the middling nobility and other subjects of worth were allowed. Beyond stretched the mass of the emperor's subjects, jostling to get a better view or present their grievances to their ruler.

This clear delineation of space does not, however, reflect the tumult and babel that seems to have accompanied these public audiences. Guards with large sticks were employed to keep the crowds in line, and all the while drums were beaten and music played from a gallery above. As his subjects pushed or cajoled their way to the emperor's attention, Jahangir's prize elephants and horses, too, were led past for his inspection – and if any appeared as if they had not been taken good care of by their keepers, there would be consequences. Justice (and punishment) was integral to the durbar – one eyewitness says that hangmen and men with whips stood at the very centre of the hall.

The durbar was public in every sense. Thomas Roe couldn't quite believe how every decision made here was immediately common knowledge, liable, he says, to be 'tossed and censured by every rascal'. Indeed, he goes on, not only were the Mughal emperor's decrees subject to public censure, his everyday routine dare not betray public expectation, 'for as all his Subjects are slaves, so is he in a kynd of reciprocal bondage'.

Jahangir, unaware that he was a harbinger of the paradoxes of twenty-first-century democracy, stuck to the task at hand, and quite amiably at that. When William Hawkins first came to his durbar, the emperor greeted him warmly, 'with a most kinde and smiling countenance he bade me most heartily welcome'; and there are many such descriptions of Jahangir's good-natured manner. Equally, however, the emperor could be frightening. He spent two hours or so in his public durbar, listening to whatever complaints made their way to him and delivering his verdicts. Edward Terry writes that the emperor's justice was swift, if often brutal: 'hangings, beheading, impaling, killing with dogges, by elephants, serpents, and other like, according to the nature of the act'. Thomas Roe describes how, once, a hundred thieves were caught and sentenced to death. As it happened, their chief and thirteen others were killed near Roe's house: twelve dogs were set upon the gang leader, to tear him to bits, while the others 'had their Necks cutt with a sword, but not quite off, and so left naked, bloody and stincking to every mans view and incomodytie.'

Such macabre execution of criminals was, arguably, a means of safeguarding the realm. A similar desire to preserve the integrity of his world – in this case, it's natural beauty – could be ascribed to Jahangir's justice vis-à-vis a wilful gardener. In a particularly beautiful garden by the Sabarmati river in Ahmedabad, the emperor was 'stunned' to hear that a gardener had chopped down some champa trees. For this 'wanton act', the gardener's index fingers were cut off – and it was only because the provincial governor, Muqarrab Khan, was entirely ignorant of the matter that he escaped punishment.

It wasn't uncommon, however, for the emperor's justice to be spurred by less public-spirited fury. William Hawkins relates the well-known anecdote of the mansabdar in charge of Jahangir's china. The poor man happened to break a plate that the emperor happened to love. When his clumsiness was discovered, he was whipped almost to death and then, at Khurram's intervention, given five thousand rupees and ordered off to China, where he was to find a copy of the plate or never return.[2]

Such was the emperor's power over the life of men that sometimes it seems as if even Jahangir was taken aback by it. Once, in the latter years of his reign, a blacksmith called Kalyan came to Jahangir's durbar. Kalyan was besotted with a widow on whom, unfortunately, 'the lovesick wretch's love had made no impression'. Jahangir, wanting to help, was trying to persuade the reluctant woman when Kalyan declared that if the emperor would only 'give her' to him, he would leap off the Shah Burj, a tower in the Agra fort. 'Just as a joke', writes Jahangir, 'I said, "Never mind the Shah Burj. If your claim of love has any truth to it, you'll have to throw yourself off the roof of this building. Then I'll give her to you by command."'

No sooner said than done: a moment later, Kalyan lay smashed on the ground below, blood trickling down his face. The emperor was distraught: 'I really regretted having spoken in jest and was dreadfully sorry.' Perhaps, growing old, he had temporarily forgotten that his word was no joking matter – or had he, perhaps, encountered the one force that could match, even surprise, the sheer enormity of imperial power: the madness of love?

So, at any rate, the emperor sat, disbursing life and death alike into the late afternoon, until he retreated into his palace once again, said his prayers, ate an elaborate meal and had his first drink of the evening. The real drinking, however, was reserved for the hall of private audience, then called the gusalkhana.

The gusalkhana, literally bathroom, was the emperor's most private chamber, open only to select amirs and only by invitation. Its odd appellation is said to derive from the fact that Sher Shah Suri, the Afghan king who toppled Humayun and almost undid the Mughal empire, would often hold meetings in his bath, because his very curly hair took longer than usual to dry. Here, Jahangir would have the rest of his strictly regimented drink – another five cups – while engaging with matters of governance, with abstract theology, with his various aesthetic passions, all of it, says Thomas Roe, 'with much Affabilitye'. He might even, in this most intimate of spaces, have his hair cut.

Then, having had his fill of conversation and his dose of opium, the emperor would fall asleep. Some hours later, past midnight, Jahangir would wake once again and eat his dinner ... then sleep, once more, till dawn.[3]

It was a stringent, but stable routine, and his days passed so peacefully that, in 1613, Jahangir had time to think of redecorating his durbar hall in Agra. It seemed to him that there should be some visible difference between the two railings that marked the boundaries of the hall; for the moment, they were both made of wood, but shouldn't the one that surrounded the emperor look more grand? But of course: he had it coated in silver.

Was Jahangir getting bored? Or did he think that now, eight years into his reign, he should fulfil some of the promises of conquest he had made at the start of it? Was it the fact that Khurram had grown old enough, and seemingly able enough, to lead an army? Or did Nurjahan suggest it?

Whatever the cause, in September 1613, Jahangir decided to move his court to Ajmer, to visit Khwaja Moinuddin Chishti's shrine and to 'deal with the damn Rana'. A few months later, in December, Khurram was given 'a gold-brocaded coat with jewel-studded flowers surrounded by pearls, a gold-brocaded turban with pearl fringe, a gold-spun scarf with pearl beading', a jewel-studded sword and dagger, an elephant and a horse from Jahangir's own stable, besides twelve thousand men – and sent off to claim his victory in Mewar.

Khurram fired his first salvo as soon as he arrived. Fittingly, this was a political salvo – the Mughal campaign in Mewar (like the even more convoluted campaign in the Deccan) was marked as much by infighting between Mughal generals as by forays against the enemy. So, just as Khurram took command, rumours trickled into Ajmer, whispering to Jahangir of the uncooperative and 'displeasing' manner of the previous commander, Aziz Koka. The rumours were soon followed by a message from Khurram himself, who wrote 'that it was entirely inappropriate for [Aziz Koka] to be there and that he was spoiling things purely on account of the relationship he had to Khusro'. The young prince couldn't have put it more clearly. Now that eight years had passed since Khusro's rebellion, Jahangir had begun to soften towards his eldest son. He had even commanded that Khusro come and meet him every day. Still, Jahangir would not have forgotten how Khusro's father-in-law – that old wolf Aziz Koka – had supported Khusro's bid for the throne. To bring up that old wound may have incensed the emperor. Immediately, he gave orders for Mahabat Khan to arrest Aziz Koka and bring him to court.

When he reached Ajmer, Aziz Koka was reprimanded and imprisoned in Gwalior, though not, it seems, without some embarrassment to the emperor, who writes that he made sure 'the necessities of leisure and comfort such

as food and clothing were . . . made available to him'.
(Indeed, Jahangir's shame at imprisoning his father's
favourite foster brother for no real fault must have been
acute; a few months later, he dreamt of Akbar telling
him, 'Baba, for my sake forgive Aziz'. When, the year
after, the old man was brought before him, Jahangir was
abashed, writing that although 'I was perfectly justified in
everything I had done to him, when . . . my eye fell upon
him, I felt more embarrassed than he did.' He gave him
the shawl he was wearing, and set him free. Aziz Koka's
own spirit, meanwhile, was uncrushed. While setting
him free, Jahangir had laid down the condition that the
uninhibited amir was not to speak unless spoken to, and
for this he asked Aziz Koka's son to stand guarantee.
The son refused, declaring, 'I am his security for everything
. . . but I cannot be surety for his tongue'.[4])

For the moment, however, Aziz Koka's fortunes were
of no real consequence. Soon after he was rid of the gruff
commander and only two months after he had left for
Mewar, Sultan Khurram sent news that he had captured
the rana's favourite elephant, Alam-Guman . . . and 'soon
its owner would be captured too'.

True enough. Within a year, Jahangir was writing
'Good news!' Khurram had achieved what he had set out
to. He spearheaded a ferocious, unflagging campaign,
driving both the rana's Rajputs and his own soldiers
past the limits of endurance until the rana realized, in
Jahangir's words, that 'he would either be driven from his
kingdom or be captured'. He sued for peace. Rana Amar
Singh would agree to pay tribute and 'render service' to
the empire; he would even pay homage personally to

Khurram (bringing his seven remaining elephants as offering, besides a famously large ruby) but he would not (pleading old age) go to Jahangir's court. In his stead, he would send his eldest son and heir, Karan Singh.

Some days later, when Khurram returned to Ajmer, Karan in tow, the delighted emperor showered both princes with every possible favour. All the amirs were ordered to greet Khurram with gifts on the outskirts of the town. The next day, Jahangir greeted his son with embraces, 'kissed his head and face, singling him out for particular affection and kindness'.[5]

Of the other, equally proud prince, Jahangir writes that 'it was necessary to win Karan's affection' – and proceeded to do so with a most magnificent display of gifts and favours, unfolding day after day during the course of the year or so that Karan spent in the imperial court. Over the generations, various ranas of Mewar had been defeated in battle by Mughal forces, but none had been subdued. Obtaining Rana Amar Singh's fealty was something that even Akbar hadn't managed to achieve: this was the very mission that Jahangir had twice disdained as a prince. To have won now, even if by proxy through his son, delighted him.

On the day they first met, Jahangir gave Karan 'a sumptuous robe of honour and a jewel-studded sword'. Thereafter, he writes, 'I showed him a new favour every day'. So, on his second day in Ajmer, Karan got a jewelled dagger; the day after, a Persian horse mounted with a jewelled saddle. On some days, Karan might receive gifts from both the emperor and his queen, Nurjahan. On the same day that Jahangir gave him the Persian horse, for

example, Nurjahan gave him not only another horse but
also an elephant caparisoned in gold, besides a robe of
honour and a jewelled sword. The day after, the emperor,
too, gave him an elephant.

'Since I had it in my mind to give him something of
every sort,' Jahangir writes, 'I bestowed upon him three
hawks, three falcons, a personal sword, a coat of mail, a
breastplate belonging to me, and two rings, one set with
a ruby and the other set with an emerald.' When Karan
had been in Ajmer about a month, Jahangir arranged
a gift-giving extravaganza. Soldiers marched into the
durbar hall carrying trays heaped with brocades and felts,
carpets and bolsters, golden flasks full of attar . . . all of
it to be given to the Rajput prince.

Jahangir's wooing of the prince wasn't limited to gifts
alone. He gave him his own company, too; and Jahangir's
company, as more than one source has claimed, could be
very pleasing. Once, for example, he took him on a hunt
for a lioness, telling Kunwar Karan he would shoot the
animal wherever the young man said. *Between the eyes*
was Karan's challenge. As they approached the animal,
however, a strong wind rose, and Jahangir's elephant made
things worse with his nervous prancing around the wild
beast. It was a tricky situation, but fortunately, writes
Jahangir, 'God in His grace did not shame me before the
raja's son'. He shot the lioness exactly as agreed; then, for
good measure, he gave Karan one of his own guns.

When the Mewar prince finally returned home, in June
1615, Jahangir's record keepers calculated that 'the total
worth of the cash, goods, gems, and jewelled vessels I had
given him . . . was two lakhs of rupees, 110 horses, and

five elephants, not counting what my son Baba Khurram had given him at various times' – not too bad a haul, one might say, for having lost.

While these two princes, Khurram and Karan were basking in the glow of imperial favour, there was a third whose plight had grown even darker than before. Soon after he arrested and imprisoned Aziz Koka, Jahangir stopped Khusro's daily visits, too. 'There were never any signs of gladness or happiness in his face,' wrote the emperor, and he always appeared 'bored and preoccupied'. Why, with so much more convivial company around him, should Jahangir waste time on a gloomy rebel?

It is unlikely that Khurram felt any sympathy for his elder brother's banishment. His own star was streaking through the sky. In April 1615, just before Karan's departure, Khurram's rank was made equal to that of his other elder brother, Parvez; the year after, he would outrank him. Jahangir would soon be referring to Khurram as 'my favourite son', his growing affection treading the line between love and a kind of awe.

The emperor could hardly believe it, for example, when Khurram turned twenty-four in January 1616 that, though fully adult, married, the father already of Dara Shikoh, he had yet to have a drink! Jahangir chose to interpret this as well-mannered deference to the lack, so far, of explicit parental (and imperial) permission.

As with food, Jahangir's attitude to drink is both clear and bafflingly fuzzy. In his memoirs, he writes

with unselfconscious ease about his drinking, never shy
of admitting his excesses nor of how much he enjoys the
pleasures of alcohol. Its pages are full of merry parties in
which all are served their fill; he mourns, with no little
empathy, those of his amirs who die of drink. And yet,
as Thomas Roe writes with some bemusement, 'though
drunckennes be a Common and a glorious vice, and an
exercise of the kinges, yet it is soe strictly forbidden that
no man can enter ... wher the king sitts, but the Porters
smell his breath'. Should these porters sense the slightest
trace of alcohol in an amir, he would be denied entry
and, quite possibly, whipped. William Hawkins learnt
of this convention to his cost; a happy tippler himself,
the evidence of his breath cost him his pride of place in
Jahangir's gusalkhana, a humiliation that led, eventually,
to the English khan's return to England.

Why such double standards? William Foster, editor
of both Roe's journal and *Early Travels in India*, writes
that Jahangir made occasional 'attempts to abstain' from
drink and that it was in one such 'fit of temperance' that he
ordered these breath tests. But Jahangir's mixed feelings
about alcohol might equally have derived from the
mullah's prohibition on drink, the alcoholic's affliction of
self-loathing, or both. Besides, what defined an emperor
was that he did what no one else was allowed to; in that
sense, the prohibition was only another demonstration
of imperial authority.

Now, however, it was Khurram's very abstinence that
rankled. 'Baba has children, and monarchs and princes
have always drunk,' Jahangir declared on Khurram's
birthday, adding demurely, 'today ... I let you drink wine

and give you permission to drink on festival days, on Nauroz, and on great occasions, but you must keep to the path of moderation.' There must, after all, be some 'profit and benefit in drinking', the emperor argued; hadn't the great physician Avicenna himself written, 'Wine is an enemy to the drunk and a friend to the sober'? The lecture fell on indifferent ears. As the emperor notes wryly, 'it took great persistence to get him to drink'.

But even if he was reluctant to join him in a goblet or two, Khurram knew other ways of pleasing his father. A few months after Khurram's birthday celebration, Jahangir found himself in a strange kind of distress. On his return from Mewar, Khurram had given his father a 'fine, brilliant ruby' that he had received from Rana Amar Singh, and Jahangir had been wanting to wear it around his arm ever since. The problem was, he also needed 'two . . . lustrous matched pearls worthy to sit with this ruby'. Recently, during Nauroz, Muqarrab Khan, the expert bloodletter, had brought one such 'superb pearl' for Jahangir, and this only increased the emperor's restlessness. If only he could find another, he would have the makings of 'a perfect arm band'!

It was Khurram who came to the rescue, declaring that he had seen exactly such a pearl on an old headband of his grandfather's. A search was launched, a 'big old turban ornament' was found, and yes, indeed, it was fitted with 'a pearl of exactly the right size and shape'. The armband finally wrapped around him, an overjoyed Jahangir prostrated himself in prayer 'to render thanks to the lord'.

Was Khurram pleased, watching his father's delight? Or was he contemptuous? Was his father a fastidious aesthete, in Khurram's eyes, or a drunken sot to be wrapped around his finger? Whatever his feelings may have been, Khurram kept them to his own sober self. Soon, his gifts to the emperor would eclipse that ruby and pearl, and Jahangir's joy would transform his love into something close to adoration.

There are those who would say that as the emperor, by chance or providence, lost his friends, and as his many indulgences weakened him without weakening his appetite for indulgence itself, he grew ever more dependent on an increasingly small circle of friends and advisers. Among such commentators would be Thomas Roe, who paints a rather pathetic picture of Jahangir, 'gentle, soft, and good of disposition' wholly in thrall to his wife and her 'bewitching flattery', with Nurjahan herself the leading force in what Roe would describe as a Faction of four: the queen, her father I'timaduddawla, her brother Asaf Khan, and her stepson Khurram.[6]

The ambassador's negotiations for trade concessions had not been proceeding well, blocked and delayed with expert civility by Asaf Khan, and rather more imperiously by Khurram.[7] To know that their instructions might be coming from the enigmatic – and to Roe, unapproachable – Nurjahan must have galled. Perhaps partly as a result, Roe developed a great fondness for the imprisoned Khusro and imagined how he might one day write a full history of the court intrigues around the 'noble Prince ...a Crafty stepmother, an ambitious sonne, a Cunning favorite: all reconciled by a Patient king; whose hart was not understood by any of all these'.

In Roe's account, Khusro is not only part saint but also a popular (and viable) contender for the throne, still 'extreamly beloved and honored . . . almost adored'. Therefore, he says, it was hardly any wonder that the Faction wanted to get rid of him, knowing that 'it was not possible for them to stand if the Prince Sultan [Khusro] lived . . . whose delivery or life would Punish their ambitions in tyme'. Sometime in 1616, therefore, the year that Khurram had his first drink, the Faction, writes Roe, decided to poison his brother.

Having made their ungodly plan, the Faction's first gambit was Nurjahan's 'false teares', with which she tried to convince the emperor that Khusro was not safe where he was, in the keeping of a Rajput raja called Ani Rai Singhdalan. This was too subtle a ploy for Jahangir, however; he didn't (or wouldn't) follow the queen's drift. So, one evening when the emperor was drunk, the three men – I'timaduddawla, Asaf Khan and Khurram – came to him with a deluge of arguments to convince him to transfer Khusro from Ani Rai to 'his deare brother' Khurram's charge. In his cups and tiring of the harangue, Jahangir agreed and promptly fell asleep.

That very night, says Roe, Asaf Khan and his guards marched to Ani Rai and demanded he give up the eldest prince. But Ani Rai was made of stern stuff. Once, he had quite literally wrestled a wild lion with bare hands to protect Jahangir (who had fallen to the ground and was being trampled by servants trying to escape). His title, Singhdalan, means lion-crusher. Denying the powerful Asaf Khan may have required as much courage as fighting a wounded beast, but the raja was up to it. With diplomatic finesse, he agreed to relinquish Khusro – but only to the man who had given him charge of the prisoner, the emperor himself. 'This answere,' writes Roe, 'Coold all'.

The next morning, Ani Rai met Jahangir, told him what had happened and declared that he would rather 'dye at the Gate' than give up Khusro to his enemies. Thomas Roe was obviously not party to this secret (and possibly fictional) meeting, but he gives Jahangir a most eloquent reply: 'You have done honestly, faythfully: you have answered discretly: Continew your Purpose and take noe knowledge of any Commandes: I will not seeme to know this, neyther doe you stirr farther: hould your fayth and lett us see how farr they will prosecute yt.'

That is, Jahangir would not bring up the subject of Khusro's guardianship, and nor, therefore, would the worried Faction. For the moment, Khusro was safe.

But not for long.

The Faction resumed its persuasions within days. If not to Khurram, let Khusro at least be transferred to Asaf Khan's charge. 'The King, who had yeeilded himself into the handes of a woman, could not defend his sonne from their Practises,' said Roe. The harem, Jahangir's own sisters, erupted in protest; they cried that if Khusro was killed, a hundred of them would 'burne for him in memorye of the kinges bloudines to his woorthyest sonne'. Embarrassed, Jahangir sent Nurjahan to soothe the women but they heaped her with curses and would not let her in. The 'people' meanwhile were in a tizzy, convinced that by giving up Khusro, the emperor had more or less abdicated his own life 'into the handes of an Ambitious Prince and a treacherous faction'. All the court, Roe continued, was 'in a whisper; the Nobility sadd; the Multitude ... full of tumor and Noyce, without head or foote.'

For all Roe's lamentation, however, there was no plan to kill Jahangir and Khusro was not poisoned; he had years to live and at least one more shot at the throne. But even so, Roe was right: the plot had certainly begun to thicken. On 15 October 1616, Jahangir took up his pen and jotted down yet another of the year's events: 'I turned over Khusro, whom Ani Rai Singhdalan had been assigned to keep an eye on, to Asaf Khan.'

Sometime in the late summer of that same year, 1616, Jahangir had recorded his intention of transferring command of the Deccan campaign from Parvez to Khurram. So now, on the last day of October, Khurram was given all kinds of rich gifts and the title 'Shah' – an unprecedented honour – and he began his march southwards.

Whether this was Jahangir's own idea or the Faction's doing may not really matter. Parvez had been stationed in Burhanpur since 1610, and the Deccan campaign itself predated Jahangir's reign.[8] Historians have argued, in fact, that the 'Deccan campaign' as an idea predated the Mughal dynasty; as Beni Prasad writes, it was 'a legacy of two thousand years of Indian history'.

Something about the very geography of the region made it so. The Satpura and Vindhya ranges that divided north from south were a topographical tease. In Beni Prasad's words, once again, 'if the Vindhyas had resembled the Eastern Ghats, India might have developed into one strong united nation. If they had resembled the Himalayas, the country might have been effectively partitioned into two nations, each homogenous within itself. As it was, they divided the north from the south, and yet . . . encouraged either to domineer over the other.' From the Mauryas on, crossing this central mountain range was part of any self-respecting imperial agenda.

The greatest empire of the Deccan itself had been that of the Bahmani sultans, which lasted 150 years from 1347 to 1498 and covered, at its peak, almost all of present-day Maharashtra, Telangana, northern Karnataka and small tracts of southern Madhya Pradesh and western Chhattisgarh. By the time the Mughals were strong enough to follow their historically mandated course into the Deccan, the Bahmani empire had long broken up into several small sultanates: Khandesh, Golconda, Bijapur and Ahmednagar (which had annexed a fifth kingdom, Berar). Akbar's last campaign, in Asirgarh, had subjugated the northernmost of these, Khandesh, but the strength of the rest only seemed to increase in Jahangir's reign. Ahmednagar, which comprised most of what is now Maharashtra, was the most redoubtable: not only did it boast the legendary Deccani commander Malik Ambar, but it had also begun to attract increasingly formidable troops of mercenary soldiers – the Marathas.

Though Parvez's approach to military duty may have resembled his father's, the imperial forces in the Deccan had not lacked for effective commanders of their own, amongst them the highly regarded Abdur Rahim Khan Khanan himself. Unfortunately, as in Mewar, accusations and counter-accusations flew as fast as bullets across Mughal camps, invigorated by the great riches of the Deccan kingdoms. The khan khanan, rumoured to have succumbed to gems and gold, was summoned to Jahangir's court; when the campaign fared only worse without him, he was sent back. The khan khanan was hardly the only officer whose fortunes ricocheted thus during the protracted war. Early in his command, when one of Parvez's trusted men, Keshav Das, was recalled for no clear reason, the prince sent along a complaint: 'You will report these few words from my mouth,' he said to Keshav Das, 'when His Majesty summons my chief servants for any reason, it causes demoralisation and depression in others'.⁹

But too much morale could also backfire. Once, for example, the imperial forces had planned a pincer attack: two divisions led by experienced commanders (Raja Man Singh and others on one side, Abdullah Khan on the other) were to advance upon the same target from different directions and trap it. 'Had they followed this procedure and been united, and had selfish interests not intervened,' writes Jahangir, 'it is most probable that God would have granted them victory.' Instead, Abdullah Khan decided he wanted all the triumph for himself. 'He was obsessed with this thought,' says Jahangir, and no one could dissuade him from attacking alone. The enemy, seeing him advance unprotected, attacked: 'By day they engaged in skirmishes with him, and by night they threw every type of rocket and explosive they had at him.' Finally, Abdullah Khan retreated – in fact, he was chased out ('all the way as far as the frontier of their own territory the Deccanis followed them') – and Man Singh's troops, hearing of the rout, abandoned the plan.

But if Mughal plans were volatile, the Deccan was hardly a united front either. Malik Ambar, the Ethiopian general of Ahmednagar who had perfected guerrilla tactics to flummox the far larger Mughal army, wasn't fighting imperial forces alone, but also rival Deccani kingdoms, particularly Bijapur. Loyalties could be shattered by a breeze. A few months before Shah Khurram set out from Ajmer, for example, news came that the Marathas who formed some of Malik Ambar's most deadly troops (and also, in Jahangir's words, a 'wellspring of mischief and foolhardiness in that land') had felt insulted in some way by the Ethiopian and therefore joined the Mughals. As a result, the imperial army managed to inflict a damaging, though not conclusive, victory on the Ethiopian.

Malik Ambar was so much a bugbear of the Mughals, in fact, that one of Jahangir's best-known allegorical paintings has the emperor shooting an arrow at Malik Ambar's severed, impaled and bleeding head. Malik Ambar wasn't killed by the Mughals, however, let alone by Jahangir; in fact, he died of ripe old age at eighty. It is modern historians, once again, who look at this painting in a way that lifts it far above the somewhat comical vainglory it otherwise evokes.

On the last Friday of October 1616, Shah Khurram was to begin his march to the Deccan, taking fresh blood and strategies with him and soon to bring, it was hoped, tidings of victory and reward. On the night before his departure, Jahangir was in the gusalkhana, chatting with his amirs, when an owl flew over them and landed on the roof. It was late night and the owl was barely visible, but owls are considered birds of ill omen and, on the eve of such an eventful journey, it was absolutely imperative that its portent be destroyed. Jahangir took up a gun, aimed with a steady hand and fired. 'The ball hit the ill-omened bird like a decree from heaven and blew it to pieces,' writes the emperor; around him, the men burst into applause and praise.

If one looks at that painting with this fact in mind, it begins to reveal its real meaning. As the art historian Robert Skelton first pointed out and A. Azfar Moin later elaborated, Malik Ambar's severed head is not the only lifeless thing in the image. There is also an owl dropping dead along the pole on which the Ethiopian's head is impaled – and against which leans a gun.

It seems that Jahangir wasn't, after all, living out a vain fantasy of killing Malik Ambar without ever engaging him in battle; instead, it was his messianic self that was clearing the way of bad luck for Mughal forces heading towards the Deccan – the painting, in Skelton's words, an attempt 'to influence fate by sympathetic magic'.[10]

And who knows, perhaps there was something to it. The next morning, Shah Khurram set out for the south, unencumbered by ill portents; within the year, he would send word of triumph.

Jahangir, meanwhile, decided to follow his son, at least up to Mandu. The idea was that imperial proximity would boost the morale of his troops and awe the Deccanis. As it turned out, this was also the most enjoyable journey Jahangir had yet undertaken, and for the most part, it seems, because he undertook it with Nurjahan.

Even Thomas Roe concedes that Nurjahan was 'not incapable of Conducting busines, nor herselfe voyd of witt and subtiltye'. Another contemporary writer, Mu'tamad Khan, wrote a history of Jahangir after the emperor died, when his widowed queen had not only lost all power but was also much maligned. Naturally, then, Mu'tamad Khan writes of how coins were struck in Nurjahan's name, how imperial farmans were signed with it; of how she would sit on her balcony, behind a lattice screen, 'while the nobles would present themselves, and listen to her dictates'; of how, indeed, 'day by day her influence and dignity increased ... [until] the King was such only in name'. It is Mu'tamad Khan who records the sentence most infamously associated with Jahangir and Nurjahan: 'Repeatedly,' he writes, the emperor 'gave out that he had bestowed the sovereignty on Nurjahan Begum, and would say, "I require nothing beyond a seer of wine and half a seer of meat."'

But Mu'tamad Khan, too, concedes that Nurjahan knew how to rule. 'It is impossible,' writes the historian, 'to describe the beauty and wisdom of the Queen. In any matter that was presented to her, if a difficulty arose, she immediately solved it.' Her generosity was well known; she went out of her way to arrange dowries for destitute orphan girls; she would invariably help anyone who 'threw himself upon her protection'.

And anyone who reads Jahangir's account of their travels down to Mandu cannot doubt the fact that she loved her husband. This was their honeymoon. From Ajmer to Mandu took them forty-six days' march and seventy-eight days' halt, a leisurely pace interrupted by stops at whatever spot caught their fancy. Once, for example, they camped by the Chambal river for three days 'because the place was so lovely and the weather was so delightful. Every day we got in boats, hunted waterfowl, and toured up and down the river'. Not once, writes Jahangir, were they tired or uncomfortable; 'it was as if we were progressing from garden to garden'. Along the way, a courier arrived carrying several gardens' worth of fruit for the travellers: melons and pears from Badakhshan, apples and grapes from Samarkand and Kabul, pomegranates from Yazd, apricots from Farah, pineapples from the Portuguese.

The ruined palaces of Mandu, meanwhile, had been repaired and rebuilt at a cost of three lakh rupees; when its royal guests arrived, the long-abandoned fortress shone with its old grandeur, its beautiful palaces and lakes perfect for picnics and parties. One Thursday, Nurjahan organized such a wonderful party, in fact, that Jahangir renamed the day itself. It was held in a pavilion in the centre of a lake; wine and other intoxicants flowed freely, along with fruits and roasted meats of all kinds. 'As night fell, lanterns and torches were lit around the lake and the pavilions . . . All the torches and lanterns were reflected in the water and made it look as though . . . the water was a field of flame. What an incredible party!' The night breeze, the wine, the flames flickering upon the water, all of it brought a hint of sensuality, even to the emperor's writing. When all had drunk their fill and been dismissed, he writes, '[I] summoned the ladies of the harem, and stayed in that marvellous spot through the first watch of the night enjoying myself'.

As it happens, this Thursday was not only the occasion of this grand party but also the day of two important festivals in the Mughal calendar, Shab-e-Barat and Rakhi. Besides, Thursday was also the day of Jahangir's accession. With so much to recommend it, didn't the day deserve an honorific? The emperor renamed it Mubarak-shamba, 'blessed day' – and waterside parties on Mubarak-shamba became part of the emperor's routine.[11]

Nurjahan wasn't just a talented party organizer, however; this trip revealed her as a skilful shot, too. While camped by the Chambal river, in a lush green valley filled with trees, she had shot a tiny swallow, no mean feat. In Mandu, she killed four lions with six bullets. 'Until now,' wrote Jahangir, having showered his wife with gold coins, two pearls and a diamond, 'such marksmanship had not been seen – from atop an elephant and from inside a howdah she had fired six shots, not one of which missed'.

Admittedly, there are not many examples of the day-to-day relationship between the royal couple, but the few that exist betray an easy, intimate affection, the kind of tenderness that often grows between people who fall in love late – she was thirty-four, he forty-two when they married. Theirs may or may not have been a grand, scandalous romance, but it was, certainly, a sustainable fondness. Oddly enough, it is from Thomas Roe that we catch the most candid glimpse of the couple. Soon after the emperor left Mandu, Roe had one more altercation with Asaf Khan and Khurram. Impatient for an audience with Jahangir, he went to his camp only to learn that the emperor was out. Roe and Asaf Khan waited there all day, passing the time in squabbling until night fell. 'Suddenly,' writes Roe, 'newes came to put out all lights, the King was come'. It wasn't for the emperor's sake, however, that darkness had been ordered. As the ambassador peered into the black, he saw that Jahangir was driving into the camp on a bullock cart, sitting at its head, its reins in his own hands, and his empress by his side.

There is such a cheerful lack of restraint in this picture – the emperor of all Hindustan driving a bullock cart, Nurjahan perched merrily by his side – that what can you call it, but love?

It wasn't just Nurjahan that Jahangir would grow closer to, however, en route to and in Mandu. This was also the journey in which I'timaduddawla was made an 'intimate' of the imperial harem: allowed into the women's quarters, that is, and the women not obliged to veil themselves from him. There was no greater honour an amir of the state could expect. And it was in Mandu, too, that Shah Khurram's fortunes finally peaked.[12]

In July 1617, just nine months after he'd left with such pomp to conquer the Deccan, Shah Khurram sent word that he had done it. Jahangir's favourite son had made quick work of the Deccani resistance, and Thomas Roe would have us know that there was something suspicious about it. According to the ambassador's sensational account of the affair, not only had Khurram instigated Parvez's removal from command, he also asked for the khan khanan to be dismissed. The khan khanan refused; he had already been removed and reinstated once and, besides, he was Jahangir's former tutor. Perhaps he felt he still had some authority with the emperor. Not only did he refuse, he sent word that Khurram be replaced by one of the prince's younger brothers, maybe Shahryar, still a boy. At this, says Roe, the furious prince suggested an alliance to the self-aggrandizing Abdullah Khan, promising him the khan khanan's position. Meanwhile, the khan khanan was getting worried that his game was up, so he offered a deal to the Deccanis, telling them to pretend to submit so that the prince and the emperor would leave. The Deccanis agreed, says Roe, and even sent ambassadors to this effect, but Khurram was nobody's fool. The prince refused to accept any terms until his army was in the Deccan, declaring that he would not allow the khan khanan to 'beguile him of the honour of finishing that warr'.

The modern historian Beni Prasad, unencumbered by Roe's visceral dislike for Khurram ('his Pride is such as may teach Lucifer'), has a more dispassionate account. Having reached the Deccan front, it was Khurram, in fact, who sent ambassadors of his own, Afzal Khan and

Raja Bikramjit, to the two main powers in that region, Ahmednagar and Bijapur. 'The Deccanis,' writes Prasad, 'must have realized that the advent of Shah Khurram and the approach of the Emperor would . . . extinguish the advantage which they had so far gained from the mutual dissensions of Mughal officers.' Besides, the Deccanis were embroiled in dissension themselves at this point, and could not afford a war with Shah Khurram's indisputably superior forces.

They agreed to a truce.

His son's 'campaign' in the Deccan would not make it to the more distinguished annals of military history, but that did not diminish its worth in Jahangir's eyes. When Khurram sent word (via yet another Sayyid of Barha[13]) that 'all the [Deccani] rulers . . . had surrendered and turned over the keys to their fortresses and strongholds' the emperor turned 'in humility to the divine court, and . . . had the drums of rejoicing beaten'.[14]

That October, exactly eleven months and eleven days after they had parted, Khurram appeared before his father in Mandu. Jahangir could not restrain his joy. When the prince had performed the formal salutation, Jahangir invited him into his jharokha and, 'out of sheer love and yearning', he says, he got up and hugged him. If this was unusual, far more was to come. Khurram's rank was increased to 30,000, far above anyone else's in the realm, and he was given his own chair by the throne and allowed to sit with the emperor. 'This was a special favour for my son,' writes Jahangir, 'for prior to this there had been no such custom in our dynasty'. Indeed, other than abdicating on the spot in his son's favour, there is little more Jahangir could have done to show his son how pleased he was.

The next week, Nurjahan arranged a grand celebration in the prince's honour, at which he was given all kinds of jewelled clothes and weapons, horses, elephants, even presents for his amirs. The whole thing cost three lakh rupees (to put that in perspective, this was how much it cost to renovate all of Mandu).

Whatever the scale of Nurjahan's party might have been, however, it was nothing compared to the bounty that Khurram had brought with him from the overflowing treasuries of the kingdoms he had subdued. The treasure was so enormous that it took him a few weeks to arrange it all, but finally, on 22 October 1617, Jahangir was invited to inspect his son's offerings – arranged in a courtyard glittering with gems of infinite worth, so impressive that, for the second time that month, the emperor got up from his throne and walked down to inspect his prize at closer hand.

How could he even list it all? There was a ruby of 400 carats (Jahangir had never seen one larger than 250); a sapphire of 130 carats (none 'so large or valuable with such good colour and brilliance' had ever been seen); the Chamkora diamond, 20 carats, named for a patch of 'sag chamkora'[15] in which it was found; pearls 'perfectly round and flawless' – not to mention dozens of prize elephants and horses. In addition, Khurram's gifts to Nurjahan amounted to a staggering 22 lakh worth (his other stepmothers and his wives shared a rather measly sixty thousand rupees between them).

'No such presentation had ever been made before in this eternal empire,' wrote Jahangir, 'truly he is a son worthy of kindness and affection, and I am highly pleased with him. May God grant him long life and success.'

Jahangir himself, in these joyous days, was willing to grant the prince whatever he willed. He gave him, for example, the ruby that Hamida Banu Begum had given Jahangir at his birth – an heirloom for the prince who was, no doubt about it, his heir. Another significant honour bestowed upon him was a new title. Khurram had progressed from Baba to Sultan to Shah without missing a step; now, Jahangir declared him Shahjahan, king of the world, and gave him the name by which the world would know him. For the emperor himself, however, his favourite son would not remain Shahjahan for long, and in his last years Jahangir was denouncing the prince, with bitter rage, Bedawlat.

That Wretch.

Part VI

The Aesthete

Both night and day his delight was very much to talke with me, both of the affairs of England and other countries, as also many demands of the West Indies, whereof hee had notice long before, being in doubt if there were any such place till he had spoken with me, who had beene in the country.

William Hawkins, *Early Travels in India*

In 1617, when Shahjahan subdued the Deccan, Jahangir was at the exact middle of his reign. He had ruled eleven years since his accession in 1605, and he would rule eleven more. And so far, his rule had been a tremendous success. Mewar was his. The Deccan was his.[1] From the fact that he had not had to face any major rebellions, he might gauge that his mansabdars were, on the whole, satisfied. And Jahangir, for his part, was truly enjoying himself.

His memoirs are proof of it. Variously called the *Jahangirnama* and the *Tuzuh-i-Jahangiri*, these writings contain character sketches, descriptions of cities, detailed accounts of gifts received and promotions given, even some quite thrilling accounts of battles – but at heart, the memoirs are an account of one man's interests and pleasures. Fortunately, Jahangir was the sort of man who took his interests and pleasures seriously. And besides, not only was he possessed of an observant, curious and sceptical mind, he also had a talent for writing with infectious enthusiasm, so it is virtually impossible not to be as carried away as he is when, say, he has the idea of milking a lioness.

'It had been heard from physicians that lion's milk is extremely beneficial for the brightness of the eye', the emperor once observed. Lions being part of the Mughal menagerie, he thought he might test the theory, but unfortunately, 'however much we tried to get some milk to appear in her breasts, we couldn't'. While a more commonplace mind may wonder how the men charged with milking a lioness escaped with their lives, the emperor was trying to make sense of their failure. 'It occurs to me,' he wrote, 'that since it is an animal of an irascible nature, either milk is produced in the breasts of mothers out of the affection they feel ... when the cubs drink and suck, or else when its breasts are squeezed to produce milk, its irascibility increases and its breasts dry up'.

The mysteries of nature were, in fact, an endless source of wonder for Jahangir. It might be, for example, that two of his elephants died after being bitten by a mad dog. Jahangir was astounded that 'an animal with a body so large and big could be affected so by . . . an animal so small'. It might be that, having just shot a lion, the emperor was possessed of the idea of locating its courage in its entrails. 'I wanted to open it up and have a look,' he writes; and, indeed, it was discovered that 'unlike other animals, whose gall bladders are outside the liver, lions' . . . gall bladders are located inside.' This, Jahangir proposed, might hold the key to the animal's brave heart.

Dissecting animals became something of an obsession with Jahangir, in fact; besides examining their innards, he also liked to know what animals ate. In one ghastly but hilarious incident, the emperor came upon a snake swallowing a rabbit. Wanting to observe the process at close hand, Jahangir ordered his scouts to pick up the snake, with its meal, and bring both to him. Naturally, the startled reptile dropped its prey, but Jahangir was unperturbed. He ordered the scouts to stuff the rabbit back in the snake's mouth, 'but no matter how hard they tried they couldn't get it back in; in fact, they used so much force they tore a corner of the snake's mouth'. Now that the snake was unlikely to ever lunch again, they might as well cut open its belly. They found another rabbit in it; one the snake had managed to swallow before it was so rudely interrupted. Soon after, Jahangir happened to shoot a pregnant antelope. When this animal was cut open, it revealed two fully formed fawns, which the emperor had cooked into a do pyaza. The result, he writes, 'was quite delicious'.

As he grew older, this obsession also began to affect how Jahangir rated the 'cleanliness' or otherwise of any animal (and potential food). In his words, 'because of the fastidiousness and caution I have in such matters, I order [animals] cleaned in my presence, and I take it upon myself to inspect their stomachs in order to ascertain what they have eaten'. Should it be that they had eaten anything 'disgusting', Jahangir would strike the species off his menu. Such was the case with drakes ('I saw a domestic drake eating disgusting worms'); waterfowl generally ('from its stomach came . . . a bug so big that if I hadn't seen it with my own eyes I wouldn't have believed anything so large could be swallowed'); and herons ('ten bugs came out of its stomach, and they were so revolting that I shudder to think about them').

Sometimes, such dissections were prompted by another kind of curiosity altogether. Once, Jahangir's head scout found a quail lacking the markings that usually tell the difference between male and female in the species. The emperor, however, was clear it was a female. Naturally, they cut it open. The bird was, indeed, female: its little belly spilled out several half-formed eggs.

'How did you know?' everyone asked Jahangir.

'The female's head and beak are smaller than the male's,' replied the emperor, adding modestly 'with much observation and perseverance one gets the knack.'[2]

Jahangir's observation and perseverance were indisputable. Henry Beveridge, editor of Alexander Rogers's nineteenth-century translation of the memoirs, writes that the fourth Mughal would have been a 'better and happier' man if he had been the 'head of a Natural History Museum' instead of an empire. Modern historians have a different take on the matter. Ebba Koch, for example, presents Jahangir as an ideal of Solomonic kingship: a ruler who, as in many of his paintings, brings peace between the lion and the lamb, and in his life 'observes and records nature'.[3] Jahangir's atelier did, in fact, produce some of the most exact and beautiful paintings of natural life. From turkeys to zebras, Jahangir documented every kind of animal that came to his court; his dodo, writes Koch, is the most accurate representation of the extinct bird that exists. His desire to have everything documented and measured – and as often painted – from a dodo to a zebra, a hermit's cave to a large peach, was possibly a way of measuring (and so knowing, and ruling) his dominions.[4] Besides, as another historian, Corrine Lefèvre has noted, the emperor's curiosity was not so much 'scientific' but rather 'driven by an aesthetic sense which matched beauty (husn) with strangeness: at the core of his curiosity lay the marvels of the Creation known as 'ajaib in the medieval Islamic world and as mirabilia in the contemporary Occident.'[5]

And nowhere, perhaps, is Jahangir's fascination with the miracles of nature more apparent than in the emperor's detailed, episodic narrative of his two pet cranes.

Laila and Majnu, as they were named, were saras cranes brought to the court as chicks. Five years later, the eunuch who took care of them told Jahangir that he had seen them mate. The emperor ordered the caretaker to let him know if they ever did it again and sure enough, one dawn, the eunuch hurried in. 'I immediately ran out to watch', writes Jahangir, and provides this wonderfully lucid picture of what he saw: 'The female stretched her legs straight and then bent them slightly. First the male lifted one of his legs off the ground and put it on her back, and then the other. The instant he was seated on her back they mated. Then he got down, stretched out his neck, put his beak on the ground, and circled once around the female. It is possible that they have produced an egg and young will be brought forth.'

In fact, they had two eggs, not one. The emperor, thrilled, watched how the mother sat 'on the eggs by herself all night' while the father stood guard. 'Once a large weasel appeared, and he ran at it with great vehemence'. At dawn, the father would go to the mother and scratch her with his beak, telling her that it was his turn for nesting their eggs.

One gets the sense that Jahangir would have sat on those eggs himself if he could. When they hatched, the emperor was as protective of the chicks as their parents, maybe even more so. He wanted to see them as often as he could, ordering them 'brought very carefully so they wouldn't be hurt'. Once, noticing the male's tendency to carry his chicks upside down, Jahangir had him kept away until his bona fides were established and 'it was obvious that its action had been affectionate'.

The emperor's minute observation encompassed not only the animal world, but the human, too. Once, famously, a hard-drinking mansabdar called Inayat Khan fell so ill that he asked for permission to leave the imperial retinue and go home. When Inayat Khan came before him, Jahangir couldn't believe his eyes. 'Even his bones had begun to disintegrate,' he exclaimed. 'Whereas painters employ great exaggeration when they depict skinny people, nothing remotely resembling him had ever been seen. Good God! how can a human being remain alive in this shape?'

Of course, the emperor let the poor man go; he even gave him a thousand rupees for his journey – but first, 'it was so strange,' writes Jahangir, 'I ordered the artists to draw his likeness'.

The resulting sketch is one of the many unique contributions of Jahangir's artists – and the emperor's patronage – to Indian art. Jahangir wasn't shy to admit his pleasure in painting, nor his expertise; he claimed he could tell one brushstroke from another, 'even if it is a scene of several figures and each face is by a different master, I can tell who did which face'. It is very likely he could. The emperor's writings themselves reveal a highly developed visual sense.

Here, for example, is Jahangir passing by a tank full of water lilies, a sight that prompted this utterly beautiful – almost cinematic – meditation on the lily, the lotus and the bumble bee, and the haunting tradition of Indian poetry that unites them all: 'It is a fact,' wrote Jahangir, 'that the lotus opens by day and closes into a bud by night, whereas the water lily is a bud by day and opens at night. The black bee the people of India call bhaunra always alights on both these flowers and goes inside to suck the nectar inside them. The lotus flower often closes up and traps the bhaunra inside for the whole night. It also happens with the water lily. But when they open it comes out and flies away. Because the black bee is a constant visitor to these flowers, the Hindi poets consider it to be like the nightingale in love with the rose, and they produce marvellous poetic conceits based on it.'[6]

The water lilies were among the sights that caught Jahangir's eye on his way to Gujarat. Having enjoyed his trip to Mandu so much, he had decided, once the Deccan campaign was done, to visit his western ports; to take a ride upon the 'salty sea' and also to witness the monsoon rains in that region, of which he had heard wonderful reports. For a while, things went well. At Cambay, Jahangir sailed awhile upon the sea; he ate a sea fish that was almost (if not quite) as good as rohu; he tried a khichri made with Gujarati bajra and 'rather liked it'. He camped by the sea and gave away horses, robes, grants and other kinds of alms and aid to the people of the port town.

Jahangir's many grants, alms and charities are well documented, both by himself and by others. In the *Jahangirnama*, for example, he records how, in the fifteenth year of his reign (1620–21), his alms 'to the poor and deserving' included 85,000 bighas of land, fourteen villages, two fields, 2327 rupees, 6200 drabs, 7880 charans, and 10,000 dams,[7] 1512 tolas of gold and silver and a garden – all distributed in the emperor's presence. Some years earlier, Thomas Coryat had watched Jahangir, Nurjahan and other women from the harem serve langar to thousands at the urs of Moinuddin Chishti at Ajmer and had been impressed enough by such Christian charity in a non-Christian ruler to issue a challenge to his faith: 'Cracke mee this nut, all [ye] Papal charitie vaunters'.

Gift-giving, for all that it might have perplexed Thomas Roe, was evidently integral to the Mughal – and Hindustani – economy; and its reciprocity wasn't limited to the emperor and his subjects. When Pietro Della Valle landed in Gujarat, for example, he noticed how the wealthy and powerful made water tanks 'for the publick benefit, and as works of Charity' – what might be called philanthropy today.[8]

The anonymously authored *Intikhab-i Jahangir Shahi* records how, once, the emperor's accountants protested at his excessive liberality but Jahangir 'replied that these petitioners were like an army to pray for him' and the accountants should, therefore, endeavour only to increase their number. Jahangir, too, would pray for his subjects: in

Mandu, his entourage was suffering from a severe lack of water so, writes the emperor, 'I turned in all humility to the divine court' and, though it was not yet the monsoon season, a heavy rain did soon fall.

The give and take of gifts and prayers may not have created an economically equal society, but it did seem to hold the realm in a balance, between the people, their ruler and their gods.

From Cambay, the emperor marched to Ahmedabad. He had heard that the 'urbanity of Ahmedabad', Gujarat's chief city, 'was beyond comparison with Mandu' and was looking forward to a halt there. Unfortunately, Ahmedabad was a great disappointment. Why would anyone, he grumbled, spend 'their precious lives in this dust heap?' Not only was it dusty and dry, the water tasted bad, and the air was particularly 'poisonous'. To make matters worse, the emperor fell ill and was advised to substitute his wine with watery khichri. 'No matter how hard they tried to get me to drink some lentil and rice soup,' he protested, 'I couldn't make myself do it.' He hadn't had to eat such khichri since he was a child and hoped he never would again. In normal circumstances, the imperial camp would have made an immediate about-turn for Agra, but a plague was ravaging that city so Jahangir was stuck where he was.

It was only the emperor's observational bent of mind, complemented by his itch to experiment, that kept him amused. Thus, ill and trapped, Jahangir ordered an air quality index test. He had two sheep killed, skinned and hung up: one by the Kankaria lake near Ahmedabad, the other in Mahmudabad (now in Uttar Pradesh). Soon, Jahangir's dissatisfaction with Ahmedabad's air was proven correct: the Kankaria sheep began to rot in eight hours, while the other lasted, unspoiled, for fourteen.

There's a ruthlessness to this act – as, indeed, there is a ruthlessness to the painting of Inayat Khan (he died two days after), or to the force-feeding of that poor snake – a ruthlessness that is the prerogative of artists and emperors. Jahangir was born to command, after all, to crush as much as to exalt, to both punish and reward. At the same time, like many who exercise authority with ease but find the negotiations of affection more tricky terrain, Jahangir sometimes appears happiest in the company of animals and little children. A lovely example that combines many aspects of the emperor's personality is that of his experiment in cross-breeding two kinds of goats: markhor and Barbari. The result was a grand success. 'What can be written of their playfulness, the funny things they do, and their leaping and bounding about?' writes Jahangir. 'They do things that make one want to watch them in spite of oneself . . . I enjoyed them so much I ordered them always to be kept nearby, and each of them was given a suitable name.' Jahangir even thought of cross-breeding on a larger scale, and predicted that they would be more valuable should their offspring breed in turn. He observed that normal goat kids would bleat and cry before suckling, but these 'do not cry at all but act extremely independent'. And finally, for all their cute antics, the emperor wasn't so sentimental that he wasn't also looking forward to eating them, for 'their meat may also be quite delicious'.

When it came to his grandchildren, Jahangir could, naturally, become even more attached than he became to baby goats or saras chicks. There was a granddaughter in particular, a child of Shahjahan's, whom Jahangir loved so much that when she died, still a baby, the emperor couldn't bring himself to write about it. Instead, he gave the pen to I'timaduddawla who describes the child's tragic death and Jahangir's inconsolable sorrow. 'What am I to write of the grief that afflicted His Majesty the Shadow of God?' For two days, he met no one 'and it was ordered that the room where that bird from paradise had lived should be walled up, never to be seen again.' When Jahangir finally emerged, it was to go to his son's house, 'tears pour[ing] from his blessed eyes' all along the way, and for several weeks thereafter, any small memory of her would make him weep.

To set the seal of his anger and grief upon the event, Jahangir renamed the very day on which she died: from then on, he would refer to Wednesday, Chahar-shamba, as Gum-shamba instead, the day of loss.

It may be that the birth of another grandchild soon after, Shahjahan's son Shah Shuja, helped the emperor recover. Soon, the boy was the joy of his heart. In his account of how Shah Shuja, too, fell seriously ill, Jahangir's anxiety leaps off the page. 'He was unconscious for a long time ... and his unconsciousness robbed me of my consciousness.' The emperor prayed for his recovery and, remembering the vow that Akbar had made when Jahangir himself fell still in his mother's womb, Jahangir made his own 'solemn and honest undertaking with God'. If only the child were spared, Jahangir would never hunt with a gun again, nor harm any of God's creatures with his own hands. Shah Shuja's illness passed.

Barely two years later, the then four-year-old Shah Shuja fell out of a palace window in Kashmir and was found dazed but unhurt by Rai Man (that intrepid procurer of rohu). 'I was taking a rest when the dreadful news was reported to me,' writes Jahangir. 'I ran out in terror, and when I saw him like that, my head began to spin. I clasped him affectionately to my bosom for a long time, totally overcome by this divine gift'. Later, the emperor had alms distributed across the city and prostrated himself again and again, in grateful prayer for his grandson's life.

But Shah Shuja was obviously a child of chequered destiny. The next year, he caught smallpox. He couldn't even swallow water, and Jahangir despaired. This time, it was the emperor's favourite astrologer, one Jyotik Rai, who came to the rescue, assuring Jahangir that his beloved grandson would survive: 'Since you are so fond of him, it follows that no harm will befall him, and it will be another son who dies,' he said. That was exactly what happened. Shah Shuja recovered and a grandson in Burhanpur died in his place.

Jyotik Rai was rewarded with his weight in gold, and if there is something cold about this proffered exchange, one grandson's life for another's, that isn't any more surprising than Jahangir's ruthlessness about those hybrid goats cooked into curries. Children and grandchildren were aplenty in the imperial family; no one person could be attached to them all. It isn't surprising that Jahangir could be clinically disengaged from a grandchild in Burhanpur, one whom he had possibly never met. What is surprising, though, is how clinically disengaged he would soon become from the darling Shah Shuja himself.

Part VII

Blood

As usual, he reported the victory to his father in a pompous form. He compared his achievement to that of Akbar in Gujarat and tried to convince Jahangir that his work was even superior. It is amusing to read the puerile arguments advanced by him in support of his claims; nevertheless he was at the zenith of his power ...

Banarsi Prasad Saksena on Shahjahan's second victory in the Deccan, *History of Shahjahan of Dihli*

After expatiating upon the dutiful tenor of his whole life, he modestly mentioned the services he had so recently performed, lamented that he should have forfeited his Majesty's parental regard, without the shadow of offence, for the gratification of the ambition of a base woman, and her degenerate son-in-law. He implored the Emperor to do him only common justice; but declared that whilst he was so unfortunate as to labour under his royal displeasure

... he only begged leave to retire to Surat, which might be considered as the door to the house of righteousness (Mecca) where he would employ his whole time in praying for his Majesty's health ...

Francis Gladwin describing Shahjahan's second letter to Jahangir, sent with Afzal Khan, in which the prince made excuses for his disobedience, *The History of Jahangir*

With a symmetry that might, in retrospect, have pleased the aesthetically minded emperor, his reign ended as it began: with a rebellion.

'The wisest foresee a rending and tearing of these kingdomes by division,' Thomas Roe once wrote, 'when the king shall pay the debt to Nature, and that all Partes wil be torn and destroyed by a Civill warr'. It was a prophecy that would have done Jyotik Rai proud.

The fifteenth year of Jahangir's reign, March 1620 to March 1621, seemed to pass as usual and well. Already, as the year began on Nauroz, the emperor was on his way to Kashmir, where he spent many months, returning only towards the onset of winter. As always, the beauty of the way elicits an almost physical response from Jahangir, especially when the beauty is that of his beloved Valley. 'Its lovely meadows and beautiful waterfalls are beyond description,' he declared. 'Red roses, violets and narcissi grow wild, there are fields after fields of all kinds of flowers'. He had come to Kashmir in the full glory of its spring, when 'mountain and plain are filled with all sorts of blossoms; gateways, walls, courtyards, and roofs of houses come ablaze with tulips'. His delight grew even greater when he travelled out of Srinagar to a famous pasture: 'As far as the eye could see there were all sorts of flowers in bloom, and flowing through the midst of the greenery . . . were streams of the purest water. You'd think it was a picture drawn by a master painter of destiny. Seeing it caused the bud of the heart to burst into blossom.'

On this visit, Jahangir's heart was also full of memories of his father. He remembered how, with Akbar, he 'often toured the saffron fields and watched the autumn harvest'; how it was Akbar who had the first cherry trees grafted in Kashmir. When he found that Akbar's favourite palace garden, Nurafza Bagh, was unkempt, he was upset and had it restored, and when the garden's cherry trees bore fruit, he enjoyed himself picking a few every day 'as a relish with my cups'.[1]

This was the visit during which Shah Shuja fell from a palace window, but once the flurry of his fall was over, Jahangir's days followed pleasurably one upon the other. He enjoyed the lovely festival in which Kashmiris celebrated the Jhelum (then Bahat) river, with lamps along its banks: 'it was a beautiful illumination. I got in a boat and watched it'. He went to the Vernag spring, the source of the Jhelum, and was pleased with the pleasure house he had had built there. He watched with delighted fascination the Kashmiri style of fishing – a group of fishermen creating a circular 'trap' with their boats, then ducking underwater to catch fish with their hands. 'There was an old boatman who caught more than two fish on every dive.'

He celebrated Dussehra. 'As is done every year, horses from the royal stable and the amirs' establishments were paraded before my view.' The festival went well, but Jahangir noticed a slight tightening of his chest, a breathlessness that was the first sign of the long and frightening illness he would suffer next year.

In the summer of 1621, Jahangir was back in Agra and, as the monsoon rains began to pour upon the city, the constriction in the emperor's chest grew suddenly much worse. Two doctors in his court tried two kinds of remedies; both failed. Finally, when Jahangir was, by his own account, 'in such a state that a heart of stone would have melted' at his plight, he summoned his most senior physician, a Persian titled Masihu'z-Zaman, messiah of the age, no less. This doctor flatly refused to treat him, claiming he did not know what to do. Another trusted hakim was so obviously 'fearful and terrified' at the thought of treating (or, presumably, mistreating) the emperor that Jahangir was too 'disgusted' to even ask for his opinion.

Suffering and annoyed, the emperor turned to the 'Absolute Physician' – this time, however, he meant not so much a Chishti saint but the bottle. 'Since drinking wine gave me some relief, I began drinking during the day, contrary to established custom, and little by little I was overdoing it.' Not surprisingly, he grew worse.

Finally, it was Nurjahan who cured him. Reading Jahangir's rather helpless and moving account of this time, one gets the sense that it wasn't only Nurjahan's remedies that helped the ailing emperor – though Jahangir does write approvingly of these, too – but also her love. 'She treated me with affection and sympathy,' he writes, and 'I now relied on her affection'. Jahangir was fully recovered for his birthday, a few weeks later, and to celebrate Nurjahan arranged a grand party 'that astonished all who saw it'. She had arranged all Jahangir's birthdays from the year they were married ('and she had considered it a pleasure to do so') but this time 'she made the celebration even more ornate and took special pains to decorate the hall and arrange the banquet'.[2]

The shortness of breath on Dussehra was not the only sign of troubles to come. While the emperor enjoyed the Kashmiri spring, his forces had been fighting successfully in Kishtwar and Kangra; both would soon be conquered. The already conquered Deccan, however, had grown restless again; and Shahjahan, once more, was dispatched to subdue it.[3] He was sent off with the usual pomp – robes of honour, jewelled swords, thousands of soldiers, a crore of rupees – but also with an ominous silence on Jahangir's part on the one thing that Shahjahan insisted he would not leave without: his brother, Khusro.

Already, when Shahjahan left for his first Deccan campaign, Thomas Roe was reporting rumours of a new 'affinitye' between Nurjahan's brother Asaf Khan and his prisoner, the eldest prince. According to Roe, the court gossip was that Khusro would be married to Nurjahan's daughter (by her first husband) Ladli Begum. 'This,' wrote Roe gleefully, 'will beget his full libertie, and our proud Masters [that is, Shahjahan's] ruine'. Pietro Della Valle, writing a few years later (and far away from the court) gives a more romantic account of the affair. According to Della Valle, though Khusro was offered Ladli Begum (and therewith his freedom and the throne), his love for his wife was so strong (and his antipathy towards Nurjahan and her daughter so great) that he refused, even though his wife, 'who lov'd him as well as he lov'd her' and lived in prison with him, begged her upright husband to accept the offer, crying she would 'live with him a slave, provided she saw him free and in a good condition' – but to no avail. Instead of his freedom, all Khusro earned was Nurjahan's enmity.

Unfortunately, Beni Prasad discredits this story; and it really would have been odd for Asaf Khan, at least, to plot with Khusro against the interests of his own son-in-law.[4] Whatever the truth may be – whether Khusro ever had a last shot at the empire or not – it is recorded by the emperor's own hand that, shortly after Shahjahan left for his second tour of the Deccan, Ladli Begum was married to Shahjahan's younger brother, Shahryar. There was a mehndi party in the house of Jahangir's mother, and the wedding itself was hosted by the bride's grandfather, I'timaduddawla. 'I went myself with the ladies of the harem,' writes Jahangir, 'and participated in the celebration.'

It is worth noting that this is only the fourth time Shahryar makes an appearance in Jahangir's diary, and the first in which he lasts longer than a line. The youngest prince was born just months before Jahangir's accession and, in the sixteen-odd years since, he had done nothing, it seems, to distinguish himself.[5] From the fleeting appearances he makes in others' accounts, it is hard to tell what kind of boy he was or life he led. Once, William Hawkins saw one of Jahangir's best elephants pick up the seven-year-old prince in his trunk and hand him to his mahout. Another story tells of how Shahryar was not afraid to touch a tame lion when ordered to do so by his father – which pleased Jahangir, though not as much as it angered him against one of his nephews, who refused. Yet another time, the emperor lost his temper at Shahryar: when the boy didn't appear suitably enthused at an invitation to travel with his father, Jahangir slapped him. The child didn't cry – saying his nurses had told him a prince must never cry – so Jahangir had a needle thrust through his cheek. Still, though he bled, he didn't weep. William Hawkins, who tells this story, concluded that 'there is great hope for this child to exceed all the rest'. An anonymous Indian historian from the time called him the most beautiful of the royal princes. Shahjahan, in the manner of elder siblings, called him Nashudani, 'good for nothing'.

For the moment, however, it looked like Nashudani might well grab the throne from under his brother's nose. Meanwhile, shifting dynamics had brought new hope for the long-forgotten prince Parvez, too. During Nauroz, in March 1621, a month before Shahryar's marriage, Jahangir suddenly remembered his 'fortunate son Shah Parvez' and sent him a robe, a jewelled belt, and a transfer from Allahabad to the greater responsibility of Bihar.

With the pieces moving thus across the board towards an endgame no one could have foretold, the very heavens,

it seems, could not contain their anxiety. At dawn on
9 April, in a village in Jalandhar, there arose 'a tremendous
noise'. Jahangir writes of how the villagers rushed out,
'frightened . . . out of their skins', and the noise grew
louder and louder, rising to a crescendo until 'something
bright fell to the earth from above . . . [like] fire . . . from
heaven'. Then, as suddenly, a hush.

The local tax collector galloped to the spot and found
an area of over eight metres burnt black and 'still hot'.
They began to dig, the earth getting hotter as they went
deeper, until finally they found a piece of iron, almost
two kilos in weight, burning 'as if it had been taken out
of a furnace'.

Normally careful to appease astronomical phenomena,
especially eclipses, Jahangir did not, this time, distribute
propitiatory alms. Instead, he had a dagger and two swords
made from the meteor. The swords 'cut beautifully', said
Jahangir, and a courtier composed a verse to mark the
day. It began, 'The world attained order from the world-
seizing monarch . . .'

Ironically, the world as Jahangir had made it unravelled
rapidly that year, the sixteenth of his reign. Shahjahan
sent word of yet another quick victory in the Deccan;
but, although his father sent him a congratulatory ruby,
he did not call him back home. Also troubling: Jahangir
began to refer to his son as merely Khurram once again.
Meanwhile, the emperor's illness grew worse and 'Shah'

Parvez, who had dutifully gone to Bihar, rushed to the emperor's bedside, circling it thrice and 'no matter how insistent I was . . . that I was all right, he wept and cried'. Touched, Jahangir 'took him by the hand, pulled him to my side, and held him close to me in love and affection'.

It wasn't Jahangir, however, who was in any immediate danger just now; it was his mother-in-law. In October 1621, six months after the meteor landed, Nurjahan's mother died. Asmat Begum does not feature prominently in the histories of the time. She appears, once, to give birth to Nurjahan; and once again, when Jahangir credits her with the invention of rose attar.[6] Now, as the emperor mourned her passing, it became evident that Nurjahan's mother was a talented and vibrant woman, loved very deeply by her family. 'I had no less consideration for her than for my real mother,' said Jahangir, while her own children were distraught and her husband devastated. 'What can be written of Nurjahan Begum's attachment to such a mother,' asks the emperor, 'when a son like Asaf Khan, with all his wisdom and learning, ripped his clothing in distraction . . . adding to the father's grief and increasing his pain by seeing his son in this state?' I'timaduddawla was heartbroken, as Jahangir could tell, even though the 'poor grief-stricken old man' tried to hide his pain. 'Forbearance,' noted the emperor with empathy, 'could not replace her as a companion.'

He was right. A little over three months later, in January, I'timaduddawla, too, died. Jahangir, who had tried his best to console his bereaved friend, who had sat for hours by his side, writes, 'What can I say of how I felt over this terrible event?' Nurjahan and Asaf Khan, having been orphaned in the space of four months, would have been desolate; but Jahangir, too, writes as if he had lost not a father-in-law but a father: 'He was not only a perfectly intelligent vizier but also a kind and wise companion.' Is it possible, perhaps, that Jahangir found in I'timaduddawla's gentle (and naturally subservient) wisdom what he had sought from his own father's too-loud voice? Or is it that the emperor understood only too well what had killed the doting husband? Jahangir, too, might not have survived long without his Nurjahan.

No matter what effect I'timaduddawla's death may have had on Jahangir, its effect on his reign was tremendous. Already, the princes were inching about the throne. Khusro was in Shahjahan's custody; Shahryar was in Nurjahan's favour; Parvez was holding his father's hand on his sickbed. Now, Jahangir added a whole new dimension to the increasingly murky layers of alliance forming around him by bestowing every last bit of I'timaduddawla's fortune upon his daughter. Nurjahan got the jagir, the staff, the treasure, for good measure, Jahangir even ordered that her drums be beaten immediately after his own. Asaf Khan got nothing.

Things could only get worse, and within a month they did. 'Around this time,'[7] writes Jahangir with a strange and cold detachment, the kind that can only, perhaps, be feigned, 'a report was received from Khurram containing the news that Khusro had died ... after an attack of colic pain.'

'Murtherer.'

This is how Della Valle describes Shahjahan. No one believed he hadn't done it or hadn't had it done. The question was only how. Was it by his own hand? Was it by poison? By sword in a fracas in a gloomy dungeon cell? By soldiers who, in Della Valle's words, 'leap'd all about him ... till at length having fell'd him to the ground they strangled him with a Bowstring'? Or did they use a lungi so as not to leave marks?[8]

Beni Prasad, from an evaluation of various contemporary accounts, including Rajput chronicles, concludes that Shahjahan did have his brother killed, though he did it discreetly, going out to hunt that day to put some distance between himself and the crime. Banarsi Prasad Saksena offers a record from Shahjahan's own reign that puts the matter beyond doubt. A historian called Muhammad Salih Kambu, who wouldn't have dared court Shahjahan's wrath, particularly not with a lie, writes unequivocally that, following the advice of his counsellors, Shahjahan moved his brother 'from the ditch of prison to the plains of non-existence'.

Though Muhammad Salih Kambu might well argue that 'it is entirely lawful for the great sovereigns to rid this mortal world of ... their brothers and other relations; whose very annihilation is conducive to common good', in the long, often violent, annals of Mughal succession, this was the first time that brother had killed brother for the throne. Even Shahjahan, Kambu admits, ordered that Khusro's body be 'taken with due honour and respect' through Burhanpur, while his tainted nobility 'accompanied the hearse chanting prayers, and muttering incantations'. A shameful hush fell over the deed, as in Jahangir's terse report of colic pains – to be broken years later by Aurangzeb, now barely three years old, who would one day taunt his father with what he had done.

For the moment, however, even those who might have been inclined to mourn Khusro's death would not have had the time. In March 1622, the many internal machinations for the empire received an external jolt – the Shah of Iran began covert operations to annex Qandahar. The shah had thought Khusro's rebellion was good cover for a takeover seventeen years ago. Now, he tried once again, and sparked Shahjahan's.

Jahangir sent his son a message, ordering him to march from Burhanpur to Qandahar and repel the Persian incursion. Shahjahan did not flatly refuse – he said he'd rather wait out the monsoon in Mandu and march in winter – but he might as well have. 'From the contents of the letter and the requests he made the aroma of goodness did not come,' writes Jahangir, 'indeed, signs of rebelliousness were apparent.' Not just that: Shahjahan had recently tried to grab a jagir that Jahangir had given Shahryar. The emperor sent a cold reply: Shahjahan could do what he liked with his time, but he was to send back the imperial army and commanders immediately. In panic, Shahjahan sent his divan, Afzal Khan, to explain, but Jahangir was so angry he wouldn't even look at the messenger. Instead, he decreed that Shahjahan should busy himself administering one of his various provinces, return the army and never again 'disobey orders, otherwise he would have cause for repentance'.

Meanwhile, just in case Shahjahan didn't fall in line,

Jahangir assigned the Qandahar campaign to Shahryar and began to gather alternative forces, too. Parvez (now 'my favourite son') was summoned, as were Abdullah Khan, Raja Bir Singh Deo and, most importantly, Zamana Beg, the old friend whom Jahangir had titled Mahabat Khan and, of late, forgotten.

The anonymous author of the *Intikhab-i Jahangir Shahi* claims that the distance between the emperor and, arguably, his most talented commander grew from Mahabat Khan's dislike of Nurjahan. 'The whole world is surprised that such a wise and sensible Emperor as Jahangir should permit a woman to have so great an influence over him,' Mahabat Khan is said to have told Jahangir. 'What will kings of the future say?' According to this chronicler, Jahangir was briefly impressed with his friend's advice and 'for some days became more reserved in his demeanour towards the Begum'. Soon, however, Mahabat Khan's warning was forgotten. 'The influence of Nurjahan Begum had wrought so much upon his mind,' the historian sighs, 'that if 200 men like Mahabat Khan had advised him simultaneously to the same effect, their words would have made no permanent impression upon him.'

However, whether or not Mahabat Khan had ever tried to save Jahangir's posthumous reputation, he would soon be called upon to save his empire; and it may well have been Nurjahan herself who advised Jahangir to summon him. The emperor was in no state to strategize. He had never quite recovered from that serious illness a few years ago, and this sudden turmoil wrecked the peace he so enjoyed. Shahjahan had taken the pleasure out of things for him, and the emperor, connoisseur of beauty, reacted with a petty ugliness. He took back the vow he had made to save Shah Shuja's life. Not only, writes Jahangir, did he take up hunting with guns again, he even ordered that no one would be allowed into the palace *without* a gun. Soon, he says, 'most of the courtiers had developed a taste for guns' and archers were beginning to worry about promotions.

This was the ugliness of despair, of weakness, a desperate flailing. So wretched was he, so agitated, that Jahangir even stopped writing his diary – a habit almost as dear to him as his hunts or his drink – and, instead, delegated the task to Mu'tamad Khan.

On the other hand, one of the last things that Jahangir recorded with his own pen was this: 'Khusro's son Dawarbakhsh was given the rank of 5000/2000'. Could it be that the emperor was not so unable to strategize, after all, that he had placed yet another pawn upon the increasingly crowded chessboard of his realm?

Almost immediately thereafter, Shahjahan rebelled, and the eighteenth year of his father's reign began with civil war. Reports came that the prince was marching to Agra, to intercept the treasury that Jahangir, perhaps remembering his own long-ago raid on the capital, had summoned to his camp. The emperor, who had left Kashmir for Lahore, displayed the burst of energy he had shown when Khusro rebelled, charging 'in continuous marches to chastise the villain'. From now on, he declared – and Mu'tamad Khan noted down – Shahjahan was no more, he was Bedawlat the Wretch.

But it was almost two decades since Jahangir had

chased Khusro down. He wasn't just older, he was old. He was also sick; and no matter what he willed, he couldn't do much more than call this son names and complain to his scribe in long, lugubrious whines. 'Of which of my pains should I write?' the emperor declaimed. 'Is it really necessary for me, with my illness and weakness, to get on a horse and gallop around in such hot weather ... running off after such an undutiful son? ... [M]ust I ... kill with my own hands so many servants I have patronized for long years ...? [W]hen my sons and loyal amirs should be endeavouring ... to further the Kandahar-Khurasan campaign ... this unhappy wretch is chopping away at the roots of his own fortune and ... complicating matters.'

In March of 1623, there was not even time for the usual parties and gift-giving of Nauroz. Instead, all the most competent soldiers and amirs of the empire were about to come face-to-face in battle.

Shahjahan's forces were led by Raja Bikramjit (previously Sundar Das, the celebrated conqueror of the Kangra fort, and now 'the hideous Sundar' in Jahangir's words), and included not only the ageing khan khanan but also his son ('the accursed Darab').[9] Raja Bhim, the fiery younger brother of Karan Singh who was now rana of Mewar, and various Maratha generals had also allied with the prince. The imperial forces marching south were commanded by Mahabat Khan, their first troop led by Abdullah Khan.

A week later, on 20 March, in the warm north Indian plains, twenty-five thousand of the emperor's men, ten thousand of them led by Abdullah Khan, marched against Raja Bikramjit's 'forces of misfortune'. They did not have a good start. No sooner had the battle begun than Abdullah Khan – 'whose hideous nature was made of rebelliousness and ingratitude' – took his ten thousand soldiers and switched sides.

To lose nearly half your army before a battle is begun doesn't bode well. However, though Jahangir's health had deserted him, his luck held out. Not only did most of Shahjahan's army not know of Abdullah Khan's proposed defection, the only one who did, their commander Raja Bikramjit, was soon shot by a stray bullet. 'Since divine protection has always and everywhere been with this supplicant', Mu'tamad Khan wrote on the emperor's behalf, the seemingly lost battle took another turn: suddenly headless – Shahjahan himself was not leading his men – the rebel army scattered. The raja's head – missing its ears, chopped off for their pearls – was sent to Jahangir who remarked how 'his gloomy expression could be seen perfectly, still unchanged'.

Shahjahan's rebellion lasted over three years, for most of which it had the flavour of this first clash – treachery, bad luck and a kind of slapstick chaos that, were it not for the bloodshed involved, would be almost funny.

After months of marking time, Parvez finally arrived at his father's side, eliciting an embarrassment of gratitude from the emperor. Parvez and Mahabat Khan were to pursue 'Bedawlat and . . . his blistering comrades'; and, for all the disparity between the drunken prince and the gifted soldier, they made a successful team. On the other side, Shahjahan and Abdullah – or La'natullah, God's curse, as he'd been rechristened – had split forces: Shahjahan was off to gather more men in Mandu, Abdullah to take over Gujarat, previously governed by the gloomy Bikramjit. As it happened, however, the divan of Gujarat, Safi Khan,[10] chose loyalty to the emperor and refused to hand over the treasury. Not only this, he also managed to capture the families of two of Abdullah's amirs, threatening their wives and children with 'all sorts of humiliation' should they not leave Abdullah's army. When Abdullah Khan found out about this, he did not arrest or execute the two amirs (and potential traitors); instead, he took them into battle, but chained to their elephants to prevent desertion. As further incentive to fight well, they were guarded by slaves with orders to kill them should Abdullah's side lose.

Despite such desperate measures – one could argue, *because* of them – Abdullah Khan lost. He fled to Bharuch, then to Surat, where he gathered as much treasure as he could before galloping off to join Shahjahan in Burhanpur.

Meanwhile, Parvez and Mahabat Khan had followed the rebel prince to Mandu. Here, finally, Shahjahan entered the fray himself, marching out of Mandu at the head of twenty thousand men and three hundred elephants. His arsenal also included Maratha regiments skilled in the guerrilla tactics Malik Ambar had perfected; these troops were sent out ahead, as a vanguard meant to ambush, confuse and weaken the imperial army.

Nothing, perhaps, reflects the sheer unpredictability of medieval battlefields like this marginal incident from that time. One evening, the imperial army was preparing to camp for the night when the captain of the rearguard, Mansur Khan Firangi, arrived with his men. Mansur Khan had spent the day with both eyes peeled for Maratha ambushes – and one hand wrapped around a bottle. He arrived at the camp 'roaring drunk', spotted a group of Marathas in the far distance, leaped right back on his horse and charged off, alone, to attack what turned out to be a battalion of several thousand soldiers. 'He fought loyally and valiantly,' wrote Mu'tamad Khan, 'as long as he had a breath of life in him'.

Fortunately for Jahangir, Mahabat Khan's strategy did not rely exclusively on Dutch courage, no matter how valiant. In fact, the general's strategy was not exclusively military: he was also threatening, bribing and wooing Shahjahan's supporters away from him. In this, Mahabat Khan's most dramatic success may have been the public defection of Barqandaz Khan.

The day finally arrived when the imperial army and Shahjahan's troops were arranged against each other. Shahjahan himself, in a decision that couldn't have done much for his men's morale, chose to observe from some three or four kilometres behind. 'The soldiers drew up their ranks', writes Mu'tamad Khan, awaiting the command that would fling them one upon the other. However, a few among them – Barqandaz Khan and his troop of musketeers – were looking for another kind of opportunity altogether. Glancing this way and that with fast-beating heart, Barqandaz Khan finally gave the signal. Suddenly, with both armies watching, Barqandaz Khan and his men tore themselves from one side and raced to the other, charging across the empty, astonished battlefield shouting 'Hail Shah Jahangir!' all the way.

As news of his defection spread, it was as if Barqandaz Khan had offered a rallying cry to all the men rapidly losing faith in their rebel prince. One after another, Shahjahan's commanders left him, both on and off the battlefield, until even the khan khanan was caught writing letters to Mahabat Khan, pleading how 'a hundred persons are keeping me under watch; otherwise I'd have flown from restlessness'.

Abandoned and afraid, pursued by Mahabat Khan's men and prey to his wiles, Shahjahan fled. Even the weather turned against him. It began to pour with rain; the prince and his men had to wade through 'mud and mire' as they retreated into the Deccan. Only the Marathas stayed with him all the way, though 'with' is an overstatement. They followed him 'for their own purposes,' writes Mu'tamad Khan, 'and marched one stage behind . . . taking possession of the goods the men abandoned in their frenzied fear for their lives'.

For all the glory he had gained against the rana of Mewar and the Deccan sultans, Shahjahan's unimpressive performance during his own rebellion, whether as soldier or as tactician, makes one suspect that his talent for warfare wasn't all that much greater than his father's. He hadn't led his men in a single battle. Except for Abdullah, he hadn't managed to get any of his father's men to join him. And here he was, now, dripping wet and 'racing pell-mell across the distances', his so-called allies feeding on the carrion of his campaign.

Still, even if Shahjahan hadn't inherited Akbar's flair for battle, he did have something of his family's tenacity. For a while, he wandered the Deccan, making humiliating and largely unsuccessful overtures to his former enemies, Malik Ambar of Ahmednagar and Adil Shah of Bijapur amongst them. When this failed, he wandered northwards, drifting rather aimlessly until Raja Bhim, son of Rana Amar Singh, injected some life into the rebellion by capturing Patna. It wasn't a great battle – the city officials fled without a fight – but it gave Shahjahan the confidence to send Abdullah Khan to besiege Allahabad.

The siege was still under way when Parvez and Mahabat Khan arrived, dispersing Abdullah Khan's men and precipitating the last battle of Shahjahan's rebellion. Having fled at the imperial army's approach, the prince and his allies had gathered forces in Banaras. With Mahabat Khan marching unstoppably towards them, there was little time to decide what to do next, and Abdullah Khan, for one, was quite sure they must retreat. They could go to Delhi, then to the Deccan – lead the massive imperial army a merry dance, in fact, until Mahabat Khan grew fed up and allowed them to negotiate for peace.

This was sometime in the summer of 1624, by which time Jahangir had lost all interest in his diary and even Mu'tamad Khan was no longer charged with recording events. Instead, Mu'tamad Khan wrote his own history of Jahangir's reign, the *Iqbalnama*, in which he claims that the Rajput Raja Bhim was both horrified and insulted by Abdullah Khan's plan. If they weren't going to fight, he said, then they needn't count on him to linger, 'for such marching and moving about was against the rules of the Rajputs'. Inspired, perhaps, by these gallant claims, Shahjahan's council agreed – and rode into a rout.

As soon as they entered the battlefield, the seven thousand or so rebel soldiers that remained were blocked on three sides by a forty-thousand-strong imperial force. 'Arrows and bullets fell like hail' upon them and although Raja Bhim, true to his words, 'charged bravely with his Rajputs' and although 'he fought fiercely', he – and much of the force – was soon outnumbered and killed.

The rebel soldiers began to flee, in such desperate hurry that many even dropped their weapons. Shahjahan's own horse was struck by an arrow; Abdullah Khan had to lead him from further danger by the bridle, then give the prince his own horse to escape on.

In the months that followed, Shahjahan tried what he could – cajoling and threatening men to his side, besieging Burhanpur – but it was no use. Eventually, even Abdullah Khan left him, giving himself to the service of God, instead, in a remote village. 'There was nothing Shahjahan could do,' Muhammad-Hadi admits, 'except withdraw'.

And, of course, surrender. Shahjahan wrote to his father, offering abject apologies, submission and two of his sons, Dara Shikoh and Aurangzeb, as guarantees of his future obedience to imperial command. Jahangir accepted.

Sadly, the emperor's thoughts on the end of his once-favourite son's shambolic, expensive and bloody civil war are not on record. Shahjahan surrendered sometime in the twentieth year of his father's reign; Jahangir's memoirs, even as they were inscribed by Mu'tamad Khan, end abruptly in the early months of the nineteenth, sometime around May 1624.

Once again, there was no grand Nauroz celebration that year; instead, Jahangir began his nineteenth year as emperor with the order 'that henceforth when I rode or came out of the palace, defective persons like the blind or those whose ears or noses had been cut off, lepers, and those with any sort of disease should not be allowed in my sight'. In his mid-fifties, had the pleasure-loving prince become a fussy old man, his aestheticism pathological, and his interests closely circumscribed by his comfort? If, after all these years, he lost interest in maintaining a record of his realm, a practice he enjoyed so much, then perhaps he had lost some interest in governing it, too? Shahjahan's capitulation must have brought him some relief, but it may not have brought him any joy – perhaps he knew, whether as emperor or not, he didn't have long left to go.

Or perhaps this is an unfair underestimation of the emperor's concern for his own empire – and his dynasty. Perhaps he was still gazing intently at that chessboard, still very much alive to the game. This might explain why, soon after Jahangir had promoted Parvez and put him in command of the army to fight Shahjahan, he conferred yet another favour on Khusro's son, Dawarbakhsh, and made him governor of Gujarat. Not just that, he also sent Aziz Koka – an old wolf, perhaps, but one of the most experienced amirs in his court – to guide the young prince. A couple of years later, Daniyal's long-forgotten sons were summoned too: Jahangir married one of them to his own daughter and the other to a daughter of Khusro's.

Unfortunately for Dawarbakhsh, Aziz Koka died soon after they reached Gujarat. The prince was recalled to court where, however, he continued to enjoy the emperor's favour. Jahangir was particularly thrilled when Dawarbakhsh brought him a strange pair of animals: a lion and a goat that shared the same cage and an 'extraordinary affection'. From Mu'tamad Khan's telling of the event, it seems that Jahangir had lost none of his interest in observing – and experimenting with – nature. First, 'it was ordered that the goat should be taken away to a distance and concealed' whereupon the lion began to fret. Then, another goat of exactly the same shape and size was thrust into the cage. The lion wasn't fooled. He took one sniff and killed it. Next, they tried a sheep, which 'was immediately torn and devoured', too. Finally, Jahangir had the original goat brought back, prompting a loving reunion between the animals (the lion 'took the goat upon its breast, and licked its face') and much applause in court.

Perhaps, then, Jahangir was not so unaware of the world around him, after all, nor unconcerned. Perhaps, with the sudden favours to previously ignored nephews and sons and grandsons, he was doing a little of what his own father had done: throwing the succession open to as wide a field of candidates as possible. But even if Jahangir was a canny observer – even participant – in this endgame, he couldn't possibly have known what fresh upheaval was soon to arrive at his very door.

He might, however, have liked to describe what happened next. He did, after all, enjoy the strange, and nothing could have been stranger than the events of the penultimate year of Jahangir's reign.

Soon after the defeat of Shahjahan, an odd sort of animosity had crept into the relationship between Mahabat Khan and the emperor – or, at least, into the emperor's decrees. This was, after all, the man who had saved Jahangir's throne – briefly, he had been made the khan khanan and Jahangir had referred to him as Madarussalatana, the axis of the sultanate – and there is no explanation for how he was treated now except the one usually proffered: Nurjahan thought he was becoming too powerful. More accurately, she thought his alliance with Parvez had been far too successful; that the older prince now had a real chance at the throne. Arguably, there was not much to choose between Parvez and Shahryar, but Shahryar was the one married to Nurjahan's daughter Ladli Begum, he was the one she could control, not Parvez; and certainly not Parvez with the shrewd and popular Mahabat Khan by his side. In this, she was supported by her brother Asaf Khan, who, while he would have hoped that Shahjahan, his son-in-law, might still become emperor, would have preferred Shahryar, his nephew-in-law after all, to Parvez. Besides, Asaf Khan and Mahabat Khan are said to have hated each other.

An order was thus issued to split the alliance: Mahabat Khan was to proceed to Bengal while Parvez stayed on in Burhanpur. At first, Parvez refused, his sudden good fortune having given the prince something of a spine. Another order followed directly, writes Mu'tamad Khan, 'warning him not to disobey'. The prince did not dare.

But Nurjahan and Asaf Khan soon overplayed their hand. Another emissary came to Mahabat Khan, demanding all the elephants he had captured during the battles of the previous three years and, even more insultingly, a settlement of accounts. Mahabat Khan decided to settle matters instead.

In March 1626, Jahangir was camped on the banks of the Jhelum, on his way from Lahore to Kabul, when Mahabat Khan arrived, leading four or five thousand Rajput soldiers, 'brave men united in one cause', as Mu'tamad Khan describes them. In fact, Mu'tamad Khan continues, many of these men had brought their families with them, to inspire them to fight not only for their general's honour, but also for their own. Not surprisingly, Mahabat Khan wasn't allowed into Jahangir's riverside court; he was told, firmly, to stay across the river and to send the conquered elephants in his stead.

Both Mu'tamad Khan and Muhammad-Hadi blame Asaf Khan for this heavy-handed humiliation. However, as Muhammad-Hadi writes, although 'Asaf Khan had made it his single-minded purpose to humiliate Mahabat Khan, strip him of his honour, ravage his women, and deprive him of life and property . . . he treated this weighty undertaking very lightly'. So, having forbidden the aggrieved soldier from approaching the imperial camp, Asaf Khan himself moved across the river, taking almost all the imperial retinue with him, leaving Jahangir behind with only Nurjahan, Mu'tamad Khan and a handful of servants and guards.

The next morning, Mahabat Khan woke up with an

angry heart and the knowledge that the emperor was
virtually unprotected. He took his Rajputs and galloped
across the bridge, leaving two thousand of them to guard
the crossing, with strict instructions not to let a fly across
– and rode into Jahangir's camp.

Mu'tamad Khan had been awake awhile. He had said
his morning prayers, greeted his various colleagues and
was inspecting the camp, no doubt to make sure that
everything was ready for their departure. Suddenly, shouts
of alarm filled the air – *Mahabat Khan is coming!*

Before Mu'tamad Khan knew what to make of this,
Mahabat Khan's own voice was ringing in his ear. The
loyal scribe drew his sword and went towards it, but
Mahabat Khan, when he saw him, was almost friendly.
'He addressed me by name,' writes Mu'tamad Khan, 'and
asked after His Majesty'. Besides, how could the lone
historian have attacked? Mahabat Khan had dozens of
Rajput soldiers behind him, their horses raising such
clouds of dust that Mu'tamad Khan couldn't make out
their faces.

Even Thomas Roe, who spent much of his time in
the empire trying not to be impressed by it, couldn't
help being impressed by Mughal camps. These elaborate
affairs Roe described as 'one of the woonders of my little
experience'; in size, they could be as large as any European
town, several kilometres in length and breadth, and set
up exactly the same way always – the emperor's red tent
and quarters at the very heart, the nobility spreading
outwards, their proximity an indication of their rank; then
orderly streets and 'all sorts of shopes' – the whole affair
'distinguished so by rule that every man knowes readely

were to seeke his wants'. Instead of the afternoon durbar, the emperor would go 'hunting or hawking' and business would be conducted later, at night, in the gusalkhana.

Although the Jhelum camp may not have been of such grand dimensions, it would have been of the same model; and Mahabat Khan would have known exactly where to go. He headed for the gusalkhana, with Mu'tamad Khan hurrying behind, scolding him for his 'presumption and temerity'. Mahabat Khan did not bother to reply; instead, his Rajputs began tearing down the wooden boards that made up the walls of the private chamber.

At this, the emperor emerged – and, in what may be an indication of how frail he had become, no sooner had he walked out than he sat down on his palki. 'Mahabat Khan advanced respectfully to the door of the palki,' writes Mu'tamad Khan, 'and said, "I have assured myself that escape from the malice and implacable hatred of Asaf Khan is impossible, and that I shall be put to death in shame and ignominy. I have therefore boldly and presumptuously thrown myself upon Your Majesty's protection. If I deserve death or punishment, give the order that I may suffer it in your presence."'

Jahangir, furious but so weak, so old, with barely two or three men by his side, the determined Mahabat Khan before him and two hundred Rajputs all around, was hardly in any position to give such orders. 'Twice,' writes Mu'tamad Khan, the emperor 'placed his hand on his sword to cleanse the world from the filthy existence of that foul dog,' but an aide by his side wisely persuaded him against any heroics at this stage. Already, in the confusion, one of his amirs had been wounded; his clothes

were growing damp with his own blood. The emperor
agreed to do whatever Mahabat Khan had in mind.

Mahabat Khan thought it might be best for Jahangir to
mount an elephant, so anyone who saw him would know
him safe and sound, perhaps even assume he was on his
way to a hunt. The emperor and his blood-spattered amir
climbed into the howdah. The elephant was about to begin
its march when one of Jahangir's personal attendants
came running up to him, insisting he would go with the
emperor, too. 'The Rajputs seized their spears, and with
their hands and arms tried to prevent him', but threats and
weapons would not deter the man. He pushed through,
grabbing hold of the howdah and, there being no space
for him to climb in, hung thus by the elephant's side as
it began to walk.

His loyalty is not, perhaps, surprising. Though
Mu'tamad Khan doesn't tell us his name, this brave man
was Jahangir's wine-bearer; even now, he carried the
emperor's goblet in one hand as he clung doggedly to
the howdah with the other.

When Mahabat Khan returned to his own camp, the
emperor effectively his prisoner, it became clear that
although he had fulfilled the basic requirement of a coup,
he had no idea of what to do next.

First of all, Mahabat Khan realized that in the
excitement of kidnapping Jahangir, he had forgotten all
about Nurjahan – so incredible a lapse that it must reveal
the general's nervous state of mind. Once again, Jahangir
was helped on to his elephant and the whole party
returned to his camp, only to find that Nurjahan had left.
The Rajput soldiers manning the bridge had been most

conscientious about not letting anyone into the imperial side, but they were rather less vigilant about letting people out. The empress, therefore, had easily walked across to her brother's camp, where she was dressing down a sheepish gathering of amirs in the most scathing terms.

'This,' she said, 'has all happened through your neglect and stupid arrangements. What never entered into the imagination of any one has come to pass, and now you stand stricken with shame for your conduct before God and man.' Abashed, the amirs cried they would battle the rebel tomorrow, free the emperor and exact bloody vengeance.

Mahabat Khan, meanwhile, had remembered Shahryar. Even if Nurjahan had escaped, they could still secure the prince! Once again, Jahangir climbed into his howdah, this time to ride to his son's tent. Shahryar, far less resourceful than his mother-in-law, was still in his quarters; and it was here that the emperor, Mahabat Khan and his men, after their long and peripatetic day, spent the night.

Asaf Khan's rescue mission was a disaster. With the bridge still guarded by Rajputs, Asaf Khan and his men had to cross through the Jhelum's rapid waters – a difficult endeavour made even more so by the tide of Rajputs riding against them. Mu'tamad Khan, who was part of the mission, wrote of it later, 'This was a time for the exhibition of discipline, resolution, and devotion. But now every one who was in front fell back ... The officers, in a panic, rushed off in disorder, not knowing whither they went, or where they led their men.'

Mu'tamad Khan himself, having crossed one branch of the river, stood dumbstruck at the head of the second, 'beholding the working of destiny' as he puts it, men on horseback and foot, on camels and in carriages, all wading through the swift current, 'jostling each other, and pressing to the opposite shore'. He was standing there still when a eunuch of Nurjahan's called Nadim came up to him. The empress had joined the battle, too, riding an elephant that carried not only herself but Shahryar's baby daughter and the daughter's nurse. 'The Begum wants to know if this is the time for delay and irresolution,' her eunuch asked Mu'tamad Khan, who was suitably embarrassed and dived quickly into the water.

Still, no matter how urgently or caustically she propelled her forces, no matter how she shamed them with this display of not herself, alone, but even her little granddaughter leading from the front, this was not a battle Nurjahan would win.[11] Her own elephant was brutally attacked, its trunk slashed by swords, its flanks wounded by spears; the nurse by her side was struck by an arrow; the eunuch Nadim was killed. It was only when her mahout took them into waters so deep that the Rajput cavalry couldn't follow that Nurjahan managed to escape.

Asaf Khan, meanwhile, ran away. 'I sought and shouted for his followers,' writes Mu'tamad Khan, 'but could not find . . . any trace of them.'

Soon enough, Asaf Khan would be caught and Nurjahan would surrender to be by her husband's side.

It would seem that Mahabat Khan had won, and won
so easily that another man might have thought that the
emperor's throne was his destiny. Mahabat Khan, however,
was not that man. Not only did he seem not to know what
to do with the power he had suddenly acquired, he didn't
even seem to want it. What else, after all, can explain the
resourceful general's utter inability to formulate a plan?

Not knowing how to proceed, but with Jahangir
securely in his custody, Mahabat Khan decided to
continue the emperor's original journey and proceed to
Kabul. It may be, as Corrine Lefèvre has suggested, that
the coup was actually Parvez's idea; that Mahabat Khan's
brief was to hold Jahangir captive until he died and then
ensure Parvez's succession. This might explain the detour
to Kabul and the general's procrastination. Even so, except
in that it gave Jahangir one last chance to visit the city of
his forefathers – did he, maybe, have another wine party
on the throne he had built to match Babur's? – this trip
was not a good idea.

For one thing, Mahabat Khan's Rajput troops were
uncomfortable so far from home. They got into a brawl
with some equally hot-headed Afghan soldiers in which
several hundred Rajputs died. Having lost a substantial
part of his army, Mahabat Khan thought of returning
to Lahore. Jahangir, meanwhile, whether from guile or
his characteristic geniality, 'had . . . become reconciled
to Mahabat Khan, and showed him great favour and
kindness'. Mu'tamad Khan suggests that this was a two-
pronged strategy of Nurjahan's – to have Jahangir create
a false sense of security while she herself plotted for help
'with money and promises'.

As Mahabat Khan and his royal captives marched back from Kabul, another of Nurjahan's eunuchs arranged for a force of two thousand men to meet them on their way. When the two 'armies' drew close, somewhere near Rohtas, Jahangir told Mahabat Khan that he was planning to hold a review of Nurjahan's cavalry the next day, and would Mahabat Khan's troops be so kind as to march a little ahead to prevent any altercation between the two? It was a most tactful way of putting it, and Mahabat Khan, who may well have been looking for such an opportunity to escape his unasked-for destiny, grabbed the hint with both hands.

Sometime in late August 1626, barely six months after his astonishing coup, Mahabat Khan and his men began to march away from the emperor – imagine them whistling nonchalantly – then burst into a gallop and disappeared into dust.

With the force of the empire – and the wrath of the empress – turned upon him, Mahabat Khan had few choices left. He might have returned to Parvez, still in Burhanpur, but only weeks after Mahabat Khan's ignominious bolt, Parvez followed the example of his uncles and died of drink, leaving the commander of Rajputs only one option.[12] He wrote to the prince he had so recently reduced to mud-sodden defeat and allied himself with Shahjahan.

The next year, 1627, was the last of Jahangir's reign. Nauroz was celebrated by the banks of the Chenab river because Jahangir, Nurjahan and several others of the imperial family were on their way to Kashmir, escaping the heat that Jahangir could no longer bear. This year, however, even Kashmir's soothing climate did not help him. He grew weaker by the day, unable to move except in his palki. Most troubling, writes Mu'tamad Khan, 'he lost all appetite for food, and rejected opium, which had been his companion for forty years'. All that he could bear any longer was wine.

Still, he survived the summer. He visited some of his favourite places, including the Vernag spring, the beauty of which had once inspired him to such vivid prose: 'What can be written of the purity of the canal or of the greenery and the plants that sprout below the spring? Bitter herbs, aromatic herbs, various dark green and pale green herbs all grow together. One bush that was seen was as multi-coloured as a peacock's tail and shimmering like wavy water'.

Perhaps he enjoyed it still.

But the emperor's ability to absorb beauty was also giving way to a debilitating anxiety. In October that year, on his way down to Lahore, Jahangir stopped for what would be his last hunt. No longer could the emperor shoot a lioness between the eyes from atop a frisky elephant, no longer could he hit an owl in the dark. Jahangir stood on the ground, resting his gun upon a makeshift wall, while his servants chased prey within his range. As the emperor took aim, one of the soldiers chasing game towards him fell off a precipice and died.

Accidental death was hardly shocking – let alone ominous – in medieval times. According to one of

Jahangir's European visitors, the elephant fights that the emperor so enjoyed watching often involved a bystander or two being trampled; Jahangir himself had noted, without apparent trauma, the sudden death of the lamplighter Salih, who had the misfortune to bump into an enraged lion. Now, however, it was as if he had 'seen the angel of death'. From that moment, writes Mu'tamad Khan, 'he had no rest or ease'. Somehow, they managed to march another day. The emperor called for a cup of wine on the way. Perhaps it was to celebrate a patch of flowers. Perhaps it was to chase away his fear. But when they put the cup to his lips, he couldn't swallow.

That night, he grew worse. At dawn the next day, aged fifty-eight, halfway through the twenty-second year of his reign, on the 28th of October 1627, Jahangir died.

The urgent and bloody intrigues that followed over the next few months unfold like a montage. With the emperor dead and destiny in the air, Asaf Khan made the quickest grab. Nurjahan sent messages for him to come and meet her but he refused. Since the empress could hardly come out to him, Asaf Khan had effectively locked her away. He sent his fastest messenger, Banarasi, to Shahjahan, giving him his own ring to carry as proof of the news. There wasn't even time to write a letter. Meanwhile, he crowned Khusro's son, Dawarbakhsh, declaring him king and all the while letting the confused nobility know that Shahjahan was on his way. Dawarbakhsh protested, he knew something was amiss, but he had no one but

Asaf Khan to trust by his side. Not only did Asaf Khan persuade the prince that his coronation was legitimate, he also made him march to Lahore, to destroy the ambitions of Shahryar.

Shahryar, that poor good-for-nothing, was more alive to his own misgivings. Besides, he had an advantage. Thanks to an embarrassing illness by which he lost all his hair, Nurjahan's son-in-law had left the imperial retinue a while ago. When Jahangir died in the hills, Shahryar was already in Lahore, able to command its vast reserves of money and weapons. Within a week, says Mu'tamad Khan, Shahryar had distributed 70 lakh rupees amongst anyone who would swear to be on his side.

Unfortunately, he spent a lot of money buying himself a lot of rubbish: his 'army' was barely a mob and it scattered almost as soon as Asaf Khan rode in sight. Shahryar, not even good at running away, went right back into the fortress of Lahore and hid himself in the zenana.

Asaf Khan had him dragged out of it. He made him swear allegiance to his new 'emperor'. A few days later, he had him blinded.

Meanwhile, Banarasi had made it from Kashmir to the Deccan in just twenty days. By an odd coincidence, the runner reached Shahjahan almost immediately after Mahabat Khan arrived at his new patron's court. It was Mahabat Khan, in fact, who gave Shahjahan the news. Immediately, Shahjahan began his journey north. The first great king to offer him tribute was Rana Karan, the prince whom Jahangir had wooed with such gifts and charm. The first great shrine at which Shahjahan offered thanksgiving was that of Moinuddin Chishti in Ajmer, walking there 'according to the practice of his great ancestor', the very Akbar who had brought Jahangir to life.

But also, since matters of such mortal importance cannot be trusted solely to God, the would-be emperor sent his father-in-law, Asaf Khan, a message, a farman in fact, 'to the effect that it would be well if Dawarbakhsh the son, and [Shahryar] the useless brother of Khusro, and the sons of Prince Daniyal, were all sent out of the world'. Nurjahan, keeping her head in more ways than one, had already bowed out of the race.[13]

So, on the 14th of February 1628, the very date on which his beloved grandfather was crowned, a new emperor rode into the great fort of Agra and ascended the throne. Unlike virtually each one of his predecessors in the dynasty, he did not have to worry about rebellions just yet; all those who might have contested his claim were dead.

He, and he alone, was King of the World.

Epilogue

I had ordered the supervisors of the royal library to ...
produce multiple copies [of the *Jahangirnama*] for me
to award to particular servants and to be sent to other
countries to be used by the rulers as a manual for ruling.
On Friday ... one of the recorders brought me a copy
completely written out and bound ... On the back of the
book I wrote in my own hand that ... I hoped a perusal
of the contents would be acceptable to the Creator and
occasion praise by the people.

Jahangir, *Jahangirnama*

One of the many tragedies of modern Indian history is that all the rest of our past is often held hostage to our current politics. The Mughals have long been vulnerable to such usage, their chronicles scoured not for what they might tell us of then but for the arguments they help us make about now. 'The memory of mankind is short,' Ebba Koch writes in an essay, 'and outside of South Asia it has been largely forgotten that the Mughals were once a superpower of Asia and of the Islamic world'. One might add the caveat that while South Asian memory of the Mughals may well be long, its imagined resentments are even longer. The renaming of New Delhi's Aurangzeb Road in 2015 is only the most obvious, and ridiculous, example of our attempts to erase the Mughals from our past, as if to teach them a lesson. Once, it seemed as if their greatest sin – at least, Aurangzeb's greatest sin – was to have been 'communal'. When even the much-vaunted 'secularism' of Akbar cannot save him (in Rajasthan's textbooks, he is no longer to be supplied with his suffix, the Great) it is increasingly clear that their greatest sin is to have been Muslim.

And, perhaps, to have compounded that error by having been and then remained unforgettable – the very word 'mogul' having entered the English lexicon as a synonym for grandeur.[1] It isn't just Akbar who was deemed 'the Great'; the first six rulers of the dynasty have long been known, collectively, as the Great Mughals.

Babur, the man who set the whole story in motion when he won the First Battle of Panipat in 1526, might not have been surprised. Born to a minor chieftain in the serene valley of Fergana, Babur was descended from both Timur and Genghis Khan and had inherited their ambition. As it happens, however, his ambition was to rule Samarkand, the city of his ancestors. This, he never quite achieved. Instead, he ruled over Kabul and, in the last few years of his life, conquered Hindustan – or, at least, a broad strip of land running south-east from Peshawar to Patna, taking in Delhi, Agra, Amer and small parts of the Malwa Plateau. His son Humayun did little to expand the fledgling empire; in fact, he lost it. There followed an interlude of about fifteen years, during which the Afghan Suri kings ruled the erstwhile Mughal realm and Humayun was in exile, mostly a guest of the Shah of Persia. Though his reputation in popular history makes him a bit of a dreamer, more absorbed by the movement of the stars than by the imperatives of rule, he did manage to win his throne back, aided by a large contingent of Persian soldiers and the brilliant Persian general Bairam Khan.

Less than a year later, Humayun died, famously tripping down the steps of his library. His son Akbar was fourteen. Many might have thought that with only a boy to lead them the Mughals would collapse again. Barely had Akbar been crowned – on a throne of brick in Punjab – when Hemu, a star commander of the Suri dynasty, marched upon Delhi and took it. There followed the Second Battle of Panipat, thirty years after the first. The first battle on this ground had been won by Babur's genius; his military strategy overcoming Ibrahim Lodi's far larger army. Now, however, Bairam Khan and Hemu were both generals of great talent and will. This time, it was luck that favoured the Mughal side. A stray arrow struck Hemu in the eye; when he fainted, his army fell with him.

Though it was luck that won that day for him, Akbar did not lack either courage or intelligence. First with Bairam Khan's help and later without, it was Akbar who transformed the Mughal kingdom into an empire. Not only did he give it the physical form most commonly associated with the empire now – almost all of the northern, north-western and eastern regions of the subcontinent, spilling over to Kabul and Qandahar – but also its character. A profusion of customs and races, languages and religions filled his gregarious court, a court in which Tansen sang to Salim Chishti on his deathbed, in which a Portuguese priest tutored a Mughal prince in his childhood.

A modern biographer of Shahjahan's, Banarsi Prasad Saksena, likens his reign to that of his grandfather Akbar: each one, he says, was an 'epoch by itself'. Even if Shahjahan had done no more than build the Taj Mahal, he would have deserved the comparison. In fact, writes Saksena, he may have built 'the most glorious epoch in the Medieval period'. Though it began with a devastating famine, most of Shahjahan's reign passed in peace and unequalled prosperity. Still, while Shahjahan built the tomb that Rabindranath Tagore famously described as a 'teardrop on the cheek of time', he also sprinkled blood upon the dynasty. Only two generations before him, Humayun had felt no fear when leaving his baby son, Akbar, in the care of Akbar's rebel uncle. Shahjahan had his nephews murdered.

It was a legacy that would come to haunt him through his own son. Aurangzeb didn't even wait for his father to die before succeeding him – he imprisoned Shahjahan, had his brothers killed and took over the throne. One cannot say, however, that Aurangzeb didn't work hard for his realm and his dynasty. By sheer dint of never leaving the plateau, he managed to expand and sustain Mughal dominion over the Deccan so much so that the Mughal empire was its largest under Aurangzeb, and its richest.

It was also at the beginning of its end.

Aurangzeb died in 1707. He was the sixth Mughal emperor; he ruled for forty-nine years. Just another half century later, however, the dynasty had crumbled down to Shah Alam II, who is considered anywhere between the thirteenth and the eighteenth Mughal ruler – depending on whether or not one leaves out those who held their thrones for just months. The most significant battle of Shah Alam II's time was not the Third (most bloody and last) Battle of Panipat, but the Battle of Buxar, in 1764, when the reduced might of the Mughal allied with the nawabs of Awadh and Bengal against the East India Company – and was defeated. British fortunes had risen dramatically since Thomas Roe arrived in Gujarat a century and a half ago and they would soon rise higher than Roe might ever have imagined. The fortunes of Shah Alam II, on the other hand, could hardly sink any further. He was blinded by a would-be usurper who ransacked the Mughal treasury and was furious at its depleted reserves. A doggerel attributed to the times goes 'Sultanat-e-Shah Alam / Az Dilli ta Palam': the empire that once ruled a subcontinent now stretched all the way from Delhi to Palam, where the city's airport stands today.

The great empire of Hindustan was no longer that of the Mughals, but of the Marathas.

And yet.

'In 1794,' writes K.M. Panikkar, 'Poona witnessed a strange and impressive ceremony.' By this time, Shah Alam II was virtually a vassal of the Marathas; he sat on the Delhi throne under the gaze and with the protection of the peshwa. Even so, writes Panikkar, 'the Peshwa, the actual head of the Great Maratha empire' ordered a ceremony in which this broken reed of an emperor sent him certain titles, which the peshwa 'received with the tokens of the highest respect, and with suitable formalities indicating the gratitude of the recipient for such imperial favours'.

Somehow, it seems, that while the Mughal empire was dead, the idea of the Mughal empire – what Panikkar calls 'the tradition of Akbar, the idea of the national State' – had escaped its own demise.

But what, meanwhile, of Jahangir? Sheikhu baba, much-beloved son; Salim unblemished and pure; Jahangir who seized the world – in the end, how does the fourth Mughal emperor survive in our times? The man who could be spellbound by a slant of sunlight falling upon a spring meadow, this was also the man who could watch without blinking as the skin was peeled off another human being. The man who loved and admired his father, who loved and admired his son, may not have been a man who was equally loved and admired by either. The man who excelled at describing the strange, how would he have described himself?

It is impossible to say, of course; but there is a stray anecdote in the *Jahangirnama* that may, perhaps, offer a clue. When Shahjahan – then only Shah Khurram – left for his first and glorious Deccan campaign, Jahangir followed behind, to camp a little closer to the action, in Mandu. Having settled down, the emperor took a tour of the many beautiful buildings that still stand in this town's vast fortress, once the seat of the Malwa sultanate. Amongst the sights was the grave of a man who was the most notorious of the Malwa sultans, a man called Nasiruddin.

Jahangir describes Nasiruddin with great animation, his many misdeeds evidently filling him with rage. Nasiruddin poisoned his own father with his own hands when the old king was eighty, scowls Jahangir. Then, having gained the throne at forty-eight, Nasiruddin declared that he would live for pleasure alone: 'Now that it is my turn, I have no desire to conquer territory. I want to spend the rest of my life in enjoyment'.[2]

So, indeed, he did. His harem was bursting at the seams with beautiful women, so much so that they created a playful township of 'artisans, governors, judges, kotwals'. Besides women, Nasiruddin's great passion was hunting: he built vast game reserves and spent much of his pleasurable thirty-two-year reign engaged in such sport.

Nasiruddin had a temper, too, and a fondness for drink – which traits eventually combined to kill him. Once, drunk, he fell into a deep tank. 'Several palace servants ran forward, grabbed him by the hair, and pulled him out of the water'. When Nasiruddin was told what had happened, he was so angry at the servants for having pulled him out in such an undignified manner that he had their hands cut off. 'The next time it happened,' writes Jahangir, 'no one dared to pull him out and he drowned'.

For all Jahangir's disapproval of Nasiruddin's reprehensible behaviour, it is hard to read this description of the Malwa sultan and not be reminded of the Mughal emperor. If anyone, after all, could empathize with Nasiruddin's plight – the king a ripe old eighty, his ageing heir within no clear sight of the throne – it would be Jahangir. If anyone understood what it was to really enjoy the unlimited self-indulgence that unlimited power allows, it was Jahangir. Even the story of hung-over cruelty has an echo in Jahangir's life. As Thomas Roe has written, no one could drink in the emperor's presence without his permission. Once, Roe says, on being told of 'the Merry night past' and having forgotten that he had commanded his nobility to drink with him, Jahangir was so incensed, he had them all fined – and those unfortunate enough to be immediately present were whipped 'with a most terrible instrument', so viciously, in fact, that one of them died.

Standing at Nasiruddin's grave, incensed by the sultan's 'hideous deed', Jahangir began to kick at the crypt, ordering those with him to kick it too. But this was not enough. 'Since this didn't satisfy me,' he writes, 'I said the grave should be opened and his unclean body thrown into the fire'. Then he paused.

From Akbar and his experimentations with faith, the Mughals inherited a sense of the sacredness of light – of the sun, of fire. The 'halo' that all Mughal emperors Jahangir onward are painted with is a symbol of this divine illumination. How then 'to sully that subtle essence by burning [Nasiruddin's] filthy body in it'? The aesthetically minded emperor thought up a more symmetrical, one might even say elegant, punishment. Just as Nasiruddin had died of drowning, so Jahangir now 'ordered his crumbling bones and decayed body thrown into the Narmada river'.

There are those who might argue that Jahangir, kicking desperately at Nasiruddin's grave, was afraid that one day history would judge him as harshly for his pleasures as he was judging the pleasure-loving sultan. In this, he would not have been wrong. Beni Prasad, for example, described Prince Salim as 'a man sunk in luxury and drink, weak in character to the point of criminality, a slave to selfish,

short-sighted counsel . . .' and so on, a condemnation
that, even four centuries later, will sting.

Beni Prasad's assessment of Jahangir the emperor,
however, is far more moderate, even favourable: '[T]o
dismiss him as a hard-hearted, fickle-minded tyrant,
soaked in wine and sunk in debauch, as more than one
modern writer has done, is at once unscientific and
unjust . . . From a review of his life as a whole, he comes
out as a sensible, kind-hearted man'. More recently,
Corrine Lefèvre has argued convincingly that Jahangir's
reputation suffered from the calculated bad press of two
ironically similar-minded forces. On the one hand, there
was Shahjahan, who would have wanted to portray his
father as weak and controlled by a villainous wife in order
to mitigate the fact of his own rebellion against him. On
the other, there was Thomas Roe, who, though he would
have been appalled to learn that in doing so he had
furthered the propaganda of the prince he so despised,
had an equal interest in portraying a weak king controlled
by a hostile faction, in order to excuse his ultimate failure
to gain the trade concessions he had gone to seek. Reading
against the grain, Lefèvre finds in the *Jahangirnama* a man
'defined . . . by a total dedication to justice',[3] his anecdotes
and maxims part of a larger tradition of akhlaqi literature,
that is, writings on ethics.

In his paintings, too, writes Ebba Koch, one finds a
man deeply engaged with ideas of rulership. She sees a
particular significance in the recurring image of the lion
and the lamb in the art of his time. Was this association
of predator and prey at peace essentially a symbol of a

just and peaceful world, also essential to Jahangir's ideal
of himself, as emperor?

How much will you let yourself see in this image of
Jahangir kicking at a grave, his emotions a little in excess
of himself? Was he kicking at what he imagined he might
become? Or was he kicking the exact opposite of himself
– the kind of man he warned against being?

Was this an akhlaqi anecdote? Was there a moral to
the tale? Or was he giving us another bit of strangeness
to contemplate?

Notes

Part I: Accession

1 All quotations from Salim's autobiography are from Thackston, *Jahangirnama*.

2 Father Monserrate, a Jesuit in Akbar's court, who wrote an account of his experiences that was translated, in 1922, as *The Commentary of Father Monserrate, S.J., on His Journey to the Court of Akbar*.

3 This and the following quotations in the scene are from the *Jahangirnama*.

4 Also young aunt of Akbar's greatest general, Raja Man Singh. Her family's kingdom, Amer (or Amber), was later named Jaipur.

5 Beveridge, *Akbarnama*.

6 This gossip is recorded in a most entertaining and censorious account of Akbar's reign by Abd'ul-Qadir Badauni, more about whom later.

7 Sometimes also called leopards. The confusion may have arisen because the two animals are similar looking (although it is the cheetah, not the leopard, that has the spots. The latter is dotted with rosettes). Indian cheetahs were sometimes called 'hunting leopards' by the British during the Raj. According to Thackston, even the *Jahangirnama* mixes up the two. As he remarks in a footnote: 'There is . . . confusion in terminology between leopards (*yuz*) and cheetahs (*chita*), and some instances of *yuz*

in the memoirs may actually mean cheetah . . . or even panther, but for lack of evidence to the contrary I have maintained consistency in translating *yuz* as leopard and reserved cheetah for *chita*. In Thackston's translation, therefore, Jahangir talks of hunting with *both* leopards and cheetahs; and here, he says that it was leopards Akbar vowed to stop hunting with, not cheetahs. However, since Akbar's love for hunting with cheetahs is well documented (and a famous painting of the emperor on such a hunt shows animals with the distinctive black streak down the eye to the snout that distinguishes cheetahs), I have stuck with cheetah here. (Tragically, the cheetah is extinct in India today.)

8 Muhammad-Hadi, who composed a preface and appendix to the *Jahangirnama* in the eighteenth century.

9 A chronogram is a line in which letters correspond to numerals and thus yield a date. The skill of the poet, naturally, would lie in turning what was essentially a code into meaningful verse.

10 Beveridge, *Akbarnama*.

11 Salim tells this story in the *Jahangirnama*.

12 Wild rue, also called harmal or aspand, is said to have medicinal properties today. It is sometimes identified with the soma herb mentioned in ancient Indian texts.

13 From *Yusuf and Zulaikha: A Poem by Jami*, translated by R.T.H. Griffith (Trübner and Co., 1882).

14 His wet nurse, the daughter of Sheikh Salim Chishti.

15 In Salim's words.

16 Badauni.

17 Beveridge, *Akbarnama*.

18 All ranks in the Mughal government, from that of the royal cup-bearer to the imperial vakil, were military ranks and were originally meant to indicate how many soldiers a rank-holder (or mansabdar) was supposed to bring into battle. It was one of Akbar's many administrative reforms to split the single rank into two: zat and suwar. Zat indicated a mansabdar's position in court (literally, in that it would also decide how near or far from the emperor he might stand) and his salary (either to be paid from

the treasury or to be extracted by the mansabdar himself from a grant of land, his jagir). Suwar was the number of troops he would bring to battle. Any mansabdar of sufficiently high zat was considered nobility, an amir.

Both zat and suwar were highly susceptible to inflation: in Akbar's time, the highest rank a prince of the blood could hold was 12,000 zat and suwar; by the end of Jahangir's reign, his then most favoured son was ranked 40,000 zat and 30,000 suwar. While the Mughal empire's burgeoning fortunes may well have been able to afford this dizzying rise in zat, the rank of suwar seems to have become more suggestion than command.

To keep things simple, and since zat is more indicative of a man's position within the hierarchy than its counterpart, I have used only zat ranks in this book.

19 And in this he wouldn't be wrong: Salim doesn't seem to have fought a battle in his life.

20 And, in Abu'l Fazl's words, 'the Divine tasks of severity and lenity'. Justice, too, would be a leitmotif of Salim's life and reign.

21 Sometimes 'Bhagwant'.

22 Though not his first child – that was a daughter, Sultanunnisa, born the year before.

23 Now in Punjab province of Pakistan.

24 The first couplet of the quatrain is: 'Through renouncement of wine bewildered am I / How to work know I not, so distracted am I.' From the *Baburnama*, translated by Annette Susannah Beveridge.

25 Beveridge, *Akbarnama*.

26 Khan khanan, or khan of khans, was one of the three highest ranks in the Mughal nobility, the other two being khan azam (greatest khan) and amir-ul-umara (amir of amirs). 'Khan' derives its meaning from 'lord' and 'amir' from 'commander'.

27 Which corresponds to what is now Baltistan, north of Kashmir and Ladakh.

28 She was also called Jodh Bai, the 'lady from Jodhpur'.

29 Because its original name, 'gilas', was a homonym for lizard.

30 Khan, 'Akbar's Personality Traits'. As Father Monserrate put it
    at the time, the emperor 'cared little that in allowing everyone
    to follow his religion he was in reality violating all'.

31 Raghavan, *Attendant Lords*.

32 I have paraphrased the translation somewhat but preserved the
    meaning.

33 Although it is hard to imagine now, in medieval times the north
    Indian plains seem to have been replete with lions; not only were
    they hunted, they were also kept as 'pets' in the Mughal court. As
    with leopards and cheetahs, lions and tigers, too, often get confused
    in translations of the *Jahangirnama*. As Thackston explains it: 'In
    Persian, lion is *sher* and tiger is *babr*; in modern Hindustani, the
    Persian word for lion, *sher*, means tiger . . . and lion is compounded
    of both words, *babr sher*. This unusual linguistic situation has led
    to confusion between the two cats in translation, but it is clear
    that in Jahangir's time *sher* still meant lion and not tiger.'

34 'At this time a kind of ink was introduced to [Akbar's] notice.
    Whatever was written with it was not obliterated by water or
    by rubbing, nor did any harm happen to the writing. Akbar
    examined it and taught the use of it to skilful persons.'

35 Beveridge, *Akbarnama*. Akbar's tone may owe much, of course,
    to Abu'l Fazl and his translator.

36 Ibid.

37 Ibid.

38 Ibid.

39 From 1585 to 1598, Akbar's court moved from Agra to Lahore,
    from where he made his three trips to Kashmir. Though this does
    not mean that Agra was no longer the 'capital' of the empire –
    the real capital was the emperor himself, after all – it did spell
    the end of the new city of Fatehpur Sikri. Once abandoned, it
    was never inhabited again; by the time William Finch got there,
    sometime between 1608 and 1611, it was 'all ruinate, lying like
    a waste desart, and very dangerous to pass through in the night,
    the buildings lying wast without inhabitants'.

40 Salim describes his de-addiction programme in meticulous detail in the *Jahangirnama*.

41 Daniyal did obey his father's summons, but Abu'l Fazl tells us that reports of his 'improper behaviour' reached the emperor before the prince could. Akbar had no reason, therefore, to put much hope in his youngest.

42 And now part of modern Maharashtra.

43 Now part of Vidarbha, Maharashtra.

44 As often as not, the past is half-lit and full of probabilities. Alam and Subrahmanyam, 'Deccan Frontier and Mughal Expansion'. For all that Murad's death by drink was the 'official' account of the time, Alam and Subrahmanyam offer an even more dramatic perspective. They describe how letters by the then Portuguese viceroy in Goa, Dom Francisco da Gama, 'suggest that the *Estado da Índia* may in fact have been implicated in the Mughal prince's death, since the viceroy believed that this death would increase internal dissensions in the Mughal camp, and draw their attention away from projects of conquest' – projects that were bringing them uncomfortably close to Portuguese territory.

45 Born on 7 June 1570, Murad died in May 1599, just weeks short of his thirtieth birthday.

46 As Abu'l Fazl described them.

47 Beveridge, *Akbarnama*.

48 Not much is known of Muhammad-Hadi except that he wrote in the early eighteenth century and may have served in the courts of Aurangzeb and his successor, Bahadur Shah I. He wrote a history of India, another of the descendants of Timur, and transcribed Salim's memoirs with a preface and conclusion called *Tatimma Waqiat–i-Jahangiri*.

49 Muhammad-Hadi.

50 The Asirgarh fort still stands, and is still as impressive, in southern Madhya Pradesh.

51 Khandesh, a region in what is now northern Maharashtra spilling into southern Madhya Pradesh, was then the northernmost

kingdom of the Deccan. Conquering Asirgarh was, therefore, key to any further conquests in the Deccan Plateau.

52 Jagirs and ranks could be given and taken away at the emperor's will, and there was no such thing as inherited nobility or rank. Instead, the Mughals had a system of escheat, by which, when an amir died, his property returned to its source – the emperor.

53 Inayatullah in Beveridge, *Akbarnama*.

54 Related by Beveridge in a footnote of this chapter in the *Akbarnama*.

55 The mir bakshi was the head of military affairs and one of the highest officers in the Mughal administration. Others included the vakil, which was the highest administrative position possible; the divan, head of financial affairs; and the qazi and sadr-us-sadr, responsible for law and religion.

56 Inayatullah in Beveridge, *Akbarnama*.

57 Ibid.

58 Ibid.

59 Ibid.

60 Some, no doubt, captured during his many hunting expeditions; others given to him as gifts, perhaps, by the grateful amirs amongst whom he had distributed generous titles.

61 Shakarunnisa and Salim shared a rather odd bond. According to Salim, following custom and Akbar's instructions, he had drunk a drop of her breast milk – so that she might be like a mother to him. The prince was also close to Aram Banu Begum, hot-headed, sharp-tongued and Akbar's favourite daughter. Salim writes of how the emperor called her his 'ladli', darling, and specifically commanded Salim to treat her well when Akbar was gone: 'Baba, for my sake, after I'm gone, treat this sister of yours . . . as I do. Tolerate her coquettishness and overlook her rudeness and impudence.'

62 Inayatullah in Beveridge, *Akbarnama*.

63 Ibid.

64 Ibid.

65 Thackston, *Jahangirnama*.

66 Inayatullah in Beveridge, *Akbarnama*.

67 Ibid.

68 Inayatullah in Beveridge, *Akbarnama*. 'Amin-ud-din Khan reported that the prince had conceived suspicions and that he could not come to court so long as the Prince-Royal was there'.

69 Muhammad-Hadi.

70 Khan, 'Akbar's Personality Traits'. The 'improper' acts that Salim was referring to were shutting down mosques and prohibiting congregational namaz. While such orders may have been greatly exaggerated, Khan finds some evidence for Akbar's ambiguity towards Islamic ritual in a query from Murad asking what he must do if anyone in his camp was caught praying. Akbar's reply, writes Khan, 'suggests that a person performing namaz was considered deserving "admonition" (nasihat) by his superiors so as to "help" him come to "the path of reason" (rah-i aql)'. On the other hand, he was not to be stopped, either, as that would go against the emperor's policy of sulh-i-kul, peace for all.

71 Muhammad-Hadi's account of the fight was written much later and he would have relied on contemporary sources such as the writings of Asad Beg, an employee of Abu'l Fazl's. Khwaja Kamgar Khan's *Ma-asir-i Jahangiri*, written after Salim's death, also contains a description of the fight.

72 Hakim Humam, whom Akbar had once accused of poisoning him and who had given Salim such unsparing advice about his alcoholism, had died some years previously.

73 Inayatullah in Beveridge, *Akbarnama*.

74 Quoted from *Zikr-i Mir: The Autobiography of the Eighteenth Century Mughal Poet: Mir Muhammad Taqi 'Mir'*, translated by C.M. Naim.

Part II: Empire

1 Prasad, *History of Jahangir*. A vast region 'from the eastern confines of Persia to the western bounds of modern Assam and Burma and from the Himalayas to a line between the Mahananda

and the Godavari' – encompassing a hundred million people –
'acknowledged the sway of one emperor'.

2   Ebba Koch's word, quoted in the Epilogue.

3   Thomas Roe landed on the coast of Gujarat in September
     1615 from where, after some weeks of sparring between the
     ambassador and the local governor whom he was trying to
     convince of his worth, Roe proceeded to Ajmer, where Jahangir
     was then camped. En route, however, he stopped in Burhanpur
     to visit the prince Parvez, who was there in charge of the Deccan
     campaign. What follows is the perfect example of how staunchly
     Thomas Roe stood upon his dignity and how amusing he might,
     therefore, have appeared.

     As was customary, Parvez was seated on a slightly elevated
     platform, three steps higher than his durbar. At the base of
     these steps, Roe saluted the prince, declared his ambassadorial
     credentials, and asked to be allowed to climb up to the platform.
     At this, it is possible Parvez laughed, replying that 'if the King of
     Persia, or the great Turke wher ther, it might not be admitted'.
     Undeterred, the ambassador demanded a chair. This request,
     too, was firmly denied. Eventually, however, perhaps because
     Parvez didn't want to spend all day haggling with the dogged
     Englishman, Roe was told that he might lean against one of the
     silver pillars that held the canopy above the prince.

     Satisfied, Roe offered Parvez the presents he had brought,
     which included a case of alcohol. The prince accepted graciously
     and even invited the ambassador for a private, more informal
     audience later in the day. Roe waited, not knowing that he would
     be hoisted by his own presents: 'after I had stayed a while I hard
     he was drunck,' writes the ambassador. He went home.

     For all that this anecdote reveals about Roe, it may also
     explain Parvez's largely missing role in history – it is possible he
     just slept through it all.

4   Not only did Indians sail ships, ports like Kutch and Cambay
     were centres of shipbuilding too. According to Panikkar, *Survey*

of Indian History, even the seafaring Portuguese bought some of their ships from India.

5   In *Millennial Sovereign*, A. Azfar Moin notes that Banarasidas was earlier discussed by Muzaffar Alam and Sanjay Subrahmanyam in their essay 'Witnessing Transition: Views on the End of the Akbari Dispensation'.

6   William Finch visited Akbar's tomb in Sikandra some years after the emperor's death and described it thus: 'Here, within a faire round coffin of gold, lieth the body of this monarch, who sometimes thought the world too little for him. The tombe is much worshipped both by the Moores and Gentiles, holding him for a great saint.' The gold is long gone from Sikandra, but even today people offer money at Akbar's grave, just as they do at shrines.

7   Specifically, this is the account of Father Fernão Guerreiro, translated in Payne, *Jahangir and the Jesuits*. Since Guerreiro (or perhaps his translator) tends to refer to the Jesuits collectively as 'the Fathers', I have followed suit.

8   Akbar came to Agra two years after his coronation, in 1558. He had the Agra fort rebuilt to its current impressive scale, a project that lasted eight years, from 1565 to 1573.

9   And a few Christians too. As the Jesuits walked about Agra, children would call out '*Padrigi salamat*', Padre salaam, much to the Fathers' delight.

10 This was, in fact, his first decree and he names two taxes in particular, the tamgah and mirbahri, each a kind of customs duty. The Jesuits, impressed with how 'His Majesty continued to show himself worthy of the name "The Just King" [Adil Padshah]', tell the story of an official who took 'some trifling toll' from merchants entering Lahore. When the merchants complained, the official's head was shaved and he was dragged through Lahore's streets. 'The poor fellow has never shown his face since.'

11 This ancient city, now in Uzbekistan, was ruled by both Genghis

Khan and Timur, the two great soldier-kings from whom Babur was descended. It was Babur's lifelong ambition to conquer Samarkand, an ambition that travelled through the generations of his dynasty, but was never fulfilled.

12 Thackston, *Jahangirnama*.

13 Jahangir's antipathy towards the Sewras did not extend to the Jains as a whole, however. Findly, *Nur Jahan: Empress of India*, lists several imperial farmans in favour of Jains including one, in 1610, 'prohibiting animal slaughter throughout the empire during the twelve days of the Jain Paryushana festival' and another, in 1616, 'allowing complete freedom of worship to monks of the Jain community throughout the empire'.

14 *History of Jahangir*. It may also be, as Francis Gladwin asserts, that the exclamation gave the rebels the impression that Jahangir himself had arrived and awed them into retreat.

15 'Intikhab-i Jahangir Shahi'.

16 Payne, *Jahangir and the Jesuits*.

17 Thackston, *Jahangirnama*.

18 Gascoigne, *History of The Great Moghuls*. So much so that, from Timur onward, it was used by the Mughals as a military training exercise, and often enough as a show of force.

19 Thackston, *Jahangirnama*. 'Vilayat means province in Persian, but it is often used in the sense of "homeland". The Timurids' original homeland was Central Asia, but when Babur uses the term vilayat, he seems generally to mean Kabul, the secondary "homeland" from which he came to the subcontinent.'

20 He also issued an order rescinding certain taxes on trade.

21 And possibly because he had only recently, in Kabul, leafed through an original manuscript of the *Baburnama*.

22 The real test of a subcontinental mango aficionado is not, of course, mere love for the fruit, but a deep-rooted parochialism about it. In this, too, Jahangir reveals himself as truly Indian. Since the emperor liked them so much, every year mangoes from across the land – the Deccan, Burhanpur, Gujarat, Malwa – would arrive at his court. Jahangir enjoyed them all but, he writes, 'for

juiciness, tastiness and digestibility, the mangoes of Chapramau in the Agra vicinity are the best of . . . Hindustan'.

23 According to the Jesuits, in fact, Khusro travelled with his father in most humiliating conditions: locked in a cage with his feet bound, flung upon an elephant for all to see.

24 On the subject of complexion, it is interesting to see how at least one European traveller to Jahangir's court was greatly confused by the colour of his skin: 'Hee is of complexion neither white nor blacke, but of a middle betwixt them; I know not how to express it with a more expressive and significant epitheton than olive; an olive colour his face presenteth.' From Thomas Coryat's struggle, it is clear why the word 'wheatish' entered the English language.

25 Saksena, *History of Shahjahan*.

Part III: Believer/Unbeliever

1 Prasad, *History of Jahangir*. Though it was his brother Murad who had had Jesuit tutors as a child, making him the first 'convent-educated' Mughal. His tutor was Father Monserrate and all the prince's exercises began with the words 'In the name of God and of Jesus Christ, the true Prophet and Son of God'.

2 The darshan itself was an idea borrowed from Hindu ritual.

3 Payne, *Jahangir and the Jesuits*.

4 Foster, *Embassy of Sir Thomas Roe*. Once, writes Roe, Khurram complained to him about the 'unruliness of the English at Suratt, of their drincking and quarrelling in the streets, and drawing swoords in the Custome house'.

5 Soon to become governor of Sindh.

6 And 'purity', therefore, not religious belief, determined a person's position in society. Grey, *Travels of Pietro Della Valle*. Della Valle, having noted the surprising liberty of conscience in the empire, also noticed the Dheds (now a scheduled caste) whom he encountered in his travels through Gujarat. In their poverty, he says, they looked like yogis, but in fact they 'were of a Race of Indians accounted by

themselves the most sordid and vile Race of all in India, because they eat everything, even the uncleanest animals, as Rats and the like; whence they are called in Persian *Halal-chor*, which signifies a Man that accounts it lawful to eat anything. The Indians call them *Der*, and all people in general abhor not onely to converse with, but even to touch them. Concerning their Religion I have heard nothing particular of them, but believe them Gentiles as the rest, or perhaps Atheists, who may possibly hold everything for lawful, as well in believing as in eating'.

7   Roughly corresponding to the Rakhine state of modern Myanmar. The Arakanese were primarily Buddhist (these were the Magh people Jahangir met) though the Arakan kingdom also acquired a Muslim population over the centuries. The descendants of the Muslim Arakanese are called the Rohingya today.

8   As Thomas Roe put it in a letter to the Bishop of Canterbury: either 'hee is the most impossible man in the world to be converted, or the most easy; for he loves to heare, and hath so little religion yet, that he can well abyde to have any decided'.

9   Sajjad Rizvi, a scholar of Islamic studies, paints a similarly dizzying impression of Jahangir through a close analysis of the punishment and subsequent death of Qazi Nurullah Shushtari, a Shia in Jahangir's court. Shushtari may (or may not) have been pretending to be Sunni to escape harassment during the early years of Jahangir's reign, when the majority Sunni factions were, perhaps, emboldened. It may (or may not) be that Jahangir had him whipped for this offence – not the pretence alone, but the shadow such pretence cast on the emperor's avowed embrace of all sects and religions. Rizvi quotes Jahangir as lamenting the fact that thanks to Shushtari, 'people have been imagining us to be a bigoted and coarse Sunni. May God preserve all from the disease of bigotry, especially us, the manifestation of the Divine!' It may also be, however, that the emperor 'found himself in an awkward position', as Rizvi describes it, forced to order the punishment from the pressures of a sectarian court, while pretending himself, even to himself, that it was not so. (Rizvi, 'Shi'i Polemics at the

Mughal Court'. I'm grateful to Professor Sanjay Subrahmanyam
for introducing me to this essay.)

10   Of this, too, it has been argued that the idea of discipleship
     had compelling administrative and political reasons. Richards,
     'Formulation of Imperial Authority'. Drawing from arguments
     by S.A.A. Rizvi, Richards has written that while Babur's
     noblemen were tied to their king through relations of blood
     and ethnicity, two generations later, Akbar's amirs were a far
     more diverse lot: from Rajputs to Persian. Sacrality was one
     way of binding these different men into what was, essentially,
     an 'exceptionally loyal and reliable cadre of nobles'.

11   The theory was proposed by J.F. Richards and has also been
     discussed by A. Azfar Moin.

12   Koch, 'My Garden Is Hindustan'.

Part IV: Sun Amongst Women

1   In the words of the contemporary historian Mu'tamad Khan,
     Ghiyas Beg 'was considered exceedingly clever and skilful, both
     in writing and in transacting business . . . and his generosity and
     beneficence to the poor was such that no one ever turned from
     his door disappointed. In taking bribes, however, he was very
     bold and daring.'

2   Findly, *Nur Jahan*.

3   For this idea of Jahangir's sociability, of which more in the Note
     on Sources, I'm grateful to Dr Anubhuti Maurya.

4   For all its lucid, free-flowing style, the *Jahangirnama* doesn't lack
     for layers of meaning. Islam Khan was loyal, yes, but he was also
     very successful and therefore increasingly powerful. According
     to J.F. Richards, 'As governor and conqueror in distant Bengal,
     Islam Khan began challenging Jahangir's imperial authority by
     adopting various royal perquisites (e.g. the "viewing", or jharokha,
     of the governor on a balcony at set times of day by the general
     populace).'

     Could this have prompted the 'Jahangirid Regulations' that

the emperor records in early 1612? 'Since it had been repeatedly heard that the amirs of the frontier were engaging in practices that did not pertain to them', he writes, Jahangir ordered that certain practices were strictly reserved for the emperor. Amirs could no longer, for example, sit in jharokhas, have commanders salute or stand guard over them, have elephant fights, have people blinded in punishment, nor cut off noses and ears, force conversion (or possibly, circumcision), give titles, seal their letters, etc. Another way of looking at Islam Khan's sacrifice, then, could be that the story was Jahangir's way of imbuing his powerful friend with a posthumous devotion that, perhaps, he did not possess adequately in life.

Part V: Ambition

1   Saksena, *History of Shahjahan*. 'Akbar used to remark that of all his grandchildren only Khurram took after him'.
2   Imprisonment seems to have been a luxury reserved for dissenting nobility (for example, Khusro) or for spiritual leaders who might pose a political threat. So, for example, Sheikh Ahmad Sirhindi and Guru Hargobind were, at different times, locked up in the Gwalior fort. Sheikh Ahmad Sirhindi was a conservative Muslim scholar who had supported Jahangir's bid for the throne but later became too big for his boots. Guru Hargobind, the son and successor of Guru Arjan Dev, whom Jahangir had had executed, was suspected of harbouring a not ill-founded grudge against the emperor. Both the sheikh and the guru were soon released. Guru Hargobind, in fact, is said to have taken fifty-two imprisoned kings with him, a legend celebrated by Sikhs on Bandi Chhor Divas (prisoners' liberation day), concurrent with Diwali.

It was also customary for the emperor to sell petty offenders to his nobility, this having the double benefit of enriching the treasury and giving the amirs an opportunity to do a good deed. When one such felon was sent to Thomas Roe, the Englishman made the breathtakingly disingenuous claim that 'in England we [have] no slaves, neither was it lawfull to make the Image of God fellow to a Beast'. (The first known English slave trader, one John Hawkins, had shipped three very profitable cargoes of slaves from Africa to the Americas a half-century ago, in the 1560s.)

3   It may be worth noting that it is the two least privileged of the early English travellers to India who were most impressed with Jahangir's justice and generosity. Nicholas Withington worked his way aboard an English ship, became a kind of clerk with the East India Company on his way, was robbed to his 'breeches' in India and eventually sent back to England in disgrace. He never met Jahangir but he writes with a kind of wonder about his 'greate justice': 'sitting three tymes a day therin himselfe'. Where Roe often lamented the Mughal's lack of 'written' law, the very idea of the Chain of Justice inspired Withington to rhetorical raptures. Anyone could ring it, he says, and should Jahangir 'fynde that the poore man bee wronged in justice, be hee the greatest nobleman about him, he presentlye takes away all his means, puttinge him either into prison . . . or cutts his throat. In fyne his greatness is such that I rather admire yt than presume to write of yt'.

Thomas Coryat, the backpacker, was almost as far from the court as Withington and recounts with similar admiration this unverified addendum to Jahangir's midnight routine: when he awoke at night, the emperor would call for 'poore and old men' – presumably ascetics – and sit and talk to them and give them clothes and money when they left.

4   Raghavan, *Attendant Lords*.

5   Before sending him to 'pay homage to his mothers and stepmothers'.

6   Writing urgently to England for presents for the empress, Roe would also admit, 'The neglect of her last yeare I haue felt heavily.'

7   Roe's diary contains an almost slapstick account of how, once, he tried to subvert Khurram and Asaf Khan by marching into the gusalkhana to complain directly to Jahangir. He was trying to catch the emperor's attention when one of Asaf Khan's men

pulled Roe's interpreter away, leaving the ambassador speechless in more ways than one. When Roe managed to locate and grab his interpreter back, Asaf Khan stood next to the hapless fellow, trying to 'awe him with winking and jogging'. Roe's anger didn't need translation, however, and Jahangir seems to have tried to soothe him with a long discussion on English horses and how these might be brought across by sea. But Roe was not to be distracted. He returned to his complaints, at which Asaf Khan tried to pull the interpreter away again but Roe, more alert this time, grabbed him right back and held on to him firmly. Watching this unseemly scuffle, Jahangir 'grew suddenly into a Choler', so much so that even Roe was cowed. Asaf Khan 'trembled' and Khurram came forward 'in great feare, humbling himself'. The emperor ordered that the three men have a civil discussion at the end of which Asaf Khan asked Roe to write down his demands so they might discuss them later. Thus, with the ambassador back, unwittingly, to square one, Jahangir retired for the night and his court disbanded.

8   Much like Parvez, the small town of Burhanpur in southern Madhya Pradesh has long been forgotten. Unlike Parvez, however, Burhanpur was once integral to Mughal advances into the Deccan; as their headquarters in the region, it was home to many Mughal emperors, princes and generals, and is dotted with remnants of its medieval grandeur. Daniyal, for example, would drink in the Ahukhana, the deer park and garden in which his grand-nephew Aurangzeb later wooed a dancing girl. It was in Burhanpur, too, that Abdur Rahim Khan Khanan designed an underground water system, hidden from potential enemy attack. The Kundi Bhandara, as it is called, still works. Burhanpur's greatest claim to fame, however, is that it was here that Khurram's beloved Arjumand died and was briefly buried. One can only wonder how the fortunes of this sadly dilapidated town would have changed if her permanent tomb, the Taj Mahal, had been built here and not in Agra.

9   Thackston, *Jahangirnama*.

10 Moin, *Millennial Sovereign.*

11 About two years later, the emperor's camp was marching from Ahmedabad to Agra when they had to stop for three days so that Khurram's wife, Arjumand, might deliver her fourth son, Aurangzeb. As a result, it was already Wednesday when they resumed their travel and not a waterbody in sight. There was nothing for it, writes Jahangir, but to march all night until 'by dawn we dismounted next to the tank at Bhagor'.

12 It was also in Mandu that, for the second time in his reign, Jahangir ordered his amirs not to give him presents for Nauroz. The idea was Khurram's; he wrote to his father saying that since 'these are days of march and campaign' he was exempting his nobility from gift-giving. Jahangir recorded this with pride ('This pleased me greatly') and decided to follow suit.

13 Sayyid Abdullah of Barha. The messenger clearly went to Nurjahan first – as good an indication as any of her paramount importance in the court. Jahangir himself makes no bones about it: 'Since the news was given to me by Nurjahan Begum, I awarded her the pargana of Toda'. Even today, one could argue, there are few men who would be able to take their wife's authority so easily in their stride.

14 Thackston, *Jahangirnama.*

15 Colocasia, or arvi patta.

Part VI: Aesthete

1 A few months before Khurram left for the Deccan, a smaller imperial force was marching upon a zamindar called Durjan Sal in Gogra, Bihar. By good fortune or ill, Durjan Sal's land was rich in diamonds, and then, as now, mineral wealth tended to catch the eye of the state. So far, however, Durjan Sal had managed to keep himself safe: his land was a thick jungle and Mughal officials were easily bribed. In early 1616, however, Jahangir noted how his newly appointed governor of Bihar, Ibrahim Khan, had captured the land 'out of that little nobody's hands', unswayed

by Durjan Sal's usual offer of diamonds and elephants. Ibrahim Khan was titled Fath Jang (victorious in battle) and 'day by day', wrote the emperor with satisfaction, 'diamonds are found and brought to court'.

2   Thackston, *Jahangirnama*.

3   Specifically, she describes him as fitting the very idea of Francis Bacon's ideal of Solomonic kingship.

4   Koch, 'Jahangir as Francis Bacon's Ideal'. 'The imperial attention becomes the measure of all things and behind it is the will to dominate the nature of his territories'.

5   Lefèvre, 'Recovering a Missing Voice'.

6   'One such poet,' he continued, 'was Tansen Kalawant, who was in my father's service and without equal in his own time – or any other for that matter. In one of his songs he likened the face of a youth to the sun and the opening of his eye to the blossoming of the lotus and the emerging of the bhaunra. In another one he likened the beloved's wink to the motion of the lotus flower when the bhaunra alights on it.'

7   Drab, charan and dam were fractions of the rupee.

8   In Cambay, Della Valle visited its famous hospital for birds, a publicly funded enterprise where he also found a litter of orphaned mice being treated by a 'venerable Old Man with a white Beard' who kept the mice in cotton wool and 'very diligently tended them with his spectacles on his nose, giving them milk to eat with a bird's feather'. There were hospitals, also, for goats and kids, sheep, cocks and peacocks, cows and calves, the last of which, he saw, sheltered a Muslim thief who had had both his hands cut off.

Part VII: Blood

1   Fruit often reminded Jahangir of his father. When that supply of exotic fruits had arrived as he marched towards Mandu, the emperor had wished Akbar were alive. 'Every time I see these

fruits,' he wrote of some new kinds of melons, pomegranates and grapes, 'I wish they had come in his time so that he could have tasted them.' The Mughal attachment to fruit wasn't just sentimental and hereditary, it had policy ramifications too: the *Jahangirnama* records that fruit orchards were exempt from tax.

2 The Mughal emperor's solar and lunar birthdays were both celebrated with a weighing ceremony, the tula-dan borrowed from Hindu custom that became integral to the Mughal calendar. Thomas Roe, who attended one of these celebrations, describes how Jahangir appeared in the durbar 'laden with Diamonds, rubies, Pearles, and other precious vanities, so great, *so* glorious! . . . his head, necke, breast, armes, above the elbowes, at the wrists, his fingers every one with at least two or three Rings, fettered with chaines; or dyalled Dyamonds, Rubies as great as Walnuts (some greater), and Pearls such as mine eyes were amazed at.' The emperor was then weighed against a vast range of goods, from silver and gold to butter and corn, all of it to be distributed among his subjects. There was also, of course, a party in the gusalkhana at night, from which Roe excused himself. He didn't want to drink, he confesses, because 'their waters are fire'.

3 Raghavan, *Attendant Lords*. Abdur Rahim threatened to commit jauhar if the emperor didn't send him reinforcements. Jahangir, in turn, tried to spur Shahjahan to action by reminding him of Akbar's lightning dash to Ahmedabad (the prince was possibly reluctant to return to the Deccan, having conquered it with such flair already).

4 It is true, on the other hand, that three years after Khusro was transferred to Asaf Khan's custody, he was pardoned. Jahangir records this in his memoirs circa October 1619. In 'Mughal Encounter', Shireen Moosvi tracing the biography of Jadrup (he was likely a Gujarati Brahmin called Chitrarupa) notes how the news of Khusro's sudden freedom appears immediately after the emperor has described another fulfilling meeting with his favourite ascetic. The two incidents are more than chronologically

connected: apparently, Mirza Aziz Koka, Khusro's father-in-law, had appealed to Jadrup to speak to Jahangir on Khusro's behalf – and Jadrup did so, successfully.

5   Prince Jahandar, born in the same month as Shahryar, led an even more shadowy existence. There are only three references to him in the *Jahangirnama*: one where Jahangir records his birth; one where he assigns him a tutor; and one where he describes him as 'congenitally crazy'.

6   Telling the story of how Asmat Begum discovered rose attar by chance, while making rose water, Jahangir remembered his father once again, wishing Akbar had lived to smell the perfume. 'In fragrance', he wrote, 'it is of such a degree that if one drop is rubbed on the palm it will perfume a whole room and make it seem more subtly fragrant than if many rosebuds had opened at once. It cheers one up and restores the soul.' Jahangir's aunt Salima Sultan named the perfume after Jahangir, and the emperor rewarded its inventor with a necklace of pearls.

7   Circa 16 February.

8   The lungi theory is from Francisco Pelsaert's account. Pelsaert also claims that Khusro was briefly worshipped as a saint or pir after his death; that there was even a shrine built for him in Agra.

9   Raghavan, *Attendant Lords*, offers a detailed account and analysis of Abdur Rahim and his family's unenviable, sometimes tragic, position in the crossfire of this civil war.

10 Like Shahjahan, Safi Khan was a son-in-law of Asaf Khan's.

11 For this idea, of Nurjahan riding into battle with her grandchild as a way of spurring on her nobility with a show of pointedly feminine valour, I want to thank Dr Anubhuti Maurya.

12 And a little help, it was suspected but never confirmed, from Shahjahan.

13 Khan, 'Iqbal-nama-i Jahangiri'. There were rumours that Dawarbakhsh escaped to Persia, though Beni Prasad deems this unlikely. Prasad notes that there were rumours, too, of Nurjahan having been executed. This, too, was not true. The former empress and her widowed daughter, Ladli Begum, lived together in long

and quiet solitude. The new emperor gave his former ally an annual allowance of two lakh rupees, less than Nurjahan had spent on a single party, long ago, to celebrate Shahjahan's Deccan victory.

Epilogue

1 Koch, 'Jahangir as Francis Bacon's Ideal'. 'The grandest rulers brought forth by mankind' as a German philosopher, Count Hermann Keyserling, described them.
2 In Jahangir's words.
3 Beni Prasad, too, discerns a 'passion for justice' in the emperor.

A Note on Sources
and Select Bibliography

A Note on Sources

Four years ago, and almost by chance, I began to read the *Baburnama*. I was thinking of how to write about Babur for children, and since Babur had written his own memoirs, of which I'd been given a copy, I began to leaf through it. I thought I might get a broad idea of his times, a reliable chronology perhaps; other than that, I wasn't sure what to expect. Certainly, I did not expect, four pages into the memoirs, to find Babur describing how the ties of his father's tunic often snapped when the rotund king forgot to hold his stomach in.

In his own 'diary', Jahangir followed his great-grandfather's easy, unselfconscious style; his talent for description, whether of a flower or a battle, is arguably even greater than Babur's, and the *Jahangirnama* is even more readable. Not being a scholar of Persian, I could only access its English versions, both of which are wonderfully engaging – though Wheeler M. Thackston's 1999 translation is far more fluid than its predecessor.

Besides its literary worth, the *Jahangirnama* is also the only truly contemporary, comprehensive and 'official' account of Jahangir's reign. Since the emperor declared he would record his own rule, no one else could take the liberty to do so, too. Sometimes, this can be marvellous. What better way to read about Abu'l Fazl's murder, for example, than from the pen of the man who commanded it? Yet, while Jahangir was disarmingly frank on some matters, he was clearly aware that his memoirs would have a powerful and interested audience, not least his own family. Not only, therefore, was Jahangir writing down his vibrant observations of life and nature, he was also creating an image of himself and his dynasty – one in which, for example, there was no place to acknowledge the possibility that one of his sons might have murdered another, nor to delve into his own rebellion against Akbar.

For that, there is the *Akbarnama* written by Abu'l Fazl, completed by Inayatullah, and wonderfully complemented by the secret grumblings of Abd'ul-Qadir Badauni in the second volume of his *Muntakhab-ut-Tawarikh* (Selections from Histories). Abu'l Fazl's loyal pen charts a discreet yet evocative narrative of the tensions that dogged Jahangir's relationship with his father. Meanwhile, Badauni not only records the most shocking bit of gossip about the imperial family – that Akbar thought his son was trying to poison him – but also a vivid portrait of Akbar's heterodoxies and the turmoil he caused amongst his more conservative courtiers. Even more than from Abu'l Fazl's hagiographic prose, it is from Badauni's possibly exaggerated and certainly biased account that one gets a sense of the energy, eclecticism and sheer breadth of vision with which Akbar governed the empire he built.

Two histories of Jahangir that were written soon after Jahangir died are extracted in *The History of India, As Told by Its Own Historians*. One is Khwaja Kamgar Khan's *Ma-asir-i Jahangiri*; the other is *Iqbal-nama-i Jahangiri* by Mu'tamad Khan, a trusted amir in Jahangir's employ. The emperor had such confidence in the amir, in fact, that the last sixteen-odd months of the *Jahangirnama* were written by Mu'tamad Khan. Later, Mu'tamad Khan wrote his own history of the reign, which is notable for his eyewitness account of Mahabat Khan's coup.

A third, anonymous, account that may well have been written by a contemporary of Jahangir's is the *Intikhab-i Jahangir Shahi* (also extracted in *The History of India*), which, too, features Mahabat Khan – in a cameo appearance that has the soldier warn Jahangir against the growing influence of his wife Nurjahan. Finally, another 'completion' of Jahangir's own history was attempted about a century later by Muhammad-Hadi.

As I have noted elsewhere in these pages, Corinne Lefèvre has proposed that Kamgar Khan's and Mu'tamad Khan's histories (both written during Shahjahan's reign) virtually created the image of Jahangir as a weak emperor, controlled by Nurjahan, as a way of excusing Shahjahan's rebellion against his father. Another book that has, unwittingly, helped Shahjahan's 'propaganda' is Thomas Roe's account of his embassy to 'the Great Mogul'.

Thomas Roe was in India circa 1615 to 1619, and

for most of this time he was in regular attendance at Jahangir's court. He had come to negotiate better trading terms for the English, in which he failed, a failure that, Lefèvre notes, may have prompted him to paint the emperor as unable to make decisions over the heads of his powerful wife and son. Roe was a better writer than he was a diplomat: his diary, much like Jahangir's, is a treasure of vignettes and anecdotes, not least about the emperor himself. Notably, the Jahangir tarnished by weakness or cupidity usually appears in the rumours Roe records, or in his own speculation; in his actual interactions with the ambassador, Jahangir is more often generous, affable, self-assured . . . even kind.

Of the early European trader-travellers who visited Jahangir's empire, only one other spent any substantial time in his court. William Hawkins was in India from 1608 to 1613; he was appointed a mansabdar of 400 rank soon after he arrived, married to the daughter of an Armenian amir* and titled the 'English Khan'. Though Hawkins's account of his time is far shorter than Roe's, it has many lively descriptions of court life and the emperor's ways.

Most European accounts from this time, however, are written from a far greater distance from the court; what

---

*Upon Jahangir's insistence. The emperor, writes Hawkins, 'was very earnest with me to take a white mayden out of his palace'. When Hawkins said he would only marry a Christian, Jahangir remembered this daughter of a deceased Armenian called Mubarak Shah. The Englishman was clearly pleased with the match, writing, 'So ever after I lived content and without feare, she being willing to goe where I went, and live as I lived.'

these may lose in their descriptions of imperial manners and intrigue, they gain in their accounts of everyday life and gossip. Many give fascinated descriptions of sati, of caste, of religions; of the bazaars and of the heat; of the houses, the food, the roads; one Nicholas Withington even relates his experience of being robbed by highwaymen in Sindh, stripped to his underwear and left to find his way back to Ahmedabad.

Finally, there is the brief account of the Jesuits who were part of a mission to Jahangir's court in its early years. The Jesuits are distinct from other Europeans partly because they were not traders, but also because they were Portuguese – and the Portuguese, having arrived in India before the Mughals and having long established their grip on India's seas, were loath to be associated in any way with the Dutch and English traders now sailing upon India's shores. The Jesuit account, too, differs substantially from the others: they are far more evidently *subject* to the emperor than, say, Thomas Roe, but also far more deeply engaged with him, often participating in long discussions on theological matters with him and his amirs. Often, however, the 'debate' seems to be at cross-purposes, with the Jesuits seemingly unable to understand how the emperor can treat his Catholic subjects with such favour, ask his Muslim scholars such provocative questions, yet not convert to Christianity.

The *Majalis-i Jahangiri* (Assemblies of Jahangir) by 'Abd al-Sattar ibn Qasim Lahauri is another account of Jahangir's theological conversations. Though it was only discovered in 2002 and hasn't yet been translated, discussions of it by, for example, Lefèvre and A. Azfar

Moin, reveal a Jahangir very different from the conundrum of the Jesuits and the aesthete of the *Jahangirnama*.

∼

Modern historians once tended to reduce Jahangir's many identities, perhaps even his mysteries, to a kind of aesthetic whimsy. Most modern historians, in fact, tended to ignore him: he was, in Ebba Koch's words, 'something of a Cinderella of text-based Mughal historical studies', thanks to the disproportionate attention bestowed on Akbar, who made the empire what it was, and on Aurangzeb, who expanded it to breaking point. Beni Prasad, the only modern scholar to have written a history of Jahangir, treats his subject with exhaustive, often affectionate, attention, but he does not challenge the idea of his innate 'weakness', of his preference for pleasure over conquest or governance.

More recently, however, scholars such as Ebba Koch, Corinne Lefèvre and A. Azfar Moin have rethought Jahangir in fascinating ways. So, for example, where Jahangir's own translator, Wheeler M. Thackston, might argue that Jahangir's 'penchant for recording minutiae of his daily schedule has produced . . . sections that, as fascinating as they are for the general reader and for all the light they shed on Jahangir's character, are of little or no historical significance', Corinne Lefèvre concludes her rereading of the text with the argument that his memoirs are 'a masterpiece of Late Renaissance imperial propaganda.'

Partly by chance and partly from the fact that my locus

in this book has been of a lay reader, not an informed scholar, my own reading and writing of this book, too, was split between these two ways of understanding Jahangir. In my first draft, I had thought of Jahangir in the older tradition, as the most engaging but also the most lightweight of the great Mughals. Before I began my second draft, however, I encountered my last, and possibly most valuable source: Dr Anubhuti Maurya. Not only did Dr Maurya offer me much lively conversation about the emperor and introduce me to the most recent scholarship on him, she also gave me a new way of thinking about him.

During the course of a conversation in which I was describing, as many have, Jahangir's drinking habit as a possible hindrance to his rule, she said, 'Well, you could think of it as his sociability.'

Sociability. It was not, after all, that Jahangir sat and drank all alone; he drank with his sons, he drank with ambassadors to his court, he drank with the men who helmed his empire. And while he drank, he talked: about theology, about matters of state, about art, about what existed in his realm and beyond. Was drinking, and the often lavish parties that accompanied the drinking, and the freewheeling conversation that was produced by the drinking – was this Jahangir's way of binding his nobility to him?

Was it, after all, his very affability that was his greatest strength?

~

To conclude, a brief digression and then a caveat. Some twenty-odd years ago, I declared, in the manner of undergraduates, that the study of English literature was a dead end; even, I might have declaimed, a delusion. For my master's degree, I wanted something 'substantial', a study of facts, not theories and interpretations. I decided I would study history. Like most undergraduates, I was partly right and mostly wrong. On the one hand, the two years I spent reading history were greatly rewarding. At the risk of sounding as affected as I would have accused literary theory of being, I felt my brain shift. It was the thrill of discovering new ways of thinking. On the other hand, the two most rewarding papers that I wrote in that time were both, as I now realize, based on close readings of texts. Substance was not so distant, after all, from interpretation.

Perhaps it is only fitting that this book, too, arose from a glitch in my engagement with literature: I was working on a novel about, amongst other things, a professor of medieval history and I ended up writing a biography of Jahangir. Once more, I felt my brain shift. Having spent much of my life trying to learn the art of writing fiction, how, now, to tell a story that is fact?

It is a fact, for example, that Salim was born on a Wednesday; it is also a fact that as emperor Jahangir renamed that day Gum-shamba, the day of loss. The fact of the emperor's account is that he did so because his beloved granddaughter died on that day – but is there not something poignant about a man who writes of his own day of birth, in an age when the auspiciousness or otherwise of dates and days was fact, 'Would that this day would always occur less often'?

Is there some kind of truth here, hidden between the facts, or is this my own fancy, a delusion? Or is the real delusion of another kind – that there is, somehow, an elemental difference between truth and story? It is of fiction, after all, that we often say that it 'rings true'.

Or call it 'narrative' – that oddly bland word – is it a synonym for momentum? This happened, and then this and then this, gathering pace until it all builds up into a life, a world, a whole ... and then, if you're lucky, a truth, and if you're luckier still, a truth that's worthwhile.

The caveat: for all my academic ambitions, I am not a historian. My sources, Jahangir onward, have given me a bounty of incident, interpretation and argument, and I hope I have managed to build from them a story that is both accurate and engaging. For any errors of fact and analysis that I have made, I am solely responsible and gladly open to correction.

As for the truth of Jahangir, all I can say is that I have had, in this book of fact as in my books of fiction, a more modest ambition: to be honest. The Jahangir I have tried to bring alive was this, and also this ... and a bit of that. It is your imagination, in the end, that will make him whole.

Select Bibliography

Akbar in his own time

Badauni, Abd'ul Qadir. *Muntakhab-ut-Tawarikh* (Selections from Histories), trans. W.H. Lowe. Vol. 2. The Asiatic Society of Bengal, 1884.

Beveridge, Henry, trans. *The Akbarnama of Abu'l Fazl* (completed by Inayatullah). Vol. 2 & 3. The Asiatic Society, 1939.

Jahangir in his own words

Beveridge, Henry, ed. *The Tuzuk-i-Jahangiri or Memoirs of Jahangir*, trans. Alexander Rogers. Vol. 1 & 2. D.K. Fine Art Press Private Limited, 1909–14.

Thackston, Wheeler M., ed. & trans. *The Jahangirnama: Memoirs of Jahangir, Emperor of India* (including a preface and appendix by Muhammad-Hadi, 18th century). Oxford University Press with the Smithsonian Institution, 1999.

Jahangir in (and around) his own time

Anonymous. 'Intikhab-i Jahangir Shahi.' In *The History of India, As Told by Its Own Historians*, translated by H.M. Elliot, edited and completed by John Dowson. Vol. 6. Trübner and Co., 1875.

Beg, Asad (early 1600s). 'Wiqaya-i-Asad Beg.' In *The History of India, As Told by Its Own Historians*, translated by H.M. Elliot, edited and completed by John Dowson. Vol. 6. Trübner and Co., 1875.

Khan, Kamgar (1630s). 'Ma-asir-i Jahangiri.' In *The History of India, As Told by Its Own Historians*, translated by H.M. Elliot, edited and completed by John Dowson. Vol. 6. Trübner and Co., 1875.

Khan, Mu'tamad (17th century). 'Iqbal-nama-i Jahangiri.' In *The History of India, As Told by Its Own Historians*, translated by H.M. Elliot, edited and completed by John Dowson. Vol. 6. Trübner and Co., 1875.

Jahangir in late medieval times

Gladwin, Francis. *The History of Jahangir*, edited with notes by Rao Bahadur K.V. Rangaswami Aiyangar. B.G. Paul and Co., 1930 (originally published in 1788).

Muhammad-Hadi's preface and appendix to *The Jahangirnama: Memoirs of Jahangir, Emperor of India*, ed. & trans. Wheeler M. Thackston. Oxford University Press with the Smithsonian Institution, 1999.

European travellers

Foster, William, ed. *Early Travels in India: 1583–1619*, with writings by Ralph Fitch, John Mildenhall, William Hawkins, William Fitch, Nicholas Withington, Thomas Coryat and Edward Terry. Low Price Publications, 1921.

Foster, William, ed. *The Embassy of Sir Thomas Roe to the Court of the Great Mogul, 1615-1619, As Narrated in His Journal and Correspondence*. Vol. 1 & 2. Forgotten Books, 1899.

Geyl, P., and W.H. Moreland, trans. *Jahangir's India:*

The Remonstrantie of Francisco Pelsaert. Low Price Publications, 1925.

Grey, Edward, ed. *The Travels of Pietro Della Valle in India*, trans. G. Havers. Vol. 1 & 2. Asian Educational Services, 1892.

Payne, C.H., trans. *Jahangir and the Jesuits: From the Relations of Father Fernão Guerreiro, S.J.* Munshiram Manoharlal Publishers Private Limited, 1930.

Modern histories and analyses

Alam, Muzaffar, and Sanjay Subrahmanyam. 'The Deccan Frontier and Mughal Expansion, c. 1600.' In *Writing the Mughal World: Studies on Culture and Politics*. Columbia University Press, 2011.

Eraly, Abraham. *The Last Spring: The Saga of the Great Mughals Part I*. Penguin Books, 1997 (reprinted in 2000).

Findly, Ellison Banks. *Nur Jahan: Empress of Mughal India*. Oxford University Press, 1993.

Gascoigne, Bamber. *A Brief History of The Great Moghuls: India's Most Flamboyant Rulers*. Constable & Robinson Limited, 1971 (reprinted in 1998).

Khan, Iqtidar Alam. 'Akbar's Personality Traits and World Outlook: A Critical Appraisal.' In *Akbar and His India*, ed. Irfan Habib. Oxford University Press, 1997.

Koch, Ebba. 'Jahangir as Francis Bacon's Ideal of the King as an Observer and Investigator of Nature.' *Journal of the Royal Asiatic Society* 3rd series, 19: 3 (July 2009).

Koch, Ebba. 'My Garden Is Hindustan: The Mughal Padshah's Realisation of a Political Metaphor.' In *Middle East Garden Traditions: Unity and Diversity*, edited by Michel Conan. Harvard University Press, 2007.

Lefèvre, Corinne. 'Messianism, Rationalism and Inter-Asian Connections: The *Majalis-i Jahangiri* (1608–11) and the Socio-Intellectual History of the Mughal 'ulama.' *The Indian Economic and Social History Review* 54: 3 (2017).

Lefèvre, Corinne. 'Recovering a Missing Voice from Mughal India: The Imperial Discourse of Jahangir (r. 1605–1627) in His Memoirs.' *Journal of the Economic and Social History of the Orient* 50: 4 (2007).

Moin, A. Azfar. *The Millennial Sovereign: Sacred Kingship & Sainthood in Islam.* Columbia University Press, 2012.

Moosvi, Shireen. 'The Mughal Encounter with Vedanta: Recovering the Biography of "Jadrup".' *Social Scientist* 30: 7/8 (July–August 2002).

Naim, C.M. 'Popular Jokes and Political History: The Case of Akbar, Birbal and Mulla Do-Piyaza.' *Economic and Political Weekly* 17 June 1995.

Panikkar, K.M. *A Survey of Indian History*. Asia Publishing House, 1947.

Prasad, Beni. *History of Jahangir*. Bharatiya Kala Prakashan, 1930 (reprinted in 2013).

Raghavan, T.C.A. *Attendant Lords: Bairam Khan and Abdur Rahim, Courtiers and Poets in Mughal India.* HarperCollins Publishers, 2017.

Richards, J.F. 'The Formulation of Imperial Authority under Akbar and Jahangir.' In *The Mughal State: 1526-1750*, edited by Muzaffar Alam and Sanjay Subrahmanyam. Oxford University Press, 1998.

Rizvi, Sajjad. 'Shi'i Polemics at the Mughal Court: The

Case of Qazi Nurullah Shushtari.' *Studies in People's History* 4: 1 (2017).

Saksena, Banarsi Prasad. *History of Shahjahan of Dihli.* Central Book Depot, 1958.

Acknowledgements

I want to thank, first of all, my publishers. Chiki Sarkar, who suggested I try my hand at writing a book about Jahangir in the first place. Nandini Mehta, whose generous appraisal of my drafts gave me that warm feeling of doing something right that writers cannot write without. Janani Ganesan, whose unsparing queries, and Jaishree Ram Mohan, whose rigorous edits improved the manuscript more than I could ever have done alone. Gavin Morris, whose beautiful cover I can only let speak for itself. And R. Sivapriya, who buoyed me through all of it: the reading and thinking, the writing, revising and related anxieties with her acute editorial interventions and her inimitable, quite wonderful calm. In sum, and while any errors it contains are my sole doing, this book would not exist were it not for Juggernaut. To all of you, my deepest gratitude.

I want to thank, also, the people who aided and abetted in the thinking about and writing of this book: Aftab and Azra Alam, Fatima, Tahseen and Shahrukh for all the conversations and kindnesses; Reena and Neeru Nanda for their encouragement and critical insights;

Sulaiman and Azra Ahmad for a lovely trip to Aligarh; Amit Mahanti, Anita Abraham, Ruchika Negi, Mallika Ghosh, Poorva Rajaram, Sarah Quraishi and Trisha Gupta for letting me hijack many a conversation into the seventeenth century; Khalid Anis Ansari, his colleagues and students for thought-provoking discussion; Mansi Midha for arranging a very last-minute photo shoot and Ali Alam for shooting the photos – and, of course, Priya Doraswamy, for being my agent.

To Anubhuti Maurya, I am both grateful and indebted. Thank you for all your help, your engagement and your time.

My thanks and my love, as always, to my mother and father, my sister and my family.

If books are like children to their authors, this one was the unplanned but rewarding surprise. I could not have predicted I would ever write a biography of Jahangir, nor how much I would enjoy doing so. Perhaps there are few better subjects for a novelist dabbling in history than the fourth Mughal emperor, with all the richness of his character and context, and I am glad to have spent this time in his exhilarating company. I hope I have done him justice, and that you will enjoy reading this book as much I enjoyed writing it.

Index

311

312 Index

Patna, 12, 243
Pelsaert, Francisco, 100, 106,
    150–51, 153
Persia, 127–28
    Persians, 162
    Shah of, 132, 163, 235, 264
Portuguese, 71, 139
Prasad, Beni, 92, 167, 194–95,
    229, 234, 203, 270–71
Pratap, Maharana of Mewar, 51
Protestant English, 71

Qandahar, 97, 101, 103, 127–28,
    235–36, 265
Qilich Khan, 51, 54, 110, 164
Qutbuddin Khan (Khubu),
    11, 53, 55, 111, 124, 161,
    165–68, 171

Rajputs, 133, 152, 178, 185, 187,
    192, 234, 244, 252, 254
Rama, 28
Ramayana, 29
religious eclecticism, 140
religious freedom, 140–42
Roe, Sir Thomas, 98, 100–01,
    103, 137, 142–47, 155–56,
    157, 177–78, 180–81, 183,
    189, 191–99, 202–03, 216,
    225, 228, 249, 267, 269, 271
Roger, Alexander, 212
Ruqaiya Begum, 24, 135
Rustam, 40–42, 48

Safi Khan, 240
Sahib Jamal, 24
Saksena, Banarsi Prasad, 52, 165,
    167, 223, 234, 265
Salih, 257
Salim. *See* Jahangir, Nuruddin
    Muhammad
Salima Sultan Begum, 49, 66–
    68, 125, 167, 171
Salivahan, Raja, 56
Samarkand, 112, 128, 132, 200,
    264
Sati, was not prohibited in
    Mughal rule, 150–51
Sayyids of Barha, 92–93, 119,
    120, 204
Shah Alam II, 266–67
Shah Shuja, 219–21, 226, 237
Shahjahan (Khurram), 25, 41–
    42, 52, 56, 81, 89–91, 114,
    125, 135–36, 147, 165, 167,
    170, 172, 177–79, 181–86,
    188–94, 197–98, 202, 206,
    209, 219, 223, 224, 228,
    230–31, 233, 234–35, 247,
    255, 257–58, 265–66, 268
ascended the throne, 259
Deccan campaigns, 194,
    197–99, 203–05, 209,
    223, 228, 229, 231, 268
Jahangir declared Khurram
    as Shahjahan, 206
had his nephews murdered,
    266

1

CRAFTED FOR MOBILE READING

Thought you would never read a book on mobile? Let us prove you wrong.

Beautiful Typography

The quality of print transferred
to your mobile. Forget ugly PDFs.

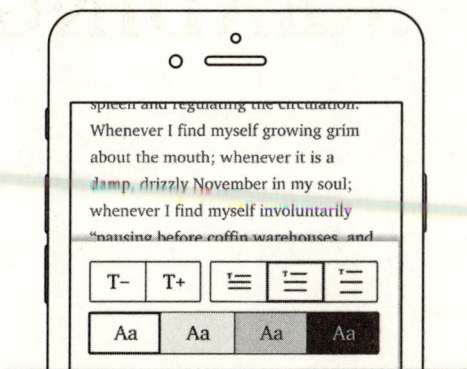

Customizable Reading

Read in the font size, spacing
and background of your liking.

AN EXTENSIVE LIBRARY

Including fresh, new, original Juggernaut books from the likes of Sunny Leone, Praveen Swami, Husain Haqqani, Umera Ahmed, Rujuta Diwekar and lots more. Plus, books from partner publishers and loads of free classics. Whichever genre you like, there's a book waiting for you.

juggernaut.in

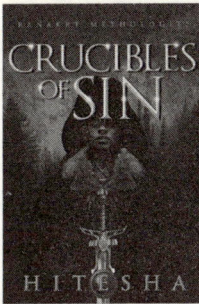

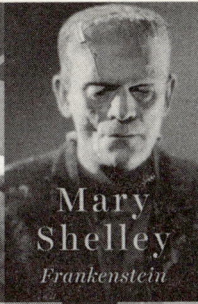

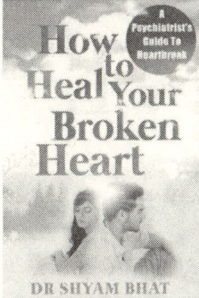
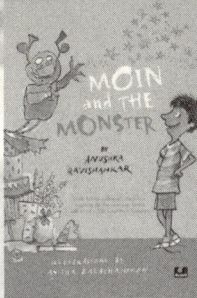
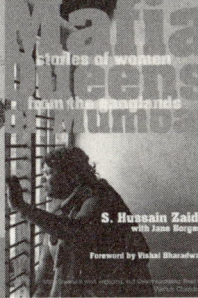
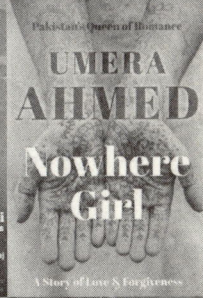
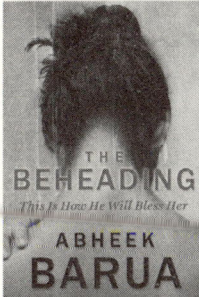
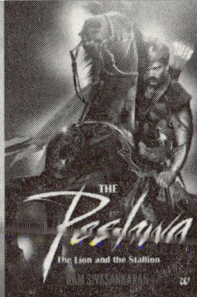
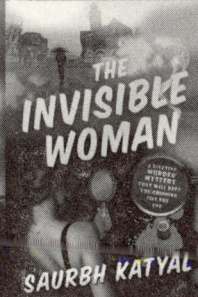

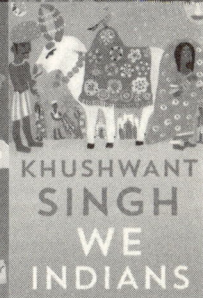

DON'T JUST READ; INTERACT

We're changing the reading experience from passive to active.

Ask authors questions

Get all your answers from the horse's mouth. Juggernaut authors actually reply to every question they can.

Rate and review

Let everyone know of your favourite reads or critique the finer points of a book – you will be heard in a community of like-minded readers.

Gift books to friends

For a book-lover, there's no nicer gift than a book personally picked. You can even do it anonymously if you like.

Enjoy new book formats

Discover serials released in parts over time, picture books including comics, and story-bundles at discounted rates. And coming soon, audiobooks.

4

LOWEST PRICES & ONE-TAP BUYING

Books start at ₹10 with regular discounts and free previews.

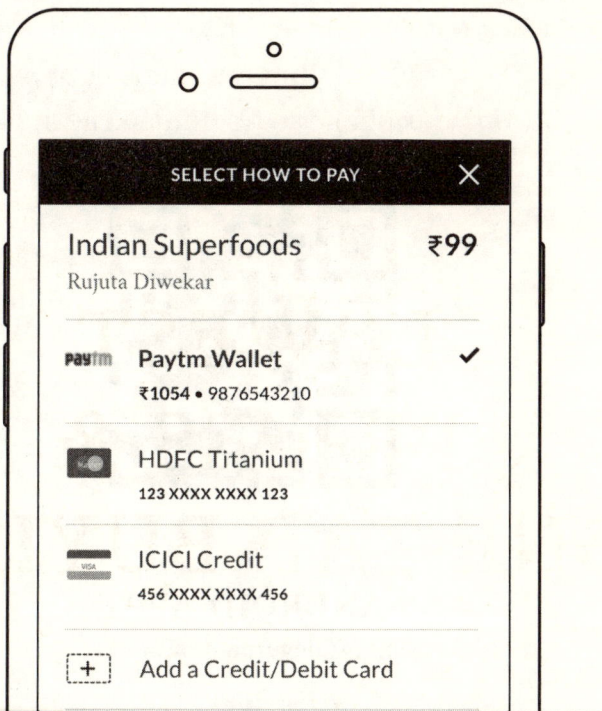

Paytm Wallet, Cards & Apple Payments

On Android, just add a Paytm Wallet once and buy any book with one tap. On iOS, pay with one tap with your iTunes-linked debit/credit card.

Click the QR Code with a QR scanner app
or type the link into the Internet browser
on your phone to download the app.

ANDROID APP
bit.ly/juggernautandroid

iOS APP
bit.ly/juggernautios

For our complete catalogue, visit www.juggernaut.in
To submit your book, send a synopsis and two
sample chapters to books@juggernaut.in
For all other queries, write to contact@juggernaut.in